FR. LÉON-DUFOUR, who is known ... his scripture studies, particularly on the gospels, pub... his masterpiece, *Les Évangiles et l'Histoire de Jésus,* in France in 1963. It was rightly regarded as one of the best statements of the problem raised by the gospels in connection with the quest for the historical Jesus, form criticism, and historicity. The present volume, an abridged and edited version of that book prepared by Fr. John McHugh of Ushaw College in England, retains all the clarity and scholarship of the original work. *The Gospels and the Jesus of History* has been highly praised by critics of all denominations, both here and abroad. A few of their comments appear below.

"Professional scripture scholars will already have this volume in its French edition, and the rest of us, familiar with Léon-Dufour's magnificent *Dictionary of Biblical Theology,* will need only the gentlest prod in order to tackle it. The same care, mastery, clarity carry us here through the forbidding maze of Form-Criticism, with an ease that is almost flattering." *America*

"[*The Gospels and the Jesus of History*] is far more than an introduction to the study of the Gospels . . . it is an excellent introduction to the Christology of the New Testament. And not the least of its merits is that it is easy to read." *Glasgow Herald*

"After a most valuable and, at times, penetrating approach to the issues involved, he concludes by reminding us that the evangelists 'were not concerned merely to set down a record of certain events, but above all to introduce their readers to a living person.' A book written in that spirit with Dr. Léon-Dufour's scholarship is bound to be worth reading." *Church of England Newspaper*

"Splendidly readable . . . it provides a sane, shrewd guide through the controversies surrounding the Jesus of history and the Christ of faith. . . . This is a book to buy." *S.P.C.K. View Review*

THE GOSPELS
AND
THE JESUS OF HISTORY

by

XAVIER LÉON-DUFOUR S.J.
Translated and edited by
JOHN MC HUGH

IMAGE BOOKS
A Division of Doubleday & Company, Inc.
Garden City, New York

Image Books edition 1970
by special arrangement with Desclee Company, Inc.

Image Books edition published February 1970

Originally published in French under the title
Les Évangiles et l'histoire de Jésus
© Editions du Seuil
This English translation © 1968 William Collins Sons
& Co., Ltd.
London and Desclee Co. Inc., New York
All rights reserved
Printed in the United States of America

Acknowledgments

The translator and publishers wish to thank the Reverend G. A. Williamson, and Penguin Books Ltd., for permission to cite from the Penguin translation of Eusebius' *History of the Church*; The Loeb Classical Library, and the Harvard University Press, for permission to quote the Loeb translation of Josephus' *Jewish Antiquities*, by Louis H. Feldman; Messrs. Darton, Longman and Todd, and the Newman Press, Westminster, Maryland, for permission to use a paragraph from the English translation (by Patrick Hepburne-Scott) of Mgr Lucien Cerfaux's *The Four Gospels*.

Abbreviations have been kept to a minimum: *PG* and *PL* stand for Migne's *Patrologia Graeca* and *Patrologia Latina* respectively, *HE* for Eusebius' *Historia Ecclesiastica*, and *ANCL* for the series *Ante-Nicene Christian Library*, published by T. and T. Clark of Edinburgh (which is referred to because it is still, after half a century, the only English translation of the early Fathers which is more or less complete and easily accessible in libraries).

Contents

PART IV

PROLEGOMENA TO A LIFE OF JESUS

Translator's Preface

Fr Xavier Léon-Dufour's book, *Les Évangiles et l'Histoire de Jésus*, has met with remarkable success in France since its publication in 1963, and it was inevitable that an English translation should be called for. It was decided (with the consent of the author and the owners of the copyright, *Les Éditions du Seuil*) to produce an abridged and edited version which would be about half the length of the original. The final text has, of course, been submitted to Fr Léon-Dufour for his approval.

It was no easy task to condense such a lengthy and detailed work of scholarship, and readers who wish to see the full documentation behind the argument will, of course, consult the French original.

A word must be said about the translation of biblical texts. It is customary in France, more than in England, for an author to supply his own translations, particularly when he wishes to bring out the force of some particular word or phrase. There were many instances in this book where none of the classical English versions would have served the author's argument adequately, and biblical texts have therefore been translated throughout from his French rendering, and compared with the original Greek.

It only remains for me to thank Fr Léon-Dufour and the French publishers for their exceptional generosity in allowing the book to be published in this form.

J. McHUGH

Ushaw College, Durham

Foreword

'What do you think of Christ?' Men have constantly asked this question over the centuries, but the question gives rise to different problems in different ages, and an answer which satisfied men in an age of religious fervour may prove very unsatisfactory in an age of unbelief. In modern times changing attitudes towards religion and the development of critical historical scholarship have both had their effect. Towards the end of the eighteenth century many writers began to attack the historical value of the four gospels, and to claim that they do not give an accurate account of the life of Jesus. Ever since that time the question has been continuously debated, and innumerable books have been written for and against the truth of the gospels. These books were all written with one purpose: to get back with real certainty to the unadorned facts, and to reconstruct what actually happened in the past. What other authors did in their day, we have to do again for our own generation; but today, anyone who attempts to write about the historical value of the gospels finds that the task is harder than ever before, for during the last forty years a new method of discussing the various problems has been steadily gaining ground.

There are two reasons for this change. First, many Christians have reacted strongly against those who claim that Jesus of Nazareth is just one among many religious teachers. Christians are not content to look upon Jesus merely as someone who lived in the past; they are not satisfied until they have made contact with One who is living, now and always. Secondly, many historians have been deeply influenced by existentialism; these men aim at being utterly impartial in their research, but they are not content merely to establish facts about the past. They consider that it is also their duty to assess the significance of the past for themselves in their own environment: in other words, they see themselves as 'involved' in history.

One cannot but admire the religious faith and the broad humanity which lead theologians and historians to think in this way. Unfortunately, some of these scholars proceed to draw conclusions which, if accepted, would undermine once more all the ground upon which any historical knowledge of Jesus must be based. For example, Professor Bultmann and some of his followers have claimed that the facts about Jesus which can be known by sound historical scholarship are minimal: some go so far as to say that we know practically nothing about the historical Jesus, and that faith must fill the gap left by history. Historians, they say, should abandon the attempt to know Jesus of Nazareth, and be satisfied (as historians) to study the faith shown by the primitive community in the risen Lord.

Conclusions of this kind seem to be quite unjustified, and in fact most contemporary scholars, Protestant as well as Catholic, refuse to accept them, on the ground that they contradict both historical evidence and traditional faith. But a refusal to accept these erroneous conclusions must not be taken to imply that the questions which Bultmann has raised should never have been asked at all. On the contrary, the whole purpose of the present book is to give a fair hearing to these new arguments. At the same time there can be no question of accepting philosophical presuppositions which determine the outcome of any inquiry from the start. If the historical value of the gospels is to be investigated along strictly scientific lines, there is no place for presuppositions of this kind.

The question which this book sets out to answer may therefore be put in these words: 'How can we know Jesus from the four gospels?' The aim is to find out, by using the critical methods of historical scholarship, the full and objective truth (as far as it can be known) about the life of Jesus of Nazareth. The results will not be minimal, for though we cannot know everything we should like to know about his life, the gospels do contain a wealth of trustworthy historical information. Indeed, the present book will endeavour to demonstrate that a thorough-going application of the principles of historical criticism does not weaken, but rather strengthens the conviction that the gospels are historically reliable. When they are studied impartially with all the techniques of modern scholarship, the picture of Jesus becomes more clearly defined, and his words take on a starker and more imperious tone: 'And you—who do you say I am?' Once the impartial inquirer has reached this point, a particular answer is already suggesting itself to his mind, an answer which is a step on the road to faith. But if a man is to reach the end of that road, his mind must remain genuinely open.

In the early Christian Church, various interpretations of the life of Jesus were current. There are some people who think that these interpretations have nothing to offer to the man who is studying the life of Jesus, but there are many others (including the present writer) who take the opposite view. We believe that the investigation of the faith of the early Church reveals an answer to the question raised by Jesus, and that this answer is not unconnected with the events of his life; indeed, we believe that it can throw light on them. That is why this book traces the gospel tradition to the very end of the apostolic age: it does not confine itself to the data supplied by the first three gospels, but includes also a discussion of the Gospel according to Saint John. The argument, of course, will not compel a man to assent; but it will face him with a problem, and with a question which demands an answer.

This present book (particularly in its English dress) is not meant to be a technical work of theology addressed to professional theologians or exegetes. Those who want a fuller statement of the case must consult the French original, and examine the literature cited there. But it is hoped that this English version will provide the general public with an up-to-date statement of the reasons which lead orthodox Christians even today to regard the gospels as historically reliable. In a synthesis of this kind, written for a wide public, it is neither possible nor desirable to encumber the text with the paraphernalia of scholarship, but the broad lines of the argument will be all the clearer for that. Obviously, some of the statements made here will one day need to be revised or qualified in the light of further research, but such modifications will not necessarily invalidate the whole argument. It is the earnest hope of the author that a general synthesis of this kind may be of service both to educated Christians and to sympathetic inquirers who want to know how modern historical methods have affected Christian attitudes towards the gospels.

In conclusion, I should like to thank Dr Rudolf Schnackenburg, Professor at the University of Würzburg, and Fr Ignace de la Potterie, S.J., Professor at the Pontifical Biblical Institute in Rome, for their helpful criticism and advice.

XAVIER LÉON-DUFOUR, sj

Introduction

1. The Person of Jesus

The life of Jesus of Nazareth cannot be discussed in the same way as the life of any other man, however famous. Men like Caesar or Napoleon, for example, had a profound effect on their own age, and may properly be said to have altered the course of history, but none of them ever claimed to give the final and definitive explanation of all that has happened, or will happen, in the course of time. Other men, like the Pharaohs of Egypt, have insisted on being worshipped as gods during their lifetime; but no one takes their claims to divinity seriously today. Quite the contrary is true when we consider the life of Jesus.

Christians have always maintained that the life and death of Jesus are of unique significance for the whole of mankind. The first Christians preached that 'there is no other Name given to men by which they may be saved' (Ac 4:12), and Jesus himself said that he had come to lay down his life for the redemption of men (Mk 10:45). And here lies the paradox of Christianity, for apart from a number of alleged miracles, there is at first sight nothing to distinguish the life of Jesus from the life of any other great religious teacher. Jesus was by birth a Jew; he lived in Palestine in the time of Augustus and Tiberius Caesar; and in the end he was crucified, like many another Jew of the time. He was not in any sense a great nationalist leader. It can even be argued that the religious doctrine which he taught is not uniquely inspiring. It is not distinguished for its moderation, like Stoicism, or for its depth, like Platonism, and there is scarcely a single saying in the gospels which cannot be paralleled in Jewish tradition or in the sayings of Eastern religions: Confucius, for example, counselled men to meet hostility with love.

Faced with this paradox, historians have every opportunity to underline the lack of proportion between the very ordinary life of Jesus (which ended in failure), and the all-embracing claims which he made. Some suggest that Jesus never made any such claims: it was his disciples, they say, who took up the story after his death, and gave the world an interpretation of his life which Jesus himself had never intended. Others have a still simpler explanation: they suggest that everything may have happened by chance, because the disciples were misled by a question which Jesus once put to them—'and you—who do you say I am?' This, then, is a crucial question: did the disciples misinterpret the significance of Jesus' life because they had misunderstood his words?

'Who do you say I am?' In the course of history, this question has been answered in two ways, and men are divided into two camps by their answers. For some men, Jesus is the Son of God; for the others, he was merely a religious genius. Believing or refusing to believe in Jesus as the Son of God involves accepting or rejecting the assertion that his life matters for each one of us. For the orthodox Christian believer, the life of Jesus, though it took place in the past, is an event which stands out from the course of events in history and provides the key to the history of the world; but for those who do not believe in him as the Son of God, his life is something over and done with in the past. Whether a man believes in Jesus or not, he is giving an answer to the question we find in the gospels: 'And you—who do you say I am?'

The Christian affirms something which is not easily acceptable to human reason: he asserts that God became man. He claims, moreover, that this God-Man underwent death, rose to life again and is now alive: this has been the constant teaching of the Church, in all its catechetical instruction and in its liturgy, from the earliest times to the present day. Assertions like these, which are of their nature incapable of empirical verification, present the historian with problems of a unique kind.

Furthermore, the Church asserts that its own life and history is for ever bound up with that of the risen Lord, and that in the Church he is present today. This belief is at the heart of the Christian faith, but it too raises a problem for the historian. How are we to distinguish in traditional Christian teaching between that which comes from Jesus and that which comes from the Church? Is it not possible that the early Church may (unconsciously) have projected on to the earthly life of its Saviour an ideal which it was trying to realize in its own life (without, of course, attaining that ideal in practice)?

No one can deny that faith may lead a man to alter the historical evidence and even to idealize events. But it is sometimes forgotten that an equally grave danger faces the unbeliever, for human reason may tend to stifle incipient movements towards faith and thus prevent them from maturing. It is an undeniable fact that there is, and always has been, a human tendency to reduce supernatural events to natural proportions. More than anyone else, Jesus of Nazareth has been the subject of charges and counter-charges: when Christians are accused of falsifying history by idealizing his life, they may legitimately reply that history is falsified if his life is reduced to merely human proportions not because of the evidence but because of philosophical objections to anything which reason cannot explain as a natural phenomenon.

This controversy dates back to the beginning of the Christian era. Celsus (*ca.* A.D. 180) and Porphyry (*ca.* A.D. 300) did their best to ridicule the contents of the Bible and even denied that there was any historical truth in the facts recorded there. Here we see two mental attitudes, one (the rationalist) claiming to represent the authentic voice of reason, and the other (the Christian) rejecting that claim in the name of faith. Celsus' ideas did not die with him, and even today they are very much alive. Voltaire was one successor of Celsus and Porphyry, and, at the time of the Enlightenment, Reimarus (1694–1768) argued that the apostles were frauds and that Jesus was a political Messiah whose plans failed. Paulus (1761–1851) was the son of a Protestant minister who practised spiritualism: the young Paulus very understandably reacted against the atmosphere of faked miracles in which he had been brought up, and consequently, in treating of the gospels, claimed to explain by natural causes all the miracles of Christ. For example, he maintained that when the apostles thought they had seen Jesus walking on the water, they must have lost their sense of direction in a fog. Paulus gave a rationalist explanation of the Resurrection also: he suggested that when Jesus was buried, he was unconscious but not dead, and that the coldness of the tomb revived him. The biblical evidence may cry aloud that this is not so, but the out-and-out rationalist is incapable of hearing what it has to say, because he has deliberately taken up his stand against the very possibility of the supernatural.

This sceptical attitude towards supernatural revelation is a human reaction which is just as instinctive as is a positive receptiveness springing from faith. But the sceptical attitude has in modern times been particularly fostered by a new science, comparative religion. It originated among men hostile to traditional Christianity, most of whom dismissed any form of religious belief as superstitious enslavement to a myth. One of its earliest exponents, D. F. Strauss, tried to find a purely rational explanation of everything in the gospels with the aid of mythology and (Hegelian) philosophy; later, Ernest Renan attempted to do the same, but with the aid of psychology, and sketched his portrait of a gentle, unworldly Galilean dreamer. In Russia, Tolstoy presented Jesus as a forerunner of socialism and of the gospel of non-violence; and in England, Matthew Arnold expounded his own version of Christianity without dogma.

What is the value of these interpretations of the life of our Lord? Rationalists always suspect Christians of being led by their piety to improve on the facts of history, but this should not deter a Christian from condemning any approach which refuses *a priori* to accept the divinity of our Lord. A truly impartial historian would no doubt fear that orthodox Christians might have been deceived into accepting an exaggerated version of a pious legend; but he would also have to condemn all the above-mentioned rationalist writers for not respecting the data given in the gospels. Impartiality demands that every possible excess, either of reason or of faith, should be severely checked, and even that is not sufficient to ensure a perfectly fair judgment. If a man claims to have a truly critical mind, then he must not uncritically accept rationalism as an unquestionable dogma; far too many people have done so in the past, and this has paralysed their thinking as soon as they encounter religious facts for which there is no neat rationalist explanation. The Christian is very glad to see anyone examining the evidence for the Christian faith in a rigorously scientific and critical way, but the examination should be conducted with an *open* mind.

2. The Sources for the Life of Jesus

Nearly everything we know about the life of our Lord comes from the four gospels, but these four books, far from providing a straightforward biography of our Saviour, seem, if read carefully, to be full of contradictions. In childhood, many of us enjoyed a *Life of Jesus* in which the whole story ran on smoothly from the Annunciation to the Resurrection. Adults, however, want something more (especially dates), and consequently lives of our Lord written for them sometimes include many precise chronological details. For example, some works will assert not only that Jesus died on 7 April, A.D. 30, but that he was baptized in January of the year 28, that the stilling of the storm took place in the December of the same year, and even that the Transfiguration took place on 6 August, A.D. 29.

Popular works are full of precise dates like these, and an educated man will often wonder how seriously he is meant to take them. When an historian finds them set down side by side with dates which are absolutely certain (*e.g.* the capture

of Jerusalem by Pompey in 63 B.C., or the assassination of
Julius Caesar in 44 B.C.), he finds himself obliged to query
them with the same severity as he queries some of the legends
about saints. At first, this questioning may seem to demolish
everything that generations of pious writers have built up,
but in the end it ensures a more solid foundation for a far
stronger building. Since the present book is meant to be a
critical study of the gospels, it will be useful to outline a
few of the problems here at the beginning, by way of introduction. This may help the reader to understand why it is
so difficult to reconstruct the life of our Lord: certainly, it is
not as simple as it might appear to be from reading the av-
erage popular *Life of Jesus*. And unless a person realizes how
complicated these questions are, he will hardly see the point
of this book.

Anyone who sets out to write a modern biography in accordance with the accepted standards of scholarship must begin by studying the general background of his subject. Now
historians cannot agree on the exact date of Jesus' birth—not
even to a year—and they argue about the date of his death:
some say he died on the 14th day of the Jewish month Nisan,
others on the 15th, and some opt for A.D. 30, while others
say it was A.D. 33. Apart from one story in St Luke's Gospel,
nothing at all is known about his childhood or youth, and
even the duration of his public ministry is hard to determine:
answers vary from one to three (or even four) years. Furthermore, within this period there are some events which it is almost impossible to date. Did Jesus drive the merchants out
of the temple at the beginning of his ministry (Jn 2:13–22),
or just before his Passion (Mt, Mk, Lk)? And if it was just
before the Passion, did it take place on the day of his solemn
entry into Jerusalem (Mt 21:12 and Lk 19:45) or on the day
after it (Mk 11:12, 15 ff.)? Was he anointed at Bethany two
days before the Jewish Passover (Mt 26:2, 6–13; Mk 14:1,
3–9) or a full week before it (Jn 12:1)? Was he scourged
before or after his condemnation by Pilate (Mt 27:26;
Jn 19:1)?

If we admit, with John, that Jesus made several visits to Jerusalem in the course of his ministry, why do the other gospels mention only one visit? And if we allow that our Lord once made a journey towards Tyre and Sidon and into the Decapolis, why does St John not mention it? Did Christ appear to his disciples after the Resurrection only in Jerusalem (Lk 24), or only in Galilee (Mt 28), or in both places (Jn 20–21)? At the end of the book we shall show that, in spite of all the uncertainties in our knowledge, it is possible to reconstruct in broad outline the story of our Lord's life, but it must be recognized from the very beginning that it is utterly impossible to write a life of our Lord of the modern, scientific type.

The essential facts are known, but many details which would be treasured by Christians simply cannot be discovered even by the most assiduous research, for the gospels record his words and actions in ways so different from one another that it is often impossible to decide which version, if any, relates the exact phrase he used or the precise circumstances of an event. A miracle which our Lord worked near Jericho provides an excellent illustration. According to Luke (18:35), he was just about to enter the town, whereas Matthew (20:29) and Mark (10:46) say that he was just leaving it. Mark (10:46) and Luke (18:35) say that one blind man was sitting by the roadside begging for alms; Matthew (20:30) says there were two. Which of these versions is closest to the real truth? It may be said that all these are minor details, but no historian can afford to neglect them. He must use his best efforts to discover which is the original narrative, or which version contains the oldest tradition, and therefore he must begin by subjecting the texts to literary analysis.

For it is not enough to examine the various ways in which the four gospels agree or disagree on details when they are relating the same story; the historian must also ask himself what type of literature he is dealing with. All four gospels claim to record history, but they do not conceal the theological purpose which underlies the historical record, and some modern readers will no doubt wonder whether it is possible to write history with a theological purpose without thereby falsifying the narrative.

In the fourth gospel, the symbolism is so intimately linked with the events recorded that it is very reasonable to ask whether some episodes have not been made up in order to illustrate a doctrine. Is it possible that John may have invented the story of the man born blind (Jn 9) in order to bring out the force of Jesus' saying, 'I am the light of the world' (8:12)? Could the raising of Lazarus from the tomb be a pious legend to illustrate what is meant by faith in him who is both 'resurrection and life' (Jn 11:25)?

Rationalist critics acknowledge that St Mark's Gospel contains the best descriptions and is the closest to the events; but even St Mark's Gospel is written to prove a point. Why does Mark say nothing about any public claim by Jesus to be the Messiah until the day when he was on trial for his life before the Sanhedrin (Mk 14:62)? Why does Mark stress that Jesus forbade his disciples to broadcast his claim? Why does Mark stress that the disciples did not understand the situation in which they were involved? It is clearly legitimate to ask whether Mark's clear-cut version is an exact record of what really happened, or whether it is the result of theological reflection. In other words, if the gospel records are dominated by apologetic considerations, can we still regard them as historical books?

The same problem becomes even more acute if we examine the way in which the Old Testament is used in the four gospels. Conservative theologians will say that the gospel narratives stress the Old Testament prophecies referring to our Lord precisely because he did fulfil these prophecies during his lifetime. But the critical historian can turn this argument round, and retort that because the evangelists believed that certain prophecies had been fulfilled, they made up episodes to illustrate the fulfilment. In that case, the gospel narratives would have originated not from real events but from a religious conviction that in Jesus prophecy had been fulfilled.

This is a problem which recurs on almost every page of the

gospels. Let us take as an example the infancy gospel in St Matthew (Mt 1-2). Matthew openly states that the virginal conception of Jesus took place to fulfil the prophecy of Isaiah (7:14): is he describing an historical event, or expounding a conviction, held by faith, that this prophecy had been fulfilled? The birth of Jesus in Bethlehem seems hard to reconcile with the fact that his native town, and his mother's home before his birth, was Nazareth: could it be that the evangelist has placed the birth of Jesus in Bethlehem in order to express his firm belief that Jesus had fulfilled the prophecy of Micah (5:1) about the birth of the Messianic king in Bethlehem? When Matthew tells of the flight into Egypt and of the return to Nazareth, is he merely saying that Jesus has fulfilled the prophecy of Hosea (11:1), 'Out of Egypt I have called my son'?

These are merely isolated instances, but similar ones recur throughout the gospels; the Passion story is written in the same style, and with the same careful attention to prophecy. There is certainly no attempt to give a coldly neutral account of what happened, as the rationalist sometimes seems to want. Now precisely because the gospels are written in this style by men wholeheartedly committed to Jesus, a host of problems arises. Did Jesus deliberately go to meet his death as the Servant of the Lord, or was he merely the victim of a miscarriage of justice? Did he himself know that by laying down his life he would win for men forgiveness of their sins, or is it merely that Christians have interpreted his death as having redemptive value? If as the Son of God he chose to lay down his life for men, then his voluntary self-sacrifice has a value reaching out beyond the boundaries of time; but there are many men who maintain that only the faith of Christians has given his death a more than passing significance.

These questions could be multiplied, and the problems they involve have given rise to what is often called, in England, the quest of the historical Jesus. In this quest we must first ask what is the value of the written sources from which all our knowledge of his earthly life derives? The reconstruction of past history depends mainly upon the extent to which

written evidence of a period survives, and the gospels teach
us a great deal about the life and beliefs of the early Christians. But is it possible to go back behind the gospels to an
earlier period, and, by using the tools of critical scholarship,
to learn about the life of Jesus on earth?[1] Before answering
that question, we must say something about the application
of scholarship to the Bible, and about its limitations.

3. Literary Criticism and Inspiration

Christians learn about our Lord in various ways—by listening to the passages from the gospels which are read aloud in
church, by reading about him, or by listening to sermons.
Most Christians become familiar with the events in the life
of Jesus in one or more of these ways; but those who are of
a critical turn of mind are not always satisfied by this alone.
They feel the need to have the sources for our knowledge of
Jesus' life examined and criticized scientifically, so that they
may fully appreciate the reasonableness of their faith. This
is not to disparage other ways of learning about our Lord,
for no Christian denies that our knowledge of him would be
incomplete if it did not include love and living faith; nor is it

[1] The fundamental work on this topic is still that of Albert
Schweitzer, first published in 1906 and re-issued in a sixth German
edition at Tübingen in 1951. An English translation appeared in
London in 1910, under the title *The Quest of the Historical Jesus:
A Critical Study of its Progress from Reimarus to Wrede*; it was
reprinted in 1954. The stream of monographs on the topic has
never ceased, *e.g.* V. H. Stanton, *The Gospels as Historical Documents*, 3 vols., Cambridge, 1909; L. de Grandmaison, *Jesus Christ:
His Person—His Message—His Credentials*, 3 vols., London, 1930,
1932, 1934; E. Hoskyns and N. Davey, *The Riddle of the New
Testament*, London, 1931, 3rd ed., 1947; C. H. Dodd, *History and
the Gospels*, London, 1938; M. Goguel, *The Life of Jesus*, London,
1954, with a 'History of the Lives of Jesus' on pp. 37–69; H. E. W.
Turner, *Jesus, Master and Lord*, London, 1953; J. M. Robinson,
A New Quest of the Historical Jesus, London, 1959, etc. See also
the *Introduction to the New Testament* edited by A. Robert and
A. Feuillet, New York, 1965.

here suggested that historical scholarship is, in matters of faith, a more reliable guide than the authoritative voice of the Church. But all the same, the desire to see the sources of our knowledge about Jesus examined scientifically is more than justified if we look closely at the Church's doctrine on revelation, and especially if we consider it in its connection with the Incarnation.

People in general, when they are asked to think about revelation, react instinctively in one of two ways: they tend either to idealize it or to rationalize it. Those who tend to idealize it are the men who have such a deep and instinctive appreciation of God's transcendence that they cannot easily conceive of God's revealing a message except by a kind of crude and very obvious intervention in history, *e.g.* by appearing in visible form. On the other hand, those who tend to rationalize revelation try to explain it as something belonging essentially to this earth. They look upon divine revelation not as the irruption of a transcendent being into this world, but as the sublimation of man's perennial desires, and sometimes suggest that the very idea of a God outside this world of time is only a projection of the human mind, a product of the imaginative powers of man. All men, they say, feel the need to posit some absolute reality which is far superior to their own finite nature and which gives them an absolute point of reference amid the vicissitudes of history. Hence they argue that we should regard revelation not just as something which once happened at a particular time and in a particular place, but as something taking place at every instant, in the depths of each human soul.

Either of these attitudes, if adopted exclusively, leads to error; but they are mutually corrective. The Fathers of the Church often spoke of the divine 'condescension'[2]; by this they meant that God 'condescended' to adopt the manner of life, of thought and of expression which was familiar to

---

[2] The term is applied to the Bible by Pope Pius XII in his encyclical letter *Divino Afflante Spiritu*, 1943 (in the English translation published by the Catholic Truth Society of London under the title 'Biblical Studies', §41).

men in order to raise men up to his own way of living and thinking. When we say, then, that the Bible is of divine origin, we do not mean that it came down ready-made from heaven by some kind of dictation; nor did the human body of our Lord come down from heaven—he was born 'from the line of David'. And just as the co-eternal Word of God took human flesh at a particular date and in a particular place, so the words of God in the Bible are clothed in human language of a particular age and a particular country. The Bible expresses in human language the Word of God, or (to put it the other way round), the Word of God is embodied in the Bible. And just as the believer has to discover the unique character of 'this Jesus' in the very acts which manifest him as completely human, so the reader of the Bible has to look for God's Word in language which both manifests and yet veils it.

This analogy between Jesus Christ, the Incarnate Word of God, and the Bible, which is the written Word of God, should prevent the Christian reader from being disturbed by the limitations, the gropings, the uncertainties and even the progress of biblical science. The disciples who lived with Jesus saw him at first as nothing more than a man, even though they occasionally caught a lightning glimpse of something in him which was more than human. Even those who were closest to him, like Peter and John, came to know the full truth about him only slowly, and after revising their estimate of him many times. They could not recognize the man from Nazareth as the Son of God until they received the gift of faith from his Father in heaven. The Christian, therefore, need not be anxious if modern minds do not grasp the full truth of the biblical message immediately.

But how are they to seek and find? The non-Christian can approach the Bible only as a human book (or rather, as a collection of books). He will, of course, want to know all that he can about it, relying solely on the best information that human scholarship can provide. All this is very reasonable, and no thinking Christian will be shocked or surprised by this approach. Believing that the Bible is the inspired Word of God does not mean treating the Bible as something too holy to be touched by human scholarship. On the contrary, just as the conviction that Jesus is Lord leads Christians to want to know more about him, so the belief that the Bible is divinely inspired spurs them to learn everything they can about the composition of those books in which God's eternal message is contained.

4. The Gospels as History

A word of explanation is needed here, to warn the reader that, if he is not to be disappointed, he must not expect too much. This book is going to discuss the 'historicity' or the 'historical value' of the gospels, but what do these terms imply? 'Historicity' is not a clearly defined concept, and its precise shade of meaning in any context will depend on the type of literature which is being discussed. Thucydides and Herodotus, Livy and Tacitus, Gibbon and Macaulay all claimed to be writing history; but would any of their works be classed as a masterpiece of historical accuracy today? This is not to assert that only twentieth-century scholars are capable of writing true history; but it is an assertion that the term 'history' can be applied to books of very different kinds. Everyone knows that it is not always easy to fit a book into a well-defined category of literature, because this involves making a judgment of its literary character, which in turn involves some knowledge of the living environment from which it came. And just as there are different types of literature, so there are different types of historical writing.

Bookshops and public libraries stock all kinds of books, but they are not all meant to be read in the same way. The man who settles down to a detective story does not work through it as if it were a piece of first-class historical scholarship, and Newman's *Parochial and Plain Sermons* would hardly satisfy the person who was looking for a travel book in breezy journalese. Moreover, different styles of writing can be found in one and the same book, and perhaps most of all in a newspaper. The sports page, the law report, the financial news, the exclusive interview, the editorial and the women's page are all written in different styles, each of which has its own rules. The point here is that each of them does have its own rules: there are only a limited number of ways of reporting a football match, a funeral or a fire, and the more a man knows about the conventions of a particular style, the better able he is to understand what is written in it.

Similar distinctions must be made when we talk about the 'historicity' or the 'historical character' of the gospels. In our modern Western civilization, certain conventions must be strictly observed by an author who wishes to write scientific history: no important fact may be omitted or overlooked, all the findings must be justified by trustworthy documentary evidence, and even the smallest details of this evidence must be rigorously checked before being used. If the work is a biography, the author must place on record all the known facts which might influence a judgment, or his work will be dismissed as tendentious. (It is clear that the gospels do not even attempt to present a biography of this modern, scientific kind.)

On the other hand, we may still call a book 'historical' even though it is not strictly scientific: in a popular work it is sufficient to relate accurately what happened. This is not meant to be a plea in favour of the positivist idea of history, as if photography were the most perfect of sciences, and the sole task of the historian to compile a catalogue of facts, without a word of interpretation. On the contrary, the bald narrative of events which for a time passed as history is long out-dated; indeed, modern historians, in their anxiety to interpret the past, have more in common with ancient historians than with their positivist predecessors of the nineteenth century. Moreover, they are far more conscious of the limits of human knowledge than were the nineteenth-century positivists: nowadays, an 'objective review' of what happened is seen to be an illusory ideal, impossible to achieve in practice. There is more sympathy today for the historian who tries to see his subject from the inside.

When, therefore, we say that the gospels are historical

works, we do not concede that they are 'less historical' than modern scientific dissertations, but we do assert that they represent a different type of historical writing. Only when this is understood can one go on to ask to what extent they supply reliable documentary evidence for the earthly life of Jesus of Nazareth.

Here the reader must be warned again not to expect too much of this book. He must not expect to find here attempted proofs for the historical character or historicity of every single episode in the gospels, or of every word our Lord spoke: that would demand a complete commentary on each of the four gospels. The purpose of the present book is to assess the historical character of the gospel tradition as a whole. Since the book aims to give an over-all view of the arguments, it cannot go into detail; but such an over-all view has its own intrinsic value. Objections may be raised against this point or that, but the convergence of arguments should enable us to reach a sure conclusion, even though we may not have certitude about each individual detail.

In order to discover the truth about Jesus of Nazareth, the historian has to put himself in the place of the authors who wrote about him, in order to see things as they saw them: he must try to put himself back mentally into the environment from which the gospels came. In practice, this means that a man who is reading the gospels must adjust his twentieth-century mind to a new type of writing, if he is to see the recorded events in their true perspective. A parallel from photography may help to illustrate this: when a lens is focused and the shutter opened to take in a wide panorama, certain details in the resulting picture may be blurred. Similarly, the blurring of some details is the price to be paid if we are to see the gospel teaching in the way its authors saw it—as a whole.

5. The Plan of the Book

The aim of this work is to know the real truth about Jesus of Nazareth. The classical way of achieving this aim was based

on sound historical principles: first one treated the question
of authenticity—proving that the gospels were written by particular authors, at a particular date. Then the authenticity
of any controverted passages was discussed, and after that
the historicity of each gospel. First external evidence was
cited, and then the internal evidence was amassed: the conclusion was that the gospels were written by well-informed,
sincere and therefore trustworthy authors.

It would be ungracious to reject this method of argument
out of hand, but it does seem that the way in which it is presented needs to be amplified and modified, if we are to take
account of changes in methods of literary criticism during
recent years. The principal contribution made by modern
biblical scholars concerns the environment in which the evangelists lived; without a knowledge of this environment, it is
difficult to appreciate the finer points of their works. Consequently, the presentation of the arguments in favour of the
gospels needs to be modified and brought up to date.

The authorship of the gospels is still to some extent under debate, but the question which mainly interests us is
whether the qualifications the writers claimed to possess
can stand up to an examination by modern critical standards.
We shall therefore not discuss authorship in detail, but instead concentrate on a new approach. Two reasons seem to
justify this fresh presentation of the evidence.

Mark and Luke, according to tradition, were not themselves witnesses of the life of Jesus of Nazareth, and to say
that Mark had his information from Peter, and Luke from
Paul, is not a sufficient guarantee of their testimony. The
author of the fourth gospel claims he was a witness, but his
gospel was written long afterwards, and is 'an utterly unique
work which belongs to no clearly-defined type of writing, in
which history, theology and mystical contemplation are all
inextricably combined'.[3] The first gospel is probably a re-
casting of a work attributed to the apostle Matthew. Conse-

---

[3] L. Venard, 'Historique (Genre)', in the *Supplément au Diction-
naire de la Bible*, 4, Paris, 1941, c. 29.

quently, not one of the four evangelists can be called a 'witness' in the sense in which the word is used by modern critical historians.

On the other hand, Matthew, Mark and Luke regarded themselves as being above all 'Servants of the Word', anxious to pass on the facts as they had received them, after checking their reliability. These facts came to them in forms which were already fixed by tradition, and each of these three evangelists fitted the facts into a general framework which had also been handed down to them. Only John dared to alter the traditional framework: the other three evangelists kept to it, and the phrases by which they link together the different narratives are so easily detected that we can work out what traditional material existed before the compilation of the Synoptic Gospels. Now are the 'authors' to be held responsible for the written material which was in existence before they wrote? Yes, in the sense that they accepted the traditions which had been handed down to them; no in another sense, for they did not claim to pass judgment on the Church which handed down those traditions. In short, the historian must examine critically the credentials of the evangelists, but above all he must examine and pass judgment on the traditions of the early Christians, for whom the evangelists were spokesmen. Only then can he decide how far the gospels teach us the truth about what really happened in the life of Jesus of Nazareth.

Our argument therefore will not follow the classical lines. Instead, we shall attempt to synthesize the data, working back from the second century to the oral tradition behind the gospels. At each stage we shall endeavour to find out all we can about the four gospels by using all the available external and internal evidence both together and separately; and by this means we shall be able to see step by step in what sense the gospels are historical. Thus the classical presentation of the argument will be seen in a new way.

In this book, therefore, the gospels will be examined in three ways:

(1) As one Gospel under four forms—what St Irenaeus calls

'the fourfold Gospel'—constituting the rule of faith for the Church. This is how the Gospel was regarded in the second century. After examining this early traditional teaching, we shall see what a modern man might think about the content of the gospels considered all together.

(2) As four separate gospels. This will involve an examination of what is meant by a 'Gospel', and internal criticism will show in what sense each of these four gospels deserves to be called an historical work.

(3) Finally we shall try to examine the tradition that was committed to writing in the gospels as we now have them. This will involve close attention to the environment in which this tradition took shape; and this in turn will enable us to say something positive about the nature of this tradition, about its value as historical evidence and about the source from which it ultimately came.

After having examined the gospels in these three ways, we shall be in a position to sketch (in the final part) an historical portrait of Jesus of Nazareth.

THE GOSPELS
AND
THE JESUS OF HISTORY

PART I

THE FOURFOLD GOSPEL

The four gospels are almost the only sources we possess for the life of Jesus. Contemporary works by non-Christian writers hardly mention his name, and when they do, they tell us next to nothing about him. Some may regret this lack of evidence from non-Christian writers, on the ground that their testimony would be more objective, less prejudiced, than that of Christians. It ought to be firmly asserted, against those who hold this view, that unbelief can affect a man's judgment just as profoundly as faith can; and that any historian who claims to weigh the evidence impartially must allow for the possible influence of either factor, faith or unbelief, when assessing the trustworthiness of sources.

Information from non-Christian sources is scanty. All that can be gathered from pagan authors is that a person did once exist whose name was Jesus or Christ, and that he was crucified in Palestine during the reign of the emperor Tiberius. The Jewish historian Flavius Josephus tells us a little, but not much, more. In the past there was much argument about the authenticity of a text in his *Jewish Antiquities* (XVIII, 3, 63–64) which refers to Jesus: some scholars held that part of it, and others that all of it, had been interpolated by a Christian hand. A recent article by Fr A. Pelletier seems to have established conclusively the original wording[1]: the text, stripped of interpolation, runs as follows:

[1] 'L'originalité du témoignage de Flavius Josèphe sur Jésus', in *Recherches de Science Religieuse*, 52 (1964), pp. 177–205: the trans-

'About this time there lived Jesus, a wise man. For he was one who wrought surprising feats, and was a teacher of such people as accept the truth gladly. He won over many Jews and many of the Greeks. When Pilate, upon hearing him accused by men of the highest standing amongst us, had condemned him to be crucified, those who had in the first place come to love him did not give up their affection for him. On the third day he appeared to them restored to life, for the prophets of God had prophesied these and countless other marvellous things about him. And the tribe of the Christians, so called after him, has still to this day not disappeared.'

This statement by Josephus is an eloquent assertion that the group known as Christians was considered to be closely connected with the community of Jesus' disciples. But it is only from the New Testament, and principally from the gospels, that we can learn any details about the life and teaching of Jesus.

In this first part of the book, which represents the first stage in an argument which must lead us back to the historical Jesus, the gospels will be considered as a whole. The reason is that the content of all four gospels taken as a whole can be examined, weighed up and checked over in general, as an outsider might see them; afterwards we shall pass on to a literary analysis of the individual gospels.

The first chapter of Part I deals with the writers of the second century of the Christian era. They certainly did not trouble themselves over problems of literary analysis, but in their own way they did raise interesting questions (as we shall see) about the gospels.

Working backwards, we shall then (in Chapter 2) examine the evidence of the epistles in the New Testament, for they were written only shortly after, or even before, the gospels, and their authors were very close to the events described.

In Chapter 3 we shall consider the content of the gospels

_____

lation above is taken from that in the Loeb edition of Josephus, vol. 9, London, 1965, pp. 49–51.

as a whole in the way in which a modern man sees them. The purpose of Chapter 3 is to show that the gospels do not contradict anything which is known from other sources.

In Part I, then, the general content of the gospels will be considered in three different ways. (1) What did men think of the story fifty or a hundred years after the gospels were written? (2) At the time when the gospels were being committed to writing, what did contemporary Christians who knew something about the events think about their content? (3) What (in general) should we think about the gospel story today? In short, the purpose of this first part is to find out whether there is a *prima facie* case for saying that the general content of the gospels has real historical value.

CHAPTER 1

The Gospels and the Gospel

Some critical historians try to assess the historical value of the gospels without giving due consideration to the evidence of tradition in the first and second centuries after Christ. Many historians begin like this, more or less by-passing the evidence of the second century, but it must be candidly confessed that they are not altogether to blame. All too often they have been led to undervalue ancient tradition by hearing certain Christian apologists claim that it provides clear proof of the truth of Christianity. We have all heard statements like 'The gospels must be historical documents because they were regarded as such by Christians in the early centuries', and 'The gospels must have been written by Matthew, Mark, Luke and John because the early Christians said they were'. Grossly over-simplified statements of this kind have prejudiced many people in the past, but on the other hand they are not entirely devoid of truth, and the fact that they are over-simplified does not justify a man in going to the other extreme and pretending that early traditions about the gospels are worthless, and of no interest to us today.

1. The Gospels and Oral Tradition

From the beginning of the second century the Church was constantly using the four gospels, basing its life on their message and keeping that message alive by its preaching. A work by St Justin written about A.D. 150 records that it was even then an ancient custom to read the 'memoirs of the Apostles which are called gospels' every Sunday, when Christians gathered to celebrate the Lord's Supper.[1] Throughout the second century those few Christians who were also writers made continual use of the gospels (especially Matthew and John), though they did not always cite them word for word.

Consequently, the disappearance of the original autograph manuscripts is not of too great importance: they were written on papyrus, a brittle and perishable material which can survive only in a climate like that of the dry sands of Egypt. The oldest complete manuscripts still surviving (e.g. the splendid copies in the Vatican Library or in the British Museum) were written in the fourth century, when parchment replaced papyrus. But even in the second century, the gospels were copied and recopied, passed on from one man to another and even translated into Latin, Syriac and Coptic: they were, in short 'real best-sellers'.[2]

As an example of their widespread popularity, we may mention the Rylands Papyrus, discovered in Upper Egypt and now in the John Rylands Library, Manchester. On one side it contains Jn 18:31–34 and on the other Jn 18:37–38: it was probably written around A.D. 130.[3]

The fact that the gospels were so widely read is impressive, but it does raise problems. Was the written text superseding that oral tradition which it was meant to embody? Were the gospels becoming more important than the Gospel?

Contrary to what we might expect, the transition from oral preaching to a written gospel was not everywhere regarded with favour. Eusebius, citing a passage from Clement of Alexandria, tells us that, when Mark put his gospel into writing, St Peter himself was slightly worried, and apprehensive of possible dangers. Eusebius tells us that those

[1] 1 *Apol.* 66, 3 = *PG* 6:429 = *ANCL* Justin, p. 64.

[2] Cf. L. Cerfaux, *The Four Gospels*, London, 1960, pp. 128–129.

[3] It was identified as a piece of the fourth gospel in 1933, and is known as Papyrus 52. See C. H. Roberts, *An unpublished fragment of the Fourth Gospel in the John Rylands Library*, Manchester, 1935.

who listened to Peter speaking with the power of the Spirit were not satisfied with the oral teaching of God's message. Like all those who had never known and never heard our Lord himself, they dreaded the time when the death of the apostles would deprive them of direct witnesses about the life of Jesus: 'they resorted to appeals of every kind to induce Mark (whose gospel we have), as he was a follower of Peter, to leave them in writing a summary of the instruction they had received by word of mouth, nor did they let him go until they had persuaded him, and thus became responsible for the writing of what is known as the Gospel according to Mark.' Peter himself, it seems, was not consulted, but presented with a *fait accompli*. 'It is said that, on learning by revelation of the spirit what had happened, the apostle was delighted at their enthusiasm and authorized the reading of the book in the churches.'[4]

However, another tradition related by Clement gives a rather different version of these events. 'Mark made his gospel available to all who wanted it, and when Peter heard about this, he made no objection and gave no special encouragement.'[5]

This is very significant. Peter was a Jew, brought up in a civilization in which writing was mainly used to help a failing memory to retain the lessons learnt orally from a master. Perhaps Peter could not bring himself to take an active part in a work whose purpose he did not really understand, but which seemed to be imposed on him by the Holy Spirit; he may have consented, just as he had agreed to receive into the Church the pagan Cornelius, because he believed it was the work of the Holy Spirit. Christianity had to tear itself away from the land of Palestine in order to penetrate the Greco-Roman world, but the transition from a civilization in which oral teaching dominated to one in which writing was the normal means of communication could not have been psy-

[4] Eusebius, *HE* II, 15 = PG 20:172. The above translation is taken from the version by G. A. Williamson in the Penguin Classics, London, 1965, p. 88.

[5] *ibid*. VI, 14, 7 = PG 20:552 = Penguin Classics, p. 254.

chologically easy for those born in Palestine. And perhaps the point of Clement's story here is that Peter had doubts about what might happen to the 'Good News', if it were set down once and for all 'on paper'.

Such fears were destined to disappear once Christianity was firmly rooted in the Roman world, but we find evidence of similar misgivings in the writings of Papias, a bishop in Asia Minor around A.D. 100. This simple and good-natured man was no genius, and his naïve credulity was not exactly appreciated by Eusebius, a critical historian who dismissed him rather too quickly as 'a man of very small intelligence'.[6] But even Eusebius has a certain respect for him, for if Papias did not have a very penetrating mind, he did at least humbly repeat what he had learnt, and could claim with justice that he had been the close friend of the famous Polycarp, who, according to St Irenaeus, had been a disciple of the apostles.

From this point of view, Papias remains a model for all who would adopt a reverent and religious attitude towards the gospels. He tells us that when he set out to write his five books entitled 'An Explanation of the Words of the Lord' he did not consult glib talkers or scholarly writings, but took great care to trace exactly the thread of tradition by which he was connected with the Lord himself: through the elders of the Church, he had contact with the disciples and the apostles. This is how he ends his account of his method: he had been careful not merely to listen to what the elders said, but 'to memorize' it accurately. 'For I did not imagine that things out of books would help me as much as the utterances of a living and abiding voice.'[7] The voice to which Papias refers was simply the voice of the Church as represented by the elders, the disciples and the apostles: it alone could bring to life what is recorded in the gospels. Papias's point was that in order to give an authentic interpretation of the gospels, one must 'be inside' that living tradition to

[6] Eusebius, HE III, 39, 13 = PG 20:300 = Penguin Classics, p. 152.

[7] ibid. III, 39, 4 = PG 20:297 = Penguin Classics, p. 150.

which the four gospels, precious and eternally valid as they are, merely bear witness.

Now at the latest in A.D. 130, and more probably from A.D. 100 onwards, Papias noticed that the gospels, within fifty years of their composition, were no longer regarded as holy books, beyond criticism, to be venerated with humble faith: they had already become a topic on which men would give free rein to their imagination and reason. Understandably, Papias felt afraid, and felt the need to justify his own commentary.

In fact, everyone who has no contact with the early witnesses of our Lord's life finds the four gospels a rather unusual kind of literature. If we consider the subject they are treating, they seem to be excessively restrained; they are full of surprising antinomies, if their doctrine does come from God; and they often seem to contradict one another when describing historical events. In short, one can say that unless the gospels are read in the light of the Church's tradition, the reader will probably want to fill out the record they give, to expurgate them to some extent, to clarify them and above all to harmonize them.

2. Apocryphal Gospels

The first temptation is to want to fill out the gospels by using legends. The four gospels, in fact, do not claim to give an exhaustive account of the life of our Saviour, as the closing words of the fourth gospel expressly state: 'Jesus did many other signs also, which are not written in this book. If they were written down one by one, the world itself, I think, would not be big enough to hold the books which would have to be written' (Jn 21:25). Yet Christians naturally want to know everything possible about Jesus' life on earth and to collect the slightest hints from any source which may contain some detail about it.

So it was that certain sayings of Jesus were carefully preserved in works other than the gospels. In the Acts of the Apostles (20:35) Paul ends his farewell speech to the elders of the Church of Ephesus by reminding them 'of the words of the Lord Jesus who himself said "It is more blessed to give than to receive"'. Certain manuscripts of the gospels (not few in number nor late in date) contain very interesting additions which might be authentic, though one cannot say so for certain. Thus the man with the withered hand (Mt 12:10) is said to have been a mason, and in Lk 6:4 a manuscript now in the University Library at Cambridge, the *Codex Bezae*, inserts a saying of Jesus: 'That same day Jesus seeing a man working on the sabbath day, said to him: Man, if you know what you are doing, you are blessed; but if you do not know, you are accursed and a transgressor of the Law'. St Justin records a detail not found in the gospels, namely, that our Lord was born in a cave near Bethlehem.[8] There is certainly much evidence to corroborate the statement in the fourth gospel that not everything was written down.

Not all these traditions, however, are authentic. Even in early times, those who tried to supplement the written text found themselves combining a great deal of pious imagination with the gospel text, and the imaginative part did not always have an historical basis. There are many points which are scarcely touched on in the canonical gospels and about which the faithful are, and always have been, curious: in order to satisfy this curiosity, various stories began to be told. They are preserved in what we call the 'apocryphal gospels'.[9]

Some of the stories attempt to make the Christian faith more credible by relating how unbelievers had themselves witnessed various mysteries. To illustrate the danger involved in this type of story, let us cite in detail the oldest apocryphal work still extant. When Papias was writing his commentary and carefully seeking out authentic witnesses, a little book (no doubt one among many) was also circulating unofficially. One fragment of it, discovered in 1886, describes the Resur-

---

[8] *Dial.* 78 = PG 6:657 = ANCL Justin, p. 196.

[9] There is a splendid English edition of these documents, edited by R. McL. Wilson: *New Testament Apocrypha*, vol. 1, *Gospels and Related Writings*, London, 1963.

rection of Christ: it is obviously meant for an unsophisticated public, and the anxiety to convince those who do not believe is very evident. Under the very eyes of the soldiers who stood on guard at the tomb, two men came down from heaven: the stone rolled back of its own accord, and the two young men entered the tomb. The soldiers went to call the centurion. 'And while they were relating what they had seen, they saw three men coming out of the tomb. Two of them were helping the third, and a cross followed them. The heads of the two reached right up to heaven, but that of him whom they were leading by the hand was higher than the heavens, and they heard a voice out of the heavens crying, "Have you preached to them that sleep?", and from the cross came the reply, "Yes". Then the soldiers decided to go and warn Pilate about these happenings.'[10]

The great mistake of the authors of the apocryphal gospels was trying to prove too much. If it is possible to prove beyond all doubt to an unbeliever that Jesus rose from the grave, there is no mystery left, nor any freedom in belief. Stories like the one just cited, when compared with the sober accounts in the four canonical gospels, can only be regarded as a profanation. Still worse are what St Jerome called the *deliramenta apocryphorum*—the wild dreams of apocryphal writers, who argued that, since Jesus was God, there was no harm in attributing to him the most fantastic miracles. The fact that the miracles were unbelievably odd was of no importance, provided that the reader was thereby inspired with a salutary fear. And so we read of the child Jesus killing children who made fun of him and shortly afterwards raising some others to life.[11]

The very fact that these apocryphal stories gained (and still do gain) an audience shows how necessary it was to fix the gospel message in writing, and for the Church to take a firm

[10] *Gospel of Peter* 10–11 or 39–43; in the edition by Wilson, vol. 1, p. 186.

[11] *The Infancy Gospel of Thomas*, 3–5; in the *New Testament Apocrypha* edited by Wilson, vol. 1, pp. 393–394.

stand by informing the faithful which gospels were genuine and which were not. This was undoubtedly a step forward. But the reader must remember that when the four gospels in the Bible were put into writing, their authors did not intend to provide a substitute for living tradition; on the contrary, the written gospels were meant to be explained by oral tradition in the Church. The gospels are unlike any other kind of writing: they are permanently related to that Holy Spirit who keeps alive tradition in the Church.

3. The Rationalist Approach: Gnosticism

Alongside these crude and naïve legends there grew up during the second century another and a very different kind of literature concerned with the teaching of the Gospel. It is called 'Gnostic literature', from the Greek *gnosis*, meaning literally 'knowledge', and the movement whose ideas it contains is called 'Gnosticism'. In the second century certain groups who called themselves Christians claimed to have secret sources of information about God and Jesus, which had been handed down within their group. Like the authors of the apocryphal legends, the authors of Gnostic literature sought to fill out the sober narratives of the canonical gospels; unlike the authors of the apocrypha, they were moved not by piety but by a desire to rationalize the faith. The results were even more disastrous.

Among these Gnostics who harnessed the Gospel revelation to the service of their own theories and led simple souls astray, there was one in particular against whom the great Christian writers of the century (Justin, Irenaeus and Tertullian) all took up arms: Marcion. Marcion, in fact, succeeded in founding a dissident Church by preaching a very coherent body of doctrine which he set out as a rule of faith.

Marcion was brought up in an environment sympathetic to Gnosticism, and was himself a man of very fixed ideas: his central conviction was that God is good, but has nothing to do with this earth, which is intrinsically evil, and the work of a secondary demi-god. God (he said) could never have been responsible for the cruel acts which the Bible attributes to him, and therefore the Old Testament could not have been divinely inspired. He added that the writings of the apostles ought to be expurgated of all traces of the Old Testament, for they must have been interpolated by Jewish-Christian forgers. 'No man can serve two masters'—the kindly God of the New Testament and the cruelly just God of the Old. 'No one pours new wine into old wine-skins': we must therefore find the true revelation by discarding the false ideas of the Old Testament.

It was not hard for Marcion to collect examples showing that the Old Testament contradicted the New: and therefore he jettisoned the Old. But even the New Testament could not be accepted in its entirety. Marcion accepted as inspired only the writings of St Paul (because Paul speaks so severely about the Mosaic Law) and the Gospel according to Luke (because it was the least Jewish of the four, the one in which God's kindness is most heavily stressed, and therefore the gospel which could most easily be restored to its 'primitive purity'). Marcion was certainly an intellectual, and tried to do the work of expurgation and reconstruction with finesse, but in the end was forced to use his blue pencil rather freely. Abraham had to be cut out of the gospel story; God was no longer the creator of this material world, and therefore had no interest in the birds of the air or the wild lilies. Jesus, too, had no connection with this earth and he was not born of a woman. Marcion therefore eliminated the first two chapters of Luke's Gospel, and claimed that Jesus came down directly from heaven.

What is the relevance of Marcion for us today? As Tertullian says, Marcion 'cut the Scriptures to pieces in order to adapt them to his own ideas'.[12] He is therefore the forerunner of all those who start with an initial conviction about Jesus and then set aside all the texts which do not harmonize with their preconceived ideas. That is rationalism.

[12] *De praescr.* 38 = PL 2:52 = ANCL Tert. II, p. 46.

4. The Tendency to Harmonize the Gospels

And yet another difficulty was felt in the second century. Apocryphal writers had tried to embellish the sober narratives in the gospels by adding colourful legendary stories, and the Gnostics had tried to rid the text of interpolated passages: a third group was worried by the partial inconsistencies found in the gospels. Consequently this group also interfered with the text, not by adding to the text or by suppressing parts of it, but by trying to harmonize texts which were partly similar and partly dissimilar.

All sorts of corrections were tried. It seemed impossible that Jesus should have taught his disciples two different versions of the Our Father, and so a number of scribes inserted into their manuscripts at Lk 11:2 the phrase from Mt 6:10: 'Thy will be done.' In this way one scribe after another, moved more by good will and piety than by a scrupulous regard for the words of the text he was copying, made changes in the original text. Origen condemned them for their 'depraved audacity',[13] and St Jerome wrote to Pope Damasus that 'the numerous errors in our manuscripts result first and foremost from the fact that those passages in the gospels which record the same event have been filled out from one another. To avoid the difficulties in the four gospels, men have taken as a model the first account they have read, and then corrected the others to bring them into line with it.'[14] In other words, the scribes tried to make the gospels say more than the text contained.

Around A.D. 160, some twenty years after Marcion, there arose a man who was not satisfied to reduce difficulties to a minimum by combining different texts from time to time, whenever there was a partial inconsistency. He took a short cut, and united the four texts into one narrative, i.e. into what we nowadays call a 'harmony'. His name was Tatian.

Tatian was born in Assyria. He was a man of wide cul-

[13] In Matt. lib. 15, 14 = PG 13:1293.
[14] Epist. ad Damasum, Praef. in evangelia = PL 29:560.

ture, thoroughly familiar with Greek thought, and was converted to Christianity by reading the Bible. But he was also a stubborn, opinionated man, who eventually left the Church and fell into heresy. His errors, however, and his personal opinions have hardly affected in any way the work by which he is mainly remembered, the 'Diatessaron' or 'Harmony' of the gospels. Taking as the basis of his work St Matthew's Gospel, he wove into it the additional information to be found in the other gospels.

Let us take as an example the story of the Temptation. Substantially, the text of Matthew (4:1–11) is retained, but Tatian decided to fill it out with details from the other Synoptics. The introduction, which is rather colourless in Matthew, is replaced by the more lively words of Mark: 'And immediately the Spirit led him into the wilderness to be tempted by Satan, and he lived with the wild beasts' (Mk 1:12–13). According to Matthew, Satan's promise was rather vague: 'I will give you all this, if you will fall down at my feet and adore me' (Mt 4:9). This verse is replaced by words from Luke: 'I will give you this power and the glory of these kingdoms, for they are given to me, and I give them to whom I choose. If you, then, will kneel down before me, you shall have them all' (Lk 4:6–7). Even St Luke's little note that the devil showed Jesus all the kingdoms of the world 'in an instant' (Lk 4:5) is incorporated into Tatian's 'Harmony'. Finally, Tatian inserts, before the ending given in Matthew, that given in Luke: 'So, having tried every kind of temptation, the devil left him until the appointed time' (Lk 4:12). The aim of Tatian's work was to omit nothing that was found in the gospel tradition, and this often led to very ingenious combinations for the work was meant to be a popular one. Over the centuries, his Diatessaron was destined to be the model for many similar works, equally popular and equally ingenious.

The Diatessaron had an incredible success in the West from the Middle Ages onwards, and it was even more popular in the East. The original was composed around 170–180, very probably in Syriac; it was translated into Greek some time before 220; and it has been translated into Armenian, Arabic, Persian, Latin, Georgian, and many other languages.

Its astounding success did not protect it from fierce attacks. The Syrian Church, for example, had a translation of the four gospels by the year 200, and perhaps even earlier. The Diatessaron or 'combined gospel' was in direct competition with the 'separate gospels', and it was not until a certain Rabbula, bishop of Edessa between 411 and 431, issued an edict in favour of the four separate gospels that the issue was settled. Somewhat later Theodoret, bishop of Cyrrhus from around 423 to 458, intervened in a still more radical manner when he discovered that about a quarter of the churches under his jurisdiction were using the Diatessaron. 'The faithful did not perceive the malice of this composition, and used it in all simplicity as an abridged version. I myself have found more than two hundred copies of it in places of honour in our churches, but I have removed the lot and put in their place the gospels of the four evangelists'.[15]

There were, then, two tendencies in the Church. The official tendency was to pay great attention to the preservation of the integral texts of the four evangelists, while the popular tendency was to make the text of the gospels more accessible by fusing them into a one harmonious narrative. The latter tendency was too deeply rooted to disappear at the command of a bishop; it was destined to flourish again in the thirteenth century, in Flanders, and for long afterwards, in the many books which have been published under the title of *A Gospel Harmony* or *Four Gospels in One*. They still have their appeal in our own day.

As an introduction to the gospels, these 'digests' have their worth, but if they are not quickly superseded by the four gospels themselves, they can lead to false notions about the true history of our Lord and about the canon of Scripture: 'Our four gospels were not made to be harmonized. Each of them draws an authentic portrait of Jesus. To mix their traits is to introduce into the divine work an element of human

[15] *Haereticarum fabularum Compendium I,* 20 = PG 83:372.

thought, a choice which cannot but be personal and arbitrary; and in any case, in proportion as one refrains from making it a personal work—and Tatian hardly attempts this—it is to substitute a blurred image for the four incomparable portraits.'[16] There is no way of reaching full knowledge of Christ our Lord except by taking seriously the four gospels as they have been handed down in the Church since apostolic times.

5. Conclusion

Although this study of the writers of the second century has not provided much in the way of concrete information about the life-story of Jesus himself, it is of first importance for anyone who wants to approach the gospels with the right attitude. It should forewarn him against the three temptations which faced the Christians of those days. Marcion and Tatian and the authors of the apocryphal gospels were all trying to come nearer to the truth, but their wayward efforts needed to be constantly rectified by the living Church. The written text cannot be brought to life except within the Church which possesses a living tradition.

The achievement of the Church in the second century was that it worked out the canon of the gospels. From the time of Irenaeus onwards, tradition on this point was firmly fixed, but this tradition can never afford to be cut off from the environment which gave it birth. Christianity is not the religion of a book, like Mahommedanism, where the teaching of the Qur'an is the sole arbiter for all time. In the course of the second century there was a continual tension between written and oral tradition, between Scripture and Tradition, between the four written gospels and the one living Gospel.

It is difficult to hold a balance between the two. But if a creative imagination tries to add to the data given in the gospels in defiance of the rule of Tradition, then the canonical text is there to provide a boundary beyond which imag-

[16] L. Cerfaux, *The Four Gospels*, London, 1963, p. 108.

ination must not go. And if a rationalist mind tries to make the book subservient to its own philosophy, the evidence of the four gospels is there to show that it cannot be done without suppressing certain texts. There is always a court of appeal from the four books to the one and only Gospel embodied in the Tradition of the Church, and this tradition embraces all four books as witnesses of one faith. St Irenaeus has traced out the correct attitude in masterly fashion. The Gospel is one, but it is expressed in the four gospels; the gospels are four in number, but they can only be understood with the aid of that Holy Spirit who unifies their teaching in the Church.

CHAPTER 2

Jesus and the Theologians
of the New Testament

During the second century the Church slowly became conscious of the 'canon' of the gospels, that is, of the fact that the Gospel according to Matthew, Mark, Luke and John contained the essential truth about the life-story of Jesus. Yet before A.D. 150, Christian writers (with one exception—St Justin) paid little attention to the written texts of the gospels: they never quote them, and never regarded them as having the authority of inspired Scripture in the same way as the Old Testament. Their attitude, however, does not diminish the value of the gospels, for it is easily explained: these men lived only one generation after the apostles—at a time, therefore, when the influence of those first witnesses was still keenly felt. Our next task, therefore, is to see what those first witnesses said. We shall limit ourselves to the witness of St Paul in his letters, to that of the epistle to the Hebrews and of the First Epistle of St John.

These writings raise two crucial questions about the unity of Christian revelation. Why do the epistles centre around the teaching of Jesus and the mystery of his personality, and not around his life on earth? How is one to explain the fact that the earthly Jesus has, so to speak, been displaced by the figure of Christ in glory? The evidence given in the last chapter led us to think that the life of Jesus on earth was the essential point in the Christian faith, and yet in the New Testament, outside the gospels, doctrinal problems seem to have commanded far greater interest than the life of Jesus on earth.

This question must be discussed briefly before we pass on to the three types of theology in the New Testament.[1]

1. The Life of Jesus in the Light of Easter Day

The most obvious answer to the question just raised is that the epistles were never meant to provide a complete statement of all that the Church taught: they are simply letters. They certainly contain teaching, but it is not arranged in an orderly catechesis; most of the epistles are letters of encouragement exhorting the Christians of a certain place to remain faithful on some point of doctrine which was being contradicted there. It would be foolish to expect the writer of such a letter to repeat over and over again the whole of the apostolic teaching.

In addition to this general answer, another fact must be underlined, for it is of first importance. Even though the interest of the authors of the epistles centres not on the earthly life of Jesus, but on the risen and glorified Christ, it is nonetheless possible to reconstruct from their writings the broad outlines of Jesus' earthly life, as follows.

Jesus was descended from Abraham (Gal 3:16), of the tribe of Judah (Heb 7:14) and of the family of David (Rom 1:3). Born of a woman, he lived under the Jewish Law (Gal 4:4; Rom 15:8), and had 'brothers' (1 Cor 9:5) of whom one was called James (Gal 1:19). The apostles, among whom were Cephas and John (1 Cor 1:12; 9:5; Gal 1:18; 2:9, 11) saw him after his Resurrection when they were gathered together (1 Cor 15:5). The only event of the public life which is mentioned is the Transfiguration: it took place on a holy mountain (2 Pet 1:16–18). On the night he was betrayed, Jesus instituted the sacrament of his sacrifice, during a last meal (1 Cor 11:23–25). Before he died, he suffered a terrible agony of soul (Heb 5:7–9); from the moment his Passion

[1] The excellent little book entitled *The Riddle of the New Testament*, by E. Hoskyns and N. Davey, London, 3rd ed., 1947, has been an inspiration not only for this chapter but for the whole of the present work.

began he was cruelly insulted (Rom 15:3), but in spite of this did not return insult for insult (1 Pet 2:23). It was under Pontius Pilate (1 Tim 6:13), about Eastertime (1 Cor 5:7), that he was put to death by the Jews (1 Thess 2:15), by crucifixion (Gal 3:1; 1 Cor 11:23; 2:2) on a wooden cross (1 Pet 2:24) outside the city gate (Heb 13:12). He was buried (1 Cor 15:4; Rom 6:4), rose again (1 Cor 15:4), appeared to many of the brethren (1 Cor 15:5–8) and ascended into heaven (Eph 4:10), where he is seated at the right hand of God (Col 3:1; Heb 1:3); from there he will come back at the end of time (1 Thess 1:10; 4:16).

These incidental references show that the epistles were addressed to people who were already familiar with the lifestory of Jesus from the preaching of the apostles. The fact is of first importance, but it does not solve completely the problem facing a historian. Why do these epistles, which along with the gospels are recognized by the Church as a 'rule of faith', pay so little attention to the events in the public life of our Lord, and why do they not frequently cite his actual words? What explanation is there for their astonishing omissions? The epistle to the Hebrews, for example, speaks at great length about Jesus' sacrifice and about the repetition of sacrifices (Heb 9:11–28; 10:5–18), but never once mentions the fact that he instituted the Holy Eucharist.

The difficulty becomes even more acute if we compare the teaching of the theologians of the New Testament with the message in the gospel. At the beginning of the century Adolf von Harnack and Albert Schweitzer suggested that there was a dichotomy between 'the gospel of Christ' (*evangelium Christi*) and 'the gospel about Christ' (*evangelium de Christo*), and each of them tried (though from totally different starting points) to argue from the second to the first, in an endeavour to go back behind Paul and John to the true historical Jesus.

It was a most attractive plan, for these brilliant scholars worked hard to find the reason for the apparent dichotomy between the epistles and the gospels, and drew conclusions which corresponded exactly with the impression left after a first reading of St Paul. Does not Paul present a picture of a Christ who is the object of faith and who has few features in common with the Jesus whose life is recorded in the Synoptic Gospels? Were there, then, two versions of Christianity, one for simple people, presented in the Synoptics, and one for more advanced Christians, worked out by the highly speculative minds of Paul or John? This idea has ever since commended itself to critical scholars—Loisy and Bultmann, for example.

For many of these men, 'Paulinism' is a speculative system of religious thought, a *'gnosis'*, derived from the Greek mystery religions. Paul preached a mystique of 'rebirth', of 'incorporation', of death and mystical life,[2] and these very terms seem to be so many clues pointing to the mysteries of Eleusis or to the Iranian myth about primordial Man. The earthly existence of Jesus is, these men say, meaningless unless it is seen as a convenient way of teaching simple-minded men about the spiritual experience of the first Christians.

Some go even further and maintain that Christianity is not essentially connected with a unique happening in past time (the life of Jesus), but is a vision in which the mystical experience common to all humanity is crystallized: this is a favourite theory of specialists in the history of religion, and of those depth psychologists who study the 'archetypes' which dominate the human mind.

The historical life-story of Jesus, considered in this way, serves only to express eternal and life-giving truths: it has the same importance as a fable or myth. According to this theory, the story of Jesus' Passion and Resurrection was told not primarily because it had in itself a redemptive significance, but because it presented Christians with a model of life to imitate. Thus the paradox of a once-for-all event (the death and resurrection of Christ) is suppressed, but the rites and symbols of Christianity are retained in order to satisfy the religious needs of mankind.

[2] See, for example, A. Schweitzer, *The Mysticism of Paul the Apostle*, 2nd ed., London, 1953.

Bultmann sums up the difference between Paul and the Synoptic Gospels by referring to the words of the Apostle himself: 'From now on I no longer want to know Christ according to the flesh, but only Christ according to the Spirit'. In practice, this is interpreted as an invitation not to trouble about the historical facts in the life of Jesus but to concentrate on sharing in the Pauline mystique of the Spirit, the mystique of the *in Christo*.

What Bultmann says of Paul, others affirm about John, saying that he plagiarized the idea of the Logos from Philo. Others again think that the epistle to the Hebrews clothed Christianity in Neo-Platonist philosophy. In either case, the Christian faith ceases to be based on an historical event.

In short, the charge is that the writers of the New Testament, even if they allude to the life of Jesus and to his teaching, have displaced the centre of gravity in Christianity from the person, Jesus, who once lived on earth, and transferred it to the spiritual figure of the Christ in whom we believe. More exactly, the charge is that the theologians of the New Testament are really responsible for Christianity as we know it, and that later centuries have disfigured it still further by idolizing the very human Jesus portrayed in the Synoptic Gospels.

This is the main objection arising out of the theological writings of the New Testament, and those who press it maintain that any '*Life of Jesus*' can be no more than a condition or a presupposition for a study of Christ as known by faith.

2. Paul and the Life of Jesus

In recent years some very distinguished scholars have openly rejected the style of interpretation launched by Harnack and Schweitzer, according to which Paul transformed the original message of Jesus by hellenizing it and giving it a mystical meaning. Maurice Goguel stated in 1948 that it would no longer be possible for him to write the work he had published in 1904 on the relation of Paul to Jesus, and several others have adopted the same view. We shall therefore set out in detail the points of contact between the teaching of Paul and the data in the gospels, but first let us try to state the distinctive characteristics of St Paul's thought.

The central point in St Paul's teaching is that the human race has been redeemed by the death and resurrection of Jesus. This statement concerns an event which took place in time: it is not the result of abstract reasoning, or of the influence of Hellenic religion. Paul's belief was rooted in an event which took place at a particular moment in time.

To support his teaching, Paul appealed to the evidence of those witnesses who had seen the risen Jesus, some of whom were at that time still alive: they said that Jesus had died, and risen again on the third day (1 Cor 15:3–4). If they had simply made up the story, he wrote, then our faith would be pointless and we should be false witnesses (15:14–15). It was impossible for him to assert more clearly that the Christian faith is by nature bound up with an historical event, and this, Paul claimed, was the tradition which he had received from the infant Church (15:3). Moreover, the death and resurrection of Jesus brought salvation and redemption through sacrifice: 'God destined Jesus to be a means of propitiation through his own blood' (Rom 3:25), 'Christ died for sinful men' (Rom 5:6), and thus 'we were reconciled to God by the death of his Son' (Rom 5:10). Paul certainly realized that this event, unique in history, had a mystical significance, but its significance was utterly different from what was found in mystery-religions. In his view, though man is already 'justified' by the death and resurrection of Jesus (Rom 5:1), no one can in fact share in this salvation unless his life conforms to that of Christ: this comes about by baptism, in which the believer is united with the crucified Christ and pledges himself to live a holy life (Rom 6:3–4, 11).

For Paul, then, the Christian faith is epitomized in the death and resurrection of Jesus Christ. As a result, he presents the mystery of the Incarnation in the context of the Redemption. Jesus came on earth to take on 'sinful flesh' (Rom 8:3–4). The whole earthly existence of Jesus Christ is presented as a voluntary self-abasement (Phil 2:5–11); the Incarnation was itself the *kenosis*—an act whereby he 'reduced himself to nothing'—which was consummated on Calvary. In the eyes of St Paul, the earthly life of Jesus was from the first instant directed towards his death; Paul therefore did not set out in detail the individual happenings of Jesus' life, but contented himself with a blurred outline—not because he thought the life of Jesus unimportant, but because he looked at it from a particular angle.

Although scholars differ in their assessment of the part that Paul played in thinking out the implications of the data received from earlier tradition, more and more they tend to agree that behind Paul, the great architect of a doctrinal system, we must see also a man firmly committed to tradition, an ambassador of Jesus. Certainly, when Paul reminded the Corinthians that the stories of the Last Supper and of the Resurrection had been handed down to him (1 Cor 11:23–26; 15:3–5), he hardly seemed to think of himself as the founder of Christianity. And indeed, throughout his epistles, if we set aside those passages in which he engages in theological systematization, and concentrate on his exhortations or on the catechetical passages, we find Paul constantly referring to the person of Jesus and to his teaching. Often enough, his references are by allusion, but the language is very similar to that used by Jesus.

Paul thought of himself as a simple 'envoy' of the Lord, and took good care to distinguish between the commands of the Lord and his own recommendations. He gave the married people of Corinth 'a command of the Lord, not of mine' (1 Cor 7:10), but shortly afterwards, speaking to the unmarried, added: 'To the rest, it is not the Lord, but I who tell you . . .' (7:12; *cf.* 7:25). To justify his right to live at the expense of the faithful, he referred to 'the rule laid down by the Lord' (1 Cor 9:14).

In addition to the sayings of Jesus which he cites explicitly, Paul has many allusions to his teaching. Ordinarily they occur in places where the apostle is expounding a catechetical theme. Thus the catechesis of the first Epistle to the Thessalonians, where Paul speaks of the return of the Lord, is evidently inspired by the gospel tradition. The passage begins with an allusion to a mysterious saying of Jesus about those who would still be alive at his coming (1 Thess 4:15); then there comes the eschatological language of Jesus himself (5:2–6). There is a reference to the thief who comes unexpectedly during the night (*cf.* Lk 12:39; Mt 24:43), to the illusion of security which men will have in those days (*cf.* Lk 12:39, 41; 21:34), to the need to stay awake and to fight off sleep (*cf.* Mt 24:42; Mk 13:27; Lk 21:34, 36), because no one knows the day or the hour (*cf.* Mt 24:36, 42; 25:13), though the day is as inescapable as the pains which come upon a woman in childbirth (*cf.* Mt 24:8).

The Epistle to the Romans (12:14–14:14) echoes the teaching of Jesus, and especially that contained in the Sermon on the Mount. Paul exhorts his hearers to bless those who persecute them (*cf.* Mt 5:44) not to repay evil with evil (*cf.* Mt 5:39–41), to give every man his due (Mt 22:15–22) and to fulfil the law by loving their brothers (*cf.* Mt 22:34–40), not by passing judgment on them (*cf.* Mk 7:1). And there are several other catechetical passages (*e.g.* Col 3:3:13–4:12) in which the presence of the Master is revealed on almost every line.

The presence of Jesus is so pervading and so real that Paul can be said to have been influenced by it not only in his mentality but even in his language. Paul's preaching was so penetrated by the images and parables of our Lord that they occur quite naturally in his writing, as when he speaks of 'fulfilling the Law' (Rom 13:8; Gal 6:2) or of 'the faith which moves mountains' (1 Cor 13:2). Paul systematized in theoretical form what Jesus had taught in images: the gratuitousness of justification, for example, is an abstract way of expressing the lesson of the parable of the Labourers in the Vineyard (Mt 20:1–16). More remarkable still is the manner in which Paul, a town-dweller familiar with Hellenistic customs and crafts, writes so often as if he were a very simple countryman. He describes the role of Jesus and of Christian missionaries by using the metaphors of sowing, of gathering fruit and of reaping a harvest (1 Cor 9:11; 2 Cor 9:6–10; 1 Cor 15:34–44; Gal 6:7–8; Rom 15:27–28). He compares the Churches with fields and vineyards (1 Cor 3:6–9), with a house which needs to be built (1 Cor 3:9–17; cf. Mt 7:24–27), or with a house in which the servant must be loyal (1 Cor 4:1–2; Lk 12:42).

Paul, not content with adopting the words and thoughts of Jesus, lived his own life in imitation of Christ, embracing poverty and humiliation as Jesus had done (2 Cor 8:9; Phil 2:8). He presented the death of Jesus as the climax of his life, imploring the Corinthians to copy that model (1 Cor 11:1). And when Paul speaks of the love with which Christ loved us (Eph 5:2; Gal 2:20), the reader cannot fail to think of Paul's love for his own converts. It is impossible to miss the human overtones in the language of this strong and passionate personality, who speaks of 'his tenderness' for his children, comparing it with that of a mother caring for her babies and with that of a father who works himself to exhaustion for his family (1 Thess 2:7–12). He tells the Philippians that he loves them 'with the tenderness of Christ Jesus' (Phil 1:8), and begs the Corinthians 'to open their hearts' (2 Cor 6:13). And when he dares to propose himself as an example to his readers, he does so because he is conscious that he himself lives in close imitation of Christ (1 Thess 1:6; 1 Cor 11:1; 2 Cor 11:1–2). For Paul, the person of the historical Jesus was anything but an abstract idea—*cor Pauli, cor Christi.*

We may now re-read the passage to which Bultmann appeals in support of his view that we must give up the attempt to know Christ according to the flesh and be content to know him according to the Spirit.

St Paul writes (2 Cor 5:16–17): 'From now on, we no longer know anyone according to the flesh; even if we have known Christ according to the flesh, now certainly we know him no longer. Anyone therefore who belongs to Christ is a new creature: ancient things have passed away, and a new order has begun.' Paul, whether he is making a real or a hypothetical concession to his adversaries, is here wholeheartedly on the attack, and argues from what they admit. At Corinth, some Christians wanted to exalt Cephas or to underline the privilege of those 'brothers of Jesus' who (by contrast with Paul) had been witnesses of the earthly life of our Lord. Paul was incessantly in conflict with these Jewish-Christians who wanted to keep Christianity as a kind of Jewish religion; he rejected their attitude with vigour.

In the passage just cited (2 Cor 5:16–17), Paul condemns all those who seek to restrict the knowledge of Jesus to out-dated forms and refuse to open their hearts to new forms, be-longing to a new order of creation. Paul, of course, does not despise the historical Jesus who once lived in Galilee, but he does sternly reject the idea that knowledge of the his-torical Jesus is itself sufficient: he insists that the knowl-edge of the earthly life of Jesus must open the path to that full knowledge of Christ as Lord which is given by the Holy Spirit. He knew all too well that it was possible to look at Jesus 'with the eyes of the flesh' alone: he himself had once done so, and had regarded him as a troublesome opponent of the Law. But from the moment of his conversion on the road to Damascus, Paul realized that Jesus had to be adored as the Lord, by the grace of the Spirit. In short, St Paul did not set aside the historical Jesus in favour of a spiritual or mysti-cal Christ: he knew only one Jesus, who was crucified, rose again and now lives for ever.

3. Jesus in the Epistle to the Hebrews

Although the Epistle to the Hebrews is full of the spirit of St Paul, modern authors agree that it was not written by him personally. Its author has not yet been identified, but he wrote perhaps in the decade preceding the Fall of Jerusalem in A.D. 70. He was therefore writing about the time when the first three gospels were being put into their final form, but there is no evidence that he had used them directly. This makes his testimony about Jesus and his life all the more interesting and worthy of recall.

Like St Paul, the author of the Epistle to the Hebrews lays

stress on the redemptive death of Jesus (Heb 13:12): Jesus, who was crucified outside the city gate (13:12), took away the sins of men by his sacrifice (9:26), which is of unique value (9:28). Several times the author repeats that this event was utterly unique (*e.g.* 10:2). And as Paul said, he who accomplished the act of redemption was the eternal Son, 'the brilliance of his Father's glory, the true image of his being' (1:3), who will return one day not as a victim for sin but as the one who brings salvation to those who wait for him (9:28; 10:37).

The author, however, was not content merely to point to the event which Paul saw as the 'Death-and-Resurrection', or to set out in detail its mystical and moral implications. By contemplating the Death-and-Resurrection of Jesus as a fact rich in significance, he grasped the truth that this event had far-reaching consequences and supplied an interpretation for all that preceded or followed it. The real triumph of our Lord after his death did not consist, strictly speaking, in the fact that his body was raised to life by the power of God, but (as we read in the Epistles to the Colossians and to the Ephesians) in the fact that he was enthroned for all eternity at the right hand of the Father: 'having purified men of their sins, he is enthroned at the right hand of God' (1:3), 'having passed through a higher tent-dwelling and entered into the sanctuary' (9:11–12).

The originality of this author is seen especially in his perception of the fact that the death of Jesus shows us the meaning of events which went before it in time. Jesus undertook to die because he willingly accepted the plan of God (Heb 10:7) from the moment he entered the world and had a body formed for him (10:5). For him, then, death was not simply the final instant of life, but the climax of a pattern of suffering, anticipated and freely embraced during the course of his earthly life. Jesus was 'crowned with glory and honour because he suffered death . . . and tasted death' (2:9), and he was 'made perfect by his sufferings' (2:10). So the author of the Epistle to the Hebrews reminds his readers that 'Jesus, when joy was placed before him, endured the cross, despised its shamefulness and is now enthroned at the right hand of God' (12:2). 'He, in the days of his earthly life, offered prayers and entreaties to the one who could save him from death, crying aloud and breaking into tears; and because of his reverential attitude, his prayer was heard. Although he was a Son, he learned obedience in the school of suffering' (5:7–8).

The author was anxious to confront his readers with the picture of a man who understood suffering. The people to whom the letter was addressed had been slow to understand the implications of their faith: they still needed milk when they should have been able to take solid food (5:11–12), and therefore after reminding them of what they had already heard (2:1), he urged them to advance to a 'perfect teaching' (6:1) and to reflect on the significance of suffering which they, apparently, had found a stumbling-block (12:3). The best way to impress on them the point of suffering was, he decided, to show them Jesus as 'the pioneer and perfecter of our faith'[3] (12:2), and to stress that Jesus was truly their brother—a man like them (2:11), with flesh and blood like their own (2:14): furthermore, he had, like them, been 'put to the test' (2:18), and surrounded by weakness (5:2). In spite of this, he had 'been made perfect' (7:28). Finally, it is stressed that Jesus, the sovereign High Priest, both God and man, to whom all things are subject, knows how to sympathize with our weaknesses (4:14–15), and that he whose life was one of perfect obedience can become for those who obey him the source of eternal salvation (5:9).

Our present concern is to evaluate the part played by the earthly life of Jesus in the theological reasoning of New Testament writers, and in the Epistle to the Hebrews his earthly life is not considered in quite the same way as in St Paul. The author of Hebrews mentions that the preaching of Jesus, witnessed by those who had heard it, had inaugurated the work of salvation (2:3), but his attention does not extend to

[3] According to A. Vanhoye, *Traduction structurée de l'Epître aux Hébreux*, Rome, 1963.

every event in the life of Jesus, only to its last moments. Revelation is here approaching the crossroads which lead to the fourth gospel.

4. Jesus in the First Epistle of St John

The question raised by St Paul's letters and by the Epistle to the Hebrews recurs when a person reads the first Epistle of St John. Whatever be the precise relationship between the first Epistle of John and the fourth gospel,[4] the author of the epistle is in the strict sense a 'theologian', for he brings the Christian message down to two fundamental principles: believing that 'God is love' and 'loving one another'.

When a theologian systematizes the content of the Christian faith around a few central principles, there is always a possibility that he may remove that teaching out of its original context, which is (and always will be) the person and the work of Jesus Christ our Lord. We must therefore ask how far the theology of the first Epistle of St John remains firmly bound up with the earthly life of Jesus.

When John writes that 'God is love' (Jn 4:8), his 'definition' of God has scarcely anything in common with the definition given by philosophers: his statement is the result of an historical experience, of an event which taught him that God loved us. This event is (as for Paul and for the author of the Epistle to the Hebrews) first and foremost the 'Death-and-Resurrection' of our Lord. 'The blood of Jesus cleanses us from all sin' (1 Jn 1:7), because Jesus was 'a victim of propitiation for our sins, and for those of the whole world' (2:2): 'he appeared to get rid of sins' (3:5) and 'to destroy the works of the devil' (3:8).

John the theologian was also head of a church, and certainly had in mind some errors which he had noticed among

[4] The present writer sides with the majority of critical scholars in admitting that one and the same author wrote both the epistle and the gospel. For further details, and for a discussion of the question, see F. M. Braun, *Jean le Théologien et son Evangile dans l'Eglise ancienne*, Paris, 1959, pp. 27–41.

those to whom his letter was addressed: he mentions men who were leading the faithful astray (2:26; 3:7) into erroneous beliefs (4:6). He probably had in mind a kind of laxism according to which the Christian could live in sin from the moment he began to believe in Jesus, and against this theory he asserts that the mystery of the Redemption entails certain consequences for the life of the believer. The Christian must first acknowledge that he has been 'saved': 'If we say we have no sin, we are deceiving ourselves, and truth is not in us; but if we admit our sins, (God) is faithful and just and will forgive us our sins and cleanse us from all iniquity' (1 Jn 1:8–9). Thereafter the Christian must endeavour to live without committing sins: 'Whoever lives in (Christ) commits no sin' (3:6), for the principal sin consists in not loving one's brother. Here we see clearly that John's theology is closely and inseparably linked with the historical event of the Redemption, and that Christians have a duty to imitate the act by which Jesus redeemed them. 'This is how we have come to know Love—by seeing that he laid down his life for us. And we too ought to lay down our lives for our brothers' (3:16).

Nevertheless, when we compare the teaching of the first Epistle of John with that of St Paul or of the Epistle to the Hebrews, we find that the originality of 1 John does not lie in his application of the mystery of the Redemption to the daily life of the Christian. For St Paul, the entry of Christ into the world was in a way only a part of the mystery of the cross. For John, Christ's coming in the flesh was not totally identified with, or ordered to, the fact of Redemption through the cross: for him 'flesh' was not something intrinsically connected with sin (this is the sense of the word 'flesh' in St Paul). For John, the term 'flesh' denotes rather the impermanence and the helplessness of mortal nature by contrast with the heavenly and spiritual world: when he writes that 'the Word became flesh' (Jn 1:14), he means that the Word became a real man belonging to this world of ours, with all the limitations that fact implies, but also with an earthly history which he lived out to the end.

Many modern scholars think that the 'anti-Christs' men-

tioned in 1 John (2:18, 22; 4:3) and the 'false prophets'
mentioned in 4:1 were Docetists of one sort or another, like
Cerinthus. Cerinthus taught that Jesus had been born an
ordinary man and had been filled with the Holy Spirit at his
baptism, only to be abandoned by the Spirit at his death:
if this were so, then God would have redeemed us under the
outward appearance of a man, but we should not have been
redeemed by an incarnate God. (Ignatius of Antioch also
thought it necessary to stress the reality of Christ's flesh
against similar forms of Gnosticism.)

John therefore began his epistle with the words: 'what we
have heard, what we have seen with our eyes, what we
have looked at and what our hands have touched—it concerned
the Word of Life' (1:1). John therefore presented himself as
a witness not only of the Redemption, but also of the Incarnation, which he understood as having a value in itself. In
this way John prepared the way for his gospel, which was
going to cover in detail the period of time between the coming of the Word to this earth and his departure from this
world at death. For John, the entry of the Word into this
world of time was already a redemptive act.

5. Conclusion

The writers of the epistles in the New Testament were not
evangelists, and it was not to be expected that they should retell the story of the earthly life of our Lord every time
they wrote a letter. Their letters were written for the benefit
of those addressed, and the writers naturally composed them
in any way they wanted to. But in these epistles we find everywhere references to an event in previous years, and this event
is not regarded as just another event—it is always seen as a
unique happening whose significance does not, and never will,
diminish. But what is this event? It is sometimes seen as just
the 'Death-and-Resurrection' of Jesus (St Paul); sometimes
it embraces all the sufferings which led up to his death
(Hebrews); and sometimes it includes the entry of the Word
into this world of time (St John). But whatever its meaning,

it prevents the Christian faith from being a '*gnosis*' or a kind of philosophy.

The person of Jesus, the Son of God incarnate and our Saviour, ensures that our faith is firmly anchored to this earth, and never in its history has the Church forgotten about the Jesus who lived in Galilee to concentrate on adoring a risen Christ without reference to his earthly life. The writings of the second century are a warning not to concentrate on the written gospels to such an extent that we forget all about the Good News and the Tradition which those written gospels enshrine. The epistles in the New Testament demand a contrary effort which prevents us from going to the other extreme: these epistles show that the Risen Christ in whom Christians believe cannot be thought of except in connection with the historical person, Jesus of Nazareth, who lived on earth, was put to death, and rose again.

The teaching in the epistles goes further than this, however, and is a preparation for understanding better the gospel message. The epistles make us concentrate our attention on the essential work of the Redemption, on the mystery of the perfect obedience of the Son to the Father. By humbling himself, by enduring suffering and by abasing himself freely and of his own will, Jesus showed men that he is 'the Man' above all others, a man 'made perfect'. He presented himself to mankind as the great High Priest, the leader of all his brothers—of all mankind, whose nature he shared in all things except sin. Today, the historian who studies the facts about Jesus finds in the epistles of the New Testament a rule of faith which throws light on the many data scattered throughout the gospels by providing a central principle which gives the key to the interpretation of the gospel message.

CHAPTER 3

The Background to
the Gospels

Modern Christians, convinced that 'the Bible is right', sometimes seek to strengthen their faith with arguments drawn
from sources other than the gospels and Christian literature,
and turn their attention, very properly, to the evidence
brought forward by sciences which have no direct connection
with religion (*e.g.* archaeology, botany, history and philol-
ogy). These sciences all have something to contribute to
exegesis, and educated Christians want to know whether they
confirm the facts stated in the Bible, and whether by 'digging
up the past' one can prove that 'the Bible is true'.[1]

The desire to compare the Bible with the findings of modern science is legitimate enough, provided that the limitations
of scientific knowledge are recognized. It would be an illusion
to think that science can discover, and provide positive proof
of, the truths which the Bible teaches. For example, botanists
have been able to identify the manna which the Hebrews ate
in the desert as the produce of a kind of desert acacia, the
tamaris mannifera, and have observed that ants eat it up as
soon as the heat of the sun has aroused them from their
night's sleep. Discoveries of this kind make it easier for us to

[1] Several popular works on these subjects were published in England between the two wars: *e.g.* Sir Leonard Woolley's *Digging up
the Past*, originally broadcast by the B.B.C. in 1930 and several times
reprinted by Penguin Books, London; Sir Charles Marston, *The Bible
is True*, London, 1934, and *The Bible Comes Alive*, London, 1937;
S. L. Saiger, *Bible and Spade*, Oxford, 1936, etc.

understand the story of the Exodus, but they do not reveal the whole truth about it, for the Book of Exodus is not a book on natural history, and the story of the manna is meant to be the story of a miraculous fact, of the divine gift of 'heavenly manna'. Those who try to explain everything in the story by human reason run the risk of missing the very message with which the book is principally concerned.

This chapter, then, will give a very summary outline of the way in which sciences connected with history can throw light on the New Testament.[2]

1. The Palestinian Background

The capture and destruction of Jerusalem by Titus in A.D. 70 provides the historian with a good point of reference for dating the content of the gospels. Thereafter, and more precisely after A.D. 66–70, Jewish society underwent a profound change. The relative peace and stability which had obtained under Valerius Gratus (procurator from A.D. 16–26) and Pontius Pilate (A.D. 27–37) were gone for ever. It was a time of continuous agitation, and after A.D. 66 life in Palestine was totally different from what it had been under Pontius Pilate. Which of the two periods is depicted in the gospel stories?

Some places mentioned in the gospels are still unidentified, (e.g. Dalmanutha, Mk 8:10; Magadan, Mt 15:39), but the sites of several others have been extensively excavated (e.g. Capernaum, Chorazin, Nain, Caesarea, Philippi, Magdala, Bethsaida). The value of such excavations for exegesis may be seen from the following example. Some years ago Loisy suggested that John the evangelist had altered a story about a pool whose boiling water cured those who bathed in it by

[2] The literature on this subject is immense. The reader in search of further information will have to consult specialist reviews like the *Revue biblique, Biblica, The Journal of Biblical Literature, The Palestine Exploration Quarterly, The Bulletin of the American Schools of Oriental Research* etc.

writing that it had five colonnades (Jn 5:2–3): the five colonnades were introduced, said Loisy, not because there were five colonnades but simply to remind the reader of the five books of the Law which Jesus had come to fulfil—as he did by curing the sick man. Recent excavations in Jerusalem, however, have shown that before A.D. 70 there was in fact a large rectangular pool there, with a colonnade along each side of the rectangle, and a fifth one running across the middle.

The Massacre of the Innocents (Mt 2:16) seems at first reading almost unbelievable, but if we remember that there were probably only about one thousand inhabitants in Bethlehem and its district, the number of Herod's victims would have been somewhere between ten and twenty. Now Josephus tells us that Herod drowned his son-in-law, assassinated his own sons Alexander and Aristobulus, strangled his wife Mariamne, had his eldest son, Antipater, executed only five days before his own death and left orders that immediately after his death all the leading people in the country were to be murdered so that there would be general mourning at his funeral. One historian has recorded the grim pun ascribed to Augustus Caesar, that it was better to be Herod's pig (in Greek, *hus*) than his son (in Greek, *huios*).[3] This character-sketch of Herod does not of course provide positive proof that the Massacre of the Innocents took place, but it does show that the cruel command was not unimaginable. Non-biblical sources cannot say the last word on this subject, but they do prepare the mind for an unbiased literary assessment of the gospel account (where other problems arise).

The study of the religious background to the gospels is even more valuable than the study of the topographical or chronological details they supply, for it enables us to recognize how firmly the gospel story is rooted in Judaism as it

---

[3] Josephus, *Antiquities of the Jews*, Books XIV–XVII. The play on words is recorded by Macrobius, a pagan historian of the fifth century, in his *Saturnalia*, II, 4, 11.

existed before A.D. 70, and to observe where it diverges from it. The gospels contain none of those anachronisms which betray the apocrypha as forgeries (*e.g. The Protevangelium of James* asserts that Mary was brought up in the Temple[4]—which would have been in defiance of all we know about Jewish customs).

At the beginning of this section we said that the destruction of Jerusalem made an excellent point of reference, for it enables us to date with certainty some of the facts concerning religious life which are mentioned in the gospels: strict observance of the Sabbath and pilgrimages to the Temple belong to the period before A.D. 70, after which they disappear. Heated controversies over points of rabbinical law, and in particular the acute rivalry between the Pharisees and the Sadducees, also belong to the period before the Fall of Jerusalem. Finally (and this is the most important fact of all), the expectation of the coming of the Messiah and of the end of the world, so clearly presupposed in the gospels, corresponds in every detail to what we know about Palestine before A.D. 70 from contemporary writings.

Before A.D. 70 the Jews were hoping for an earthly and national kingdom, and this sentiment is echoed in the gospels. The sons of Zebedee (Mt 20:21), Simon Peter when confronted with the lack of worldly success in Jesus' preaching (Mt 16:22), the disciples in general (Lk 19:11; 22:38; Ac 1:6), the people of Galilee (Jn 6:15), the crowd which welcomed Jesus into Jerusalem (Mt 21:9), the good thief (Lk 23:42) and the disciples on the road to Emmaus (Lk 24:21) are all witnesses to the fact that the Jews were at the time longing for a Messiah to deliver them from foreign domination. Perhaps one reason for this widespread attitude was that all pious Jews used to recite daily the 'Eighteen Blessings' (*Shemoneh Esreh*) of which the twelfth read: 'Hasten to uproot the kingdom of pride in our days'; similarly, in the seventeenth Psalm of Solomon (a Pharisaic hymn of the first century B.C.) a long passage begs God to send his Mes-

4 Chapter 8. In *New Testament Apocrypha*, vol. 1, pp. 378–379.

siah to cleanse Jerusalem of the pagans who defile it (vv. 21–46).[5] The same passion for the establishment of the kingdom of God inspired both the gospels and contemporary Jewish literature.

The writings recently discovered at Qumran have made the relationship between the gospels and contemporary literature more evident still, and an outline must be given of these matters, for some critics who had long maintained that the gospels were the product of Christian imagination have now gone to the other extreme and maintain that the gospels are almost entirely dependent on the thought of Qumran.

Until the Dead Sea Scrolls were discovered in 1948, we had precise information about the doctrines of the Pharisees and the Sadducees, but the Essenes, of whom Josephus speaks, were more or less unknown, and the only writing which threw any light on their sect was the *Document of Damascus*, discovered in Cairo just over half a century ago. Today, we possess a whole library of Essene literature, and from it their way of life can be known.

The monks who lived near the Dead Sea at Qumran regarded the worship conducted in the Temple at Jerusalem as defiled, because it was performed by an unworthy priesthood. They thought of themselves as the children of the New Covenant, as the holy ones, the poor, the chosen ones of Yahweh; they claimed also that to them alone certain secrets had been revealed, and that they alone knew of the hidden plan of God. They venerated the founder of their sect, whom they called 'the Teacher of Righteousness', and reverently preserved some magnificent psalms which he had composed. It is impossible not to see in their life a true *praeparatio evangelica* for the coming of our Lord; but should we go further and say that Christianity depends upon Qumran?

[5] The text is printed in *The Apocrypha and Pseudepigrapha of the Old Testament*, edited by R. H. Charles, vol. 2: *Pseudepigrapha*, Oxford, 1913, pp. 649–651.

Sometimes the situation described, or the formulas used, in the New Testament and at Qumran are very close to each other. Thus the rich young man who came to Jesus (Mt 19: 16–22) reminds us of those young men who, aspiring to be perfect, sought to enter the noviciate at Qumran. There are parallels, too, between the rules of excommunication from Qumran and those given in Mt 18: 15–18, and to the formula 'You must hate your enemy' (Mt 5:43).

It must be unequivocally stated that such close parallels are not numerous and do not touch essential matters. There are, however, major points on which Christianity differs from the religion practised at Qumran. None of the Qumran texts speak of a 'Son of Man'; the gospels present the life of the Servant of God as a life of suffering, and say that his expiatory sacrifice was of avail for others. Between Jesus and the Teacher of Righteousness there are profound differences. Both founded a community, and both underwent persecution, but all we know about the Teacher is that he was a holy priest who received from God the gift of interpreting Scripture, and the revelation of secrets concerning the end of the world.

Perhaps the relation between Christianity and Qumran should be explained in this way. After the ruin of Jerusalem, both the Christians of Palestine and the monks from Qumran became what we should now call 'displaced persons'. Perhaps they lived together in 'refugee camps' and exchanged ideas: this would partly explain why St Matthew and St John contain closer resemblances to the Qumran literature than the other gospels do. This is only an hypothesis, but it does help us to imagine the development of gospel literature at this time, and it does not detract from the originality of the Christian faith. There certainly are contacts between the New Testament and Qumran on particular points, but that is not to say that one is dependent on the other. This seems to be a reasonable assessment of the issue in the light of knowledge at present available.

2. A Comparison with the Theology of St Paul

The Fall of Jerusalem is not the only fact which helps us in dating the gospels. They can also be dated by being compared with other writings which circulated inside the Christian community, and in particular with the letters of St Paul, which were written before the gospels.[6] In St Paul's epistles, questions of theology and of church organization occupy the predominant place (though, as we have seen,[7] the same epistles contain many important references to the life of Jesus).

The question which must now be answered is this: do the gospels reflect this organization of the Church, the theology worked out by St Paul, and the whole environment of St Paul's age? We must compare the gospels with the Pauline epistles under these three heads.

In the time of St Paul, the infant Church was frequently persecuted by the Jews, as a result of which it turned its attention more and more clearly to all men without distinction of race. In the end, it began to organize itself for a long existence in the future: the Pastoral Epistles (1 and 2 Tim, Titus), which may well belong to the years 63–67, are of first importance for a study of this development. We may note also that St Paul had much trouble with nascent heresies.

The Synoptic Gospels give a picture of a very different world. A community grouped around Jesus used to meet in the synagogue, and even after Pentecost continued to frequent the Temple. Jesus and his disciples observed the Mosaic Laws. Jesus, though he foretold that persecution would be the fate of all who followed him, said nothing that would warrant even a suspicion that it had already commenced. Can one speak of the universal appeal of Christianity when

[6] The Epistle of St James does not contain any systematic theological thinking, and in spite of its date (which might be a very early one—between A.D. 35 and 50, or between 57 and 62?) we cannot take account of it here.

[7] See above, pp. 56–57.

we read that Jesus told his disciples 'not to go along pagan roads' (Mt 10:5) and said that he himself had been sent 'only to the lost sheep of the house of Israel' (Mt 15:24)? No doubt there are traces of a kind of hierarchy among the disciples, for some of them (especially Peter) received privileges which the others did not; but one could hardly speak of an 'organization'. And even if the disciples around Jesus used to argue over certain points, one can hardly call it incipient heresy. The gospels, when contrasted with the writings of St Paul, belong to another world.

The contrast is even clearer when we compare the doctrine expressed in the gospels with that in the epistles of St Paul. From A.D. 50–60, we see Paul giving a synthesis of Christian doctrine. No doubt in his eyes this synthesis was only Judaism brought to perfection, but already a doctrinal system was being worked out, providing the data and the terminology for future theology: he presents a doctrine about the pre-existent Christ, about the Saviour, about the Redemption, about the Holy Ghost, and about the Church as the Body of Christ. Finally, a reading of the Pastoral Epistles reveals the existence of technical notions destined to play a great part in Christian theology—'the deposit of faith', 'tradition', etc.

In the Synoptic Gospels, on the other hand, the language and thought are utterly simple and devoid of any attempt at systematization or harmonization. There is scarcely a word about the pre-existence of Jesus or about his relation to the Father (but *cf.* Mt 11:27 = Lk 10:22; Mk 13:32 = Mt 24:36). The terminology of the Synoptics, which was extremely primitive, was destined to disappear: later theology would almost abandon the term 'Son of man', and the word 'Church' would quickly replace the expression 'Kingdom of heaven'.

Finally, the environment revealed by the epistles of St Paul is very different from that portrayed in the Synoptics. Paul had to fight hard against Judaising tendencies, and against the forerunners of Gnosticism. Nor was he the only apostle to be troubled by these new trends: St John wrote against the same ideas in his first epistle.[8] After their death the battle became even fiercer, and the story of these controversies dominates the history of the Church during the second century.

The controversies recorded in the gospels belong to another and an earlier age. Jesus fought uninterruptedly against the legalistic mentality of the Pharisees, and against the all too human hope of a nationalist Messiah. For Christians, however, Christ by his death had put an end to all hope of an earthly kingdom; and the Church, once it had freed itself from the Jewish world, no longer needed to concern itself with the erroneous ideas of Judaism or to fear their influence.

The gospels, therefore, though they were set down in writing around the time of the Fall of Jerusalem, reflect an epoch which belongs to the years before A.D. 70, and even before A.D. 50 (the date of the first epistle of St Paul). The materials they contain were therefore old, indeed very old, at the time the gospels were written. Of course it is not impossible that men of genius might have reconstructed with brilliant accuracy the environment of Palestine around A.D. 30, but as a rule efforts of this kind are not so felicitous, and often they include too many details. This is the kind of writing which we find in the apocryphal gospels, and in certain books of the Old Testament (the stories of Tobit and of Judith, for example, are full of anachronisms). Endeavours of this kind, whether intentional or unhappy, only underline, by contrast, the historical accuracy of our canonical gospels.

3. The Language of the Gospels

The evangelists, in telling the story of Jesus, used a vocabulary and a language which were peculiar to a certain age, so that it is possible even today to date the contents of the gospels by examining their language and style.

Biblical Greek is a peculiar language, resulting from the confluence of two cultures, Greek and Jewish. Until the end

[8] See above, p. 69.

of the nineteenth century this kind of Greek was a puzzle to scholars, for it stood in sharp contrast to classical Greek and even to the Hellenistic Greek of later centuries. Many of the words used in the Greek Bible were otherwise unknown, and the oddities of its syntax provoked the mockery of pagans hostile to Christianity, such as Celsus and Porphyry. Christian apologists reacted in different ways. Some of them admitted the shortcomings of biblical Greek, but sought to justify them by saying that Jesus had not come on earth to teach men to write Greek prose. Others endeavoured to prove the artistic perfection of biblical Greek. At the time of the Renaissance, the controversy became quite acrimonious: men were classed as purists or as 'Hebraisers' according to their views on whether Hebrew constructions in a Greek text were or were not worthy of the Holy Spirit!

During the nineteenth century archaeologists discovered in Egypt several large collections of papyri, which had been preserved from destruction by being buried under the dry hot sand. These papyri contained not only well-known texts of classical authors, but also private letters, wills, receipts—in fact, writings of every kind. An examination of these writings led a great German scholar, Adolf Deissmann, to the conclusion that biblical Greek was not a special kind of language, but simply the non-literary language of the common man. Previous generations had thought that the New Testament contained 550 words otherwise unknown, i.e. 12 per cent of its total vocabulary; after the discovery of the papyri this number was reduced to 50, or 1 per cent of the total. Thus, though we cannot enter into detail on this topic, it can be confidently asserted that the gospels were written in the speech of the common people as used in the first century of the Christian era. Linguistic usage, like history and archaeology, shows that the gospels do really belong to the Palestinian culture they describe.

PART II

THE FOUR GOSPELS

No one disputes that the disciples of Jesus were full of love for their Master, and it is safe to conclude that they did not deliberately distort his message. Consequently, the historian should be on the whole favourably disposed towards the evangelists.

Yet there is no denying that the gospels are written with a definite 'slant', and that their story is related in a manner which is far from being dispassionate or impartial. Men have a right therefore to ask whether the writers were not more or less unconsciously influenced by their faith to modify, to embellish and even to idealize the true facts.

In Part I we endeavoured to show that there are no valid *a priori* objections to the trustworthiness of the gospels on purely historical grounds. Now we must examine them in closer detail: first, we shall examine each of them separately as literature, in order to assess the historical value of each (Part II); secondly, we shall try to assess the historical value of the gospel tradition as a whole (Part III).

CHAPTER 4

The Gospel According to
Saint John

1. Authorship

Tradition tells us that the fourth gospel, the last to be written down, had as its author John, the son of Zebedee, one of the Twelve. During the last hundred years the truth of this statement has been repeatedly challenged, on various grounds, but in the opinion of the present writer the modern objections have not disproved the substance and core of the ancient and classical position. At the same time, they have shown that certain qualifications must be added when we say that the fourth gospel was written by John the son of Zebedee; we should not think that he wrote the book chapter by chapter in its present form. These statements must now be explained.

Sixty years ago, there were several rationalist and anti-Christian writers who claimed that St John's Gospel could not have been composed before the middle of the second century: even in the 1930s, Loisy was teaching as an incontrovertible fact that St John's Gospel was written at the earliest between 135 and 150.[1] Yet in 1933 a fragment of papyrus (the Rylands papyrus[2]) which must be dated around A.D. 130 was discovered in Central Egypt: it has on one side Jn 18:31–33 and on the back Jn 18:37–38. This is proof that by A.D. 130 (and presumably earlier) the fourth gospel

---

[1] A. Loisy, *Les Origines du Nouveau Testament*, Paris, 1936, p. 59; the assertion is still maintained in the English translation of this work, *The Origins of the New Testament*, London, 1950, p. 193.

[2] See above, p. 42.

had been carried far beyond Palestine and Asia Minor, and indeed at the present day there is hardly a scholar in the world who would put the date of its composition later than A.D. 100. Thus the fourth gospel can certainly be said to date from apostolic times.

That a book so different from the Synoptic Gospels, both in content and in tone, should have been so widely read and generally accepted seems explicable only if it had apostolic authority. Yet it was not until nearly the end of the second century that it was ascribed to John: at least, the earliest direct witnesses of this belong to the last decades of the second century. Their evidence is not trivial and cannot be dismissed as worthless, but the problem is too complicated to be treated here; we shall therefore overlook this testimony, for positive proof that the fourth gospel was written by the son of Zebedee is not essential to our argument.

Sixty years ago, it looked as if the historicity of this gospel was inextricably linked with Johannine authorship; nearly everyone thought that the value of the fourth gospel as an historical document rested on the fact that it was written by John, a sincere and well-informed witness. Today, however, many authors[3] are agreed that this gospel (the literary unity of which is undeniable) was not written from beginning to end at one time: they hold rather that it was put together out of several earlier writings or traditions which attained a fixed form at different times. For example, some verses are easily recognizable as glosses (Jn 3:24; 4:2); two versions of the discourse after the supper were drawn up, one later than the other, and they have been combined in the gospel as we have it today; it is very likely that the discourse about the bread of life was inserted into another context; and finally chapter 21 was added (in all probability) by a disciple.

The present situation may therefore be summarized as follows. External evidence indicates that the work as it has come down to us possesses apostolic authority, and there are good

[3] Among Catholics, we may mention D. Mollat, M. E. Boismard, F. M. Braun, R. Schnackenburg and R. E. Brown.

reasons for saying that the substance of it goes back to John the Apostle (though this does not mean that he wrote every page of it). Its authorship has not been established beyond all question, but this is in the end a side-issue, for the historical trustworthiness of the book depends not on this, but on the value of the sources it incorporates. For the historian cannot in the last resort base his statements on what faith teaches about the inspiration and truthfulness of the Bible, and has a right to ask whether a book written some fifty years after the events it records has escaped all inaccuracies, either by embellishment or by a change of perspective; and he has a right to ask this question whether or not the book was written by John the Apostle. Those who believe that the fourth gospel was really written by John will no doubt feel justified in minimizing or even in dismissing such doubts, but those with critical minds, even if they accept the gospel as true because of its inspiration, will feel bound to ask what kind of historical writing it represents.

And so we must first determine the *genre littéraire* of the fourth gospel before we can discuss the question of its historicity in the right way. The historian, observing the striking differences between the fourth gospel and the first three (later on, we shall discuss them in detail), is justified in asking whether the work is not the product of pious meditation on the earlier Synoptic tradition. Is the fourth gospel, then, an historical account of events in the life of Jesus, or is it the witness of a theologian who has meditated on the meaning of the gospel message for his own day?

In order to answer this question, we must first examine the book as a piece of literature. John's conception of historical writing is far distant from the modern conception of history, but this does not mean that he has nothing to contribute. His concept of a gospel, too, is different from that of the Synoptics, and therefore his book should not be judged as a Synoptic Gospel. It is not fair to say that John's gospel is unhistorical simply because it is unlike the other three gospels; rather, we must first understand exactly what the fourth gospel intended to say.

2. The *Genre Littéraire*: a Gospel

We must never lose sight of the fact that the author of John was not writing a scientific biography of Jesus in the modern sense, but a 'gospel'. He himself says: 'Jesus did many other *signs* (*i.e.* miracles) in the sight of his disciples which are not recorded in this book. These have been recorded in order that you may *believe* that Jesus, the Messiah,[4] is the Son of God, and that *believing* you may have *life* in his name' (Jn 20:30–31). His work, therefore, is closely related to the preaching of the infant Church, for he speaks of the *faith* towards which the Church's preaching is directed, of the *life* to which faith ultimately leads, and of the *miracles* which invite men to recognize in Jesus of Nazareth the Messiah and the Son of God.

Even the structure of the gospel follows the classical pattern of apostolic preaching.[5] The starting-point is the preaching of John the Baptist (1:19), and Jesus is pointed out as the Messiah from the moment of his Baptism (1:31–34); next comes an account of the signs and teaching of Jesus, then the story of the Passion, of the Resurrection and of several appearances of the risen Christ. Throughout, events are interpreted in the light of Old Testament prophecy. These are the hallmarks of a traditional gospel.

The work, therefore, does not pretend to be an impartial record of events drawn up by a neutral and detached observer, but it is meant to be a book of history relating the life-story of Jesus of Nazareth. Of course, there are many gaps in the narrative, so that the historian cannot reconstruct an exact chronological framework or give all the details about the events, but enough indications are given to enable him to trace the broad lines of the story, and there are enough precise details to enable him to sketch out a lifelike portrait of

[4] This is the better rendering (instead of: 'you may believe that Jesus is the Messiah, the Son of God').

[5] *Cf.* C. H. Dodd, *The Interpretation of the Fourth Gospel*, Cambridge, 1953, pp. 384–389.

Jesus. We are not at the moment concerned with defending the accuracy of these biographical details, but they do indicate that the author intended not just to set out the essential points of the Easter kerygma, but to give a factual account of the earthly life and teaching of Jesus. In all probability the evangelist was seeking to help the Christian community to deepen and to communicate its faith, for he was much concerned with apologetics and with the sacraments.

It has been suggested that the fourth gospel is simply a book of missionary propaganda addressed to the Jews; without going this far, we can certainly agree that the author intended to stress the contrast between the Word, with his fullness of life, and that wisdom represented by the Mosaic Law. 'The Law was given by Moses—grace and truth came through Jesus Christ' (Jn 1:17). Apologetic considerations are visible in the treatment of John the Baptist, too. A 'Baptist movement' existed for quite a long time (in Syria, it probably survived until about A.D. 300). We know from Ac 19:1–6 that a group of followers of the Baptist existed at Ephesus in the lifetime of St Paul: this group accepted Christianity, but there were other groups which did not. The latter preached that John was the Messiah and claimed that he was greater than Jesus. The early Church had attached such importance to the Baptist that the sect found itself favoured thereby, and the author of the fourth gospel seems concerned to set the record right. That is why he emphasizes that the Baptist, though sent from God, was not the Light (1:8) nor the Messiah (1:20–21); there was another who existed before him (1:25–30), and the Baptist himself had rejoiced to see Jesus borrowing his own baptismal rite and drawing disciples away from him (3:27–30). In the fourth gospel, the Baptist is merely the forerunner, the one who bears witness to the truth (5:33; 10:41).

In this the evangelist was responding to a need of the Church at the time. It seems that he was also anxious to combat a kind of Docetism, for according to the first Epistle of John, the Church at that time had to contend with some 'anti-Christs' (1 Jn 2:18–29; 4:1–6). Though we are not too clear about the precise nature of this heresy, these ex-Christians may have claimed (like their second-century successors) that Jesus was only an ordinary man in whom a heavenly spirit had dwelt for a time. They may even have boasted (like some of their successors) that they did not need to learn about the Jesus who lived in Galilee, because they had direct access, by contemplation, to the heavenly spirit who had once dwelt in him.

Against this trend, John stressed in the strongest terms that 'he who existed from the beginning, whom we have listened to, whom we have seen with our eyes, whom we have gazed upon and whom our hands have felt' (1 Jn 1:1) was the Christ, the Word of Life. That is why he makes the very heart of his gospel the Incarnation, and stresses the most minute details of it: he tells us that Jesus was once so tired out with walking that he sat down on the edge of Jacob's well (Jn 4:6), and that Jesus shed tears as he asked to be taken to Lazarus' tomb (11:35). John's message was that men had to believe that through the crucifixion of this Jesus (3:14; 8:28; 12:32, 34) they could find eternal life and bodily resurrection (5:21; 11:25). This was his message to his contemporaries, and beyond them to men of all time.

The fourth gospel was certainly concerned with apologetics, *i.e.* with defending the faith against errors outside the Church; but it was equally, if not more, concerned with the practice of the Christian life, *i.e.* with deepening the living faith of those inside the Church. The author's intense interest in the sacraments is now commonly acknowledged: for instance, the discourse which follows the multiplication of the loaves (Jn 6) is clearly meant to be read as a homily on the practice of receiving the Holy Eucharist. In other places, a sacramental interpretation is demanded by the context: Jn 3, for example, is a kind of baptismal catechesis, for the conversation with Nicodemus forms part of a wider context wholly concerned with the sacrament of baptism (*cf.* 3:22–4:3).

In Chapter 9 the story of the cure of the man born blind

shows that baptism is also an 'enlightening': 'Arise, thou who
sleepest, and Christ will give thee light' (Eph 5:14). The
man formerly blind was cast out of the synagogue, but received with open arms by Jesus, the Good Shepherd. The
man born blind and cured of his blindness is a symbol of
every member of the Church, each one of whom was born
blind and given sight by Christ through the waters of baptism. Similarly, the cripple whose story is told in Jn 5 was
enabled to walk by Christ. Thus the Christian, as he reads
through the gospel, learns about himself—that he was only
a cripple and has just begun to walk, that he was a man born
blind, indeed that he had been a dead man and had been
brought to life, like Lazarus in his tomb (Jn 11).

The Gospel according to St John is therefore intended to
be read by men inside the Church, just as it was thought
out 'in medio Ecclesiae'. The Church, though never once
mentioned by name, is present on every page, and its presence can be detected by a number of literary clues. There is
a subtle transition from 'I' to 'we' in 3:11 (cf. 1:14); there
are brusque interruptions in the plural (19:35; 20:31; 1:51;
3:7), confessions of Christian faith which serve as choruses
to the teaching of Jesus (3:31–36, and 3:16–21), and glosses
by the evangelist which give to Jesus' words the fuller meaning they acquired, after Easter Day, under the guidance of
the Holy Spirit (2:21–22; 7:39; 12:16, 33).

For in reality it was the Church which, through the gospel,
invited its children to defend, to strengthen and to deepen
their faith in Jesus of Nazareth, the Messiah and the Son of
God. The Church provided the living background against
which the fourth gospel was written, and from which that
gospel took its own literary form.

It is essential to recognize this influence of the apostolic
Church on the presentation of the message of Jesus, but this
should not lead us to overlook another piece of evidence.
Though John was influenced by the Church in formulating
his gospel, he was himself a witness who helped to lay the
foundations of the Church's faith.

3. A Work of Witness and Interpretation

The man who edited the final chapter of St John's gospel added this note: 'This is the disciple who bears witness to these facts and has written them, and we know that his testimony is true' (Jn 21:24). He tells us also that this was the disciple who during the Last Supper leaned upon the breast of Jesus and asked him, 'Lord, who is it that will betray you?' (21:20, cf. 13:25), the disciple who is mentioned in the story of the appearance by the Lake of Tiberias (21:7) and in several other places (13:23; 19:26-27; 20:2). There is little doubt that he is also that 'other disciple' who followed Jesus into the palace of the High Priest (18:15-16) and who solemnly vouched for the truth of what happened on Calvary: 'He who has seen it has borne witness, and his testimony is true, and he knows that he is speaking the truth, so that you too may continue to believe' (19:35). Indeed, he is probably the one who, along with Andrew, first followed Jesus (1:35-40).

By contrast with the other evangelists, then, the author of the fourth gospel is presented as a 'witness'. But he was also, in Jerome's phrase, a man 'soaked in revelation' who wished to put before his readers the message which had been his own light and consolation in the days when the Jewish world was falling apart and the Christian world coming to birth. So he strove to give not just the bald facts about the life of Jesus, but also a theological interpretation of those facts. Hence his gospel is often called the 'spiritual gospel', because the Holy Spirit enlightened the author and enabled him to unfold the hidden depths of meaning in the earthly life of Jesus. He did not merely narrate what took place in the past: he also unveiled its meaning for the present. If we may be permitted a bold but modern metaphor, John was not so much recounting what had happened in the past as broadcasting live a message to which he was himself still listening; by transmitting this message to the men of his own time, he hoped to make them, like himself, true contemporaries of the Lord.

The fourth gospel, therefore, is more than the work of a trustworthy human witness: it is first and foremost the work of the Holy Spirit, who enlightened its author to perceive, more fully than any other evangelist, all the richness of teaching in Jesus' life. This is shown particularly in the discourse after the Supper. Jesus there told his disciples that the Spirit would have a double role: to throw light on the past, and to uphold the cause of Jesus throughout the ages to come. In other words, there is a sense in which revelation did not come to an end with the death of Jesus, but continued, under another form, by the activity of the unseen Spirit of God. Of course, if we think simply of what has been revealed, then there has been only one revelation, that which Jesus communicated in the name of the Father; but this once-for-all revelation took place in two successive periods, of which the second alone enables men to understand fully what was (though unseen) wholly contained in the first. The time when Jesus spoke in difficult sayings was succeeded by a time when all was made plain to those who believed.

Jesus himself explained this to his disciples after the Last Supper. He said that he had revealed everything to them (Jn 15:15) but that they had not really understood it. 'I have spoken to you in dark sayings: the hour is coming when I shall no longer speak to you in dark sayings but shall announce things clearly to you about the Father' (16:25). It would always be Jesus speaking, but in the future he would speak through the Holy Spirit. 'I have told you these things while I have been with you, but the Paraclete, the Holy Spirit whom the Father will send in my name, will teach you all things and bring to your minds everything I have said to you' (14:25–26). When Jesus left this world, his word continued to make itself heard; and it was only when the Spirit recalled the past to the minds of the disciples, or rather gave them the true interpretation of the word and events they had witnessed, that the life of Jesus began to take on its full meaning: 'when he comes, the Spirit of truth, he will lead you into all truth' (16:13).

There is a sense, then, in which Jesus did give place to another than himself (Jn 14:16), and thus we are justified in referring to two periods or two ways of revelation; but in reality it is always Jesus who is speaking and acting, for 'the Spirit does not speak on his own account, but tells men what he has heard' (16:13). John teaches that just as the Son acts on behalf of the Father (5:19, 30), so the Spirit unfolds the deeper meaning of Jesus' life. This doctrine must now be explained more fully.

(a) The Interpretation of the Past

The life of Jesus ran its course, before the Resurrection, in certain places and during a fixed period of years, and John certainly knew it as something past. John, however, did not (like Paul) argue to the moral and doctrinal consequences of the events in our Lord's life; instead, he chose to present the 'Incarnation-and-Redemption' as an event in time past which had an enduring significance for all future ages. He achieved this by using a threefold procedure, each part of which is characteristic of his writing: first he states what happened (factually) in the past, then he raises questions and gives hints about the significance of the event, and finally he unveils completely, for people living in the present, the positive message which is contained in the events of the past.

John adopted this style of writing because he was convinced that the life of Jesus could not be properly understood except by the light of the Holy Spirit. It is impossible to have a true understanding of a period of history unless one sees it as a complete whole, and so the evangelist, like the leader of the chorus in a Greek tragedy, plays an indispensable role. Knowing the end of the drama, he explains the import of events as the narrative runs along, adapting his comments to the facts narrated, to help the reader to put himself in the presence of the living Lord.

An example will illustrate his way of proceeding. When

Jesus drove the merchants out of the Temple (Jn 2:13–22) and the Jews demanded a sign showing that he had authority to do so, he answered: 'Destroy this temple and I shall rebuild it in three days.' The reader of John, like the Jews who were listening to Jesus, thinks at once of the temple in Jerusalem, and is perplexed when John offers as an authoritative interpretation the explanation that 'Jesus was speaking of the temple of his body'. (This is what we have called a 'hint'.)

The story, then, can be read at two levels of understanding: the Jews at the time would have seen in our Lord's words only a reference to the destruction and rebuilding of Herod's temple, but the Christian would see in them another reference, to the Resurrection. This raises a basic question about the meaning of the episode: must we choose between these alternative interpretations, and say that Jesus was referring either to the destruction of Herod's temple or to his own Resurrection? In fact, the evangelist tells us that Jesus was speaking of both—of the destruction of Herod's temple *and* of the Resurrection. The Jews had asked for a 'sign' that this man had authority to drive out of the temple courts all those who provided the animals necessary for sacrifice and the money needed to pay the temple taxes. Jesus' answer to them implied that his own body would be the 'new temple' spoken of by the prophets, raised up in three days after the New Covenant had been established by his sacrifice. Jesus' answer implied this, but it would not perhaps have been immediately obvious even to the Christian reader. The Christian would, of course, see a reference to the Resurrection; but what John says is that it was the resurrection of a *new temple*. That is why he does not write that 'Jesus was speaking of his body', but that 'Jesus was speaking *of the temple* of his body'. By discreet touches of this kind, John strives to teach the reader to look at the past with the eyes of faith.

In other passages John unveils a hidden meaning behind an apparently commonplace statement. Caiaphas was giving his colleagues a piece of advice which (in his mind) had a merely political reference when he said: 'You do not understand at all! Do you not see that it is better for one man to die than for the whole people and the nation to perish?' John at once adds: 'He did not say this on his own initiative, but being High Priest, uttered a prophecy that Jesus was to die for the nation, and not only for the nation, but in order that all the scattered children of God might be brought together' (11:50–52). Similarly, a text of Scripture is used to give the reason why Jesus entered Jerusalem on an ass. There is nothing surprising in this, though the text of Zechariah did not spring to the minds of the observers. 'The disciples', says John, 'did not understand this at first, but when Jesus had been glorified, they remembered that these things had been written about him and that they had done this to him' (12:16). Lastly, we may note that not only are the words of Jesus explained by the evangelist in the light of the Easter mystery (*e.g.* in 12:32–33), but that Jesus himself sometimes distinguished between what could be known at the time and what would be known later (13:7).

Moreover, we must not see the past simply as events which once took place, for in those events there is a message. The contemporaries of Jesus did not grasp the full meaning of those events, but the believer who lives in the present (the 'today') of the Church can do so, for he sees the past, historical, objective event as a demand addressed to himself.

Anyone who reads carefully the dialogues in St John will observe how fresh and lively they are, but he will also find them to be artificial compositions. They are full of questions, the purpose of which is not merely to help the dialogue along, but to underline the inability of man to grasp the revelation given by the Word. Very often, a question is introduced to keep the dialogue open, and to enable Jesus to develop an earlier statement. For example, the questions put by Nicodemus express the reaction of the contemporaries of Jesus, to whom the Spirit had not yet been given: these men could not understand, and even rejected, his message. Nicodemus' questions are, as it were, a subconscious appeal for a further and definitive revelation, and they bring out the meaning of the past. And so John, knowing the answer, is able to disclose that the real purpose of events in the past is to make men put the question to themselves: who is this who is speaking?

The strange saying of Jesus, 'No one, unless he is born again, can enter the kingdom of God' (Jn 3:3), is followed by a double question about the manner and possibility of this second birth: 'How can a man be born again? Is it even possible?' (3:4). Jesus first answers the second of these questions: it is possible, by the Spirit and water (3:5–8). Nicodemus then repeats his first question, asking how this can happen (3:9), and Jesus develops his answer (3:10–15). Thus the strange saying of Jesus in 3:3 provokes a double question and leads to a double development.

John, by adopting this manner of exposition, was merely using, very systematically, a method of teaching revealed truth which is well attested in contemporary Jewish literature and which (according to the Synoptics) was used also by Jesus himself. It was quite common to proclaim religious truths in parables or in enigmatic stories, in order to rouse the curiosity of the inquirer, and then to state more clearly the truth which the parable or story embodied.

But in the end the past does not just raise questions: to some extent, it contains within itself the answer, and therefore contributes to our understanding of the present. Indeed, one may say that it makes an indispensable contribution, for John, knowing the full meaning of the past by the grace of the Spirit, reveals that meaning very subtly by describing past events in terms applicable to the Church of his own day. We may now explain this in more detail with reference to baptism and the Holy Eucharist.

St Paul, though he showed the link between baptism and the major event of Easter Day (in which the work of Christ is summed up), did not connect the rite of baptism with the life of Jesus before his death. John revealed this connection by dwelling frequently, in his miracle stories, on the sacramental symbolism of water. This was a new element in the teaching of the Church.

Throughout his gospel the apostle loved to recall the episodes in which Jesus conferred upon water its true significance. At Cana he changed water into wine; his disciples baptized; he cured the paralysed man whom the hot water of the pool of Bethzatha could not cure; he sent the man born blind to wash in the fountain of Siloam. Finally, Jesus declared that 'a man must be born of water and the Spirit', that he alone could give living water, the water which wells up into everlasting life. At the libation of water during the feast of Tabernacles, he cried out, 'If anyone thirsts, let him come to me and drink!'

This water often recalls the rite of baptism, but it also stands for something more. John wished to reveal that in the waters of baptism Persons were present, and that they alone gave the water its power. The water symbolizes above all the Spirit which Jesus, because of his promise, was to give to whoever believed in him. That is why, in the scene of the crucifixion, the evangelist underlines the extraordinary happening which followed the opening of Jesus' side by the lance: 'There came forth blood and water' (19:34). When the sacrifice had been accomplished by the shedding of blood, water (representing the Spirit) came forth from that New Temple which was the Body of Christ (cf. Ez 47:1).

In this way the rite practised by the Church was from that moment linked with the Spirit which Jesus gave to men by his sacrifice. Because of the word of Jesus of Nazareth, those who are baptized are reborn through water and the Spirit and have within themselves a well-spring of living water which will never cease to flow.

St John also shows how the deep personal faith in Christ required by baptism gives meaning also to the rite of the Holy Eucharist. It goes without saying that in John's day, as in our own, the Church celebrated the Supper of the Lord: the narratives of the institution of the Eucharist given by the Synoptics and St Paul are proof enough. Even at that time, then, the rite had a meaning: it was a celebration, in the atmosphere of Easter, of the sacrifice of Jesus Christ. The rite, therefore, was by its very nature linked with what Jesus did on the day before his death, but it still remained to link the practice with what Jesus did during his public life, and this was John's contribution.

John had in fact been to some extent anticipated on this point by the Synoptics, for they had related the miracles of the multiplication of loaves in the very words used for the institution of the Eucharist[6]: these loaves were therefore already seen as a sign of a more abundant food. But the fourth gospel goes a step further. John, though he does not relate the story of the institution of the Eucharist (as if he saw no point in re-telling what was already well-known and commonly practised), takes great care to connect this sacramental and liturgical rite with faith, *i.e.* with a personal adherence to the mystery of Jesus. That is why he relates the discourse after the multiplication of the loaves, in which Jesus explains the true meaning of the miracle.

By placing this discourse in the public life John shows that he is not just repeating a eucharistic catechesis, but also connecting it with a past event in the life of Jesus in which faith enabled him to perceive a meaning which the contemporaries of Jesus had not seen. He makes us feel the distance between the full understanding available in the present and the lack of understanding in the past, by presenting the words of Jesus in such a way that behind the eucharistic sense the more immediate meaning (which was all that Jesus' hearers grasped) is still clear and evident. The hearers did not have to choose between believing and not believing in the Holy Eucharist (whose existence they never suspected); they chose to believe, or not to believe, in the person of Jesus and his work. Thus behind the sacramental meaning there is another meaning, which John certainly saw and wished us to see in that discourse of the public life.

It is in fact possible to read the whole discourse as a revelation of the threefold personal mystery of Jesus. Jesus came down from heaven, therefore men must believe in his Incarnation. Jesus laid down his life in sacrifice for the salvation of the world; men must therefore believe in the Redemption.

[6] See below, p. 195.

Jesus ascended into heaven, and therefore men must believe that by his Ascension, Jesus saw his work crowned by God. These three mysteries, which were a stumbling-block to the contemporaries of Jesus, can be accepted only by the grace of the Spirit, as Jesus himself said (Jn 6:63).

The discourse therefore has two meanings, one referring to the Holy Eucharist, the other to faith in the person of Jesus. But these two meanings are not set down side by side, and one must not be sacrificed to the other. The gospel tells us of the choice made by those who heard Jesus, when they were confronted with the threefold mystery, but behind this story the Church of the first century saw a deeper reference to the sacrament with which it was familiar. Thanks to St John, the Church when celebrating its Eucharist, relives the *mysterium fidei* by expressing her belief in the Incarnation, the Redemption and the Ascension. The Holy Eucharist is at one and the same time the food of believers, a sacrifice of avail for the redemption of the world, and the presence on earth of the Risen Lord.

By faith, then, the Christian can see the past of Jesus of Nazareth as something which has value for the present, and the memory of that past must therefore be kept alive with care. The Christian believer who reads the story of Jesus with the eyes of faith shares in the fullness of spiritual understanding which the Church possesses about that life, but he does not thereby cease to be concerned with what we have called the 'first period' of revelation, in which the hearers of Jesus lived, before the Spirit was given. To know about the life of Jesus is the starting-point of conversion, and the Church from the first century to our own day has always condemned those 'Gnostics' (ancient and modern) who pretend that the earthly life of Jesus may be of interest to the simple and uneducated, but is irrelevant for spiritually advanced intellectuals.

John thought it necessary to distinguish two 'periods' in revelation in order to expound in the clearest and fullest way the message of Jesus, for each of the two periods throws light on the other. The Christian who reads John's Gospel is no longer living in the days of those who heard Jesus; and therefore merely to set before him an account of the earthly life of Jesus before Easter based on purely natural knowledge would only leave in obscurity events which must be seen in the light of the Resurrection. And yet, though Easter imprints on these events their definitive meaning, we must also remember that the Second Coming of Christ has not yet taken place. And so the Christian, living his life after Easter and before the Parousia for which he is waiting, is called upon to relive (in an analogous but real fashion) the life of expectation which was that of Jesus' contemporaries.

Like them he is face to face with a mystery, and until the end of time this mystery will confront him with a choice day by day. St John invites his reader to study one period of revelation in order to understand better the other. It is true that the Christian, by his faith, has already gone further than Jesus' contemporaries, but he has not stepped out of that world for ever; he must continually go further by incessantly renewing his faith, and he must always be going back to the historical event which his faith interprets. In a word, he must repeatedly rehearse the dialectic of St John, for whom the historical event is an outline of the mystery which explains it.

(b) The Relevance of St John's Gospel Today

It is evident from the preceding pages that St John's Gospel is concerned to stress the perennial significance of the past, but so is all historical writing: *historia magistra vitae*. We must therefore discuss how the fourth gospel differs from other historical writing, and this can best be done by discussing how John's symbolism contains a message which is as relevant today as when it was first preached nearly two thousand years ago. First, then, we must say something about the symbolism in this gospel.

1 JOHANNINE SYMBOLISM. Every reader of the fourth gospel is struck from time to time by the ambiguity of some word or saying or comment, for John sees signs and symbols of

heavenly realities in the most mundane things. Even the persons mentioned in the gospel are, to him, types of mankind, and their response to Jesus illustrates the different reactions of men before the Word made flesh.

It is important not to regard this all-pervading symbolism as simply a way of teaching religious truth. Some modern writers have claimed that in the end it does not matter whether the events recorded in the gospel took place or not, provided that the religious lesson of loving God and one's neighbour is grasped and put into practice. Against these writers we must assert that John's symbolism is not just a way of teaching religious truths through picturesque stories, but that it is the most effective way of expounding the history of a very real Incarnation.

The symbolism in John is inescapable. The miracles are not simply marvellous episodes designed to arouse faith, or to prove that Jesus was the Messiah: they are 'signs' which reveal an aspect of his teaching and something of the mystery of his person. The miracles are in fact parables. Thus our Lord, when he cured the blind man, was presenting himself as the light of the world; and when he raised Lazarus to life, he was stating that he himself was both resurrection and life. His words are often full of mystery, and therefore summon us to look beyond the immediate sense for a deeper meaning. We have already discussed the text 'Destroy this temple . . .' (Jn 2:19), but there are many other texts whose meaning is equally subtle. For example, 'No man, unless he is born *anôthen* . . .' (3:3): does this mean 'born again' or 'born from on high'? 'The *pneuma* blows where he chooses' (3:8): is this a reference to the wind, or to the Holy Spirit? 'The Son of Man must be lifted up' (3:14) is explained in 12:32: it refers either to the crucifixion or to the Ascension or to both. Later (5:25) we read that 'The dead will hear the voice of the Son of God, and will live': is Jesus speaking of men who are dead in the grave, or of those who are spiritually dead? There are many similar examples.

Not only the sayings of Jesus but even the events of his life have a symbolic meaning. In the story of the Samaritan woman at the well of Jacob (Jn 4), the woman stands for the whole of heretical Samaria, which welcomes Jesus when he has been driven out of Judea; and further on we find some Greeks asking 'to see Jesus' at the very moment when the leaders of the people are deciding to get rid of him (12:20).

Though we cannot always be certain of the meaning intended by John, the symbolism of these details ceases to seem far-fetched if we regard it against the general plan of the gospel. For John, symbolism is not a literary dress for abstract truth (as it sometimes is, for example, in Plato), but a normal and necessary aspect of the life-story of the Incarnate Word of God. 'All things were made by him', and therefore everything in the world is electrified and transformed as soon as it is brought into contact with the Word, until the whole framework of our mortal world takes on a new and heavenly significance (*e.g.* the Well of Jacob, the Pool of Bethzatha, the Feast of Lights, the water which flowed from the side of Christ). By the presence of the Incarnate God, all things become a new kind of creation, and it is thus that he refashions the face of the earth.

2 THE RELEVANCE OF THESE SYMBOLS TODAY. John's symbolism, if it is to be properly understood, must never be considered in separation from the Incarnation. That does not mean, however, that we may ignore the material facts related in the gospel. Quite the contrary is true, for in John's Gospel the life-story of Jesus is firmly tied to a definite chronological development. Step by step John unfolds before the reader the spiritual challenge of the Incarnation, especially by describing how mankind responded to that challenge in Jesus' lifetime, and by summoning the reader to respond to it in his own day.

To grasp this plan, one need only examine John's vocabulary, which abounds in juridical terms like 'to judge, judgment, witness, advocate, to convict, to accuse' etc. 'Truth' is contrasted with lies or with false witness rather than with error, and John the Baptist, for instance, when the Pharisees sent a committee to interrogate him '*bore witness*' that he

was not the Christ. When the Jews challenged Jesus with acting illegally on the sabbath day (Jn 5:8–16), he replied
that he had more than the two witnesses required by the
law (Jn 5:31, 32, 33, 36, 45–46). The evangelist solemnly
claimed that he was telling the truth, and that 'his witness
was true' (19:35). The frequency of juridical terms is a reminder that the entire gospel is the account of a trial, in
which John carefully traces every step.

Chapter 5 is couched in terms of judicial procedure. Jesus,
having just cured a man on the sabbath day, is accused of
behaving as if he were equal to God: the accusation is made
in public, and the Jews demand the death sentence (Jn 5:16,
18). Jesus then makes his speech for the defence, and it falls
into three parts. First he appeals for a fair hearing (5:19–
29), underlining his appeal for belief with the words 'You
will be astounded' (5:20); next he states his technical
'defence', citing the evidence of the witnesses for the defence (5:30–38); and he concludes (5:39–47) by revealing
the prejudice of those who wish to judge him, and putting
his finger on the true source of their unbelief. Thus Jesus
turns the situation completely round: Moses, to whom his
accusers had appealed, accuses them in public, and Jesus,
whom they had sought to put on trial, becomes the judge of
his prosecutors.

The whole message of the gospel is contained in this scene,
and Chapters 7 and 8 develop the theme: again there is a
dispute about the value of Jesus' witness, then deliberation
by a jury, and the accusation rebounds upon those who seek
to put Jesus on trial. This time, however, it is Abraham, not
Moses, who comes forward as a witness in favour of Jesus,
against those who called themselves his children. After that,
Jesus can solemnly state that 'the world is now condemned'
and that 'the prince of this world is going to be cast out',
while he himself will be 'exalted' (Jn 12:31–32). And when
he cries out in triumph, 'I have conquered the world'
(16:33), he means that he has emerged victorious and justified from the trial in which he was involved with the Jews

and with the world. 'Darkness was unable to suppress the Light' (Jn 1:5).

The same notion of a trial can be perceived in the attitudes of the contemporaries of Jesus. When John uses the term 'Jews', he is not thinking ordinarily of Jews in a racial sense, but in a very general way of the enemies of Jesus. This can be seen from the fact that our Lord and John the Baptist do not speak as if they were Jews: 'It is written in *your* Law' says Jesus (Jn 8:17), while Nicodemus talks about '*our* law' (7:51). Anyone who believes in Jesus is contrasted with 'the Jews', even if he is in fact by race and religion a Jew (*e.g.* the paralytic in 5:15, and the man born blind in 9:18). By this literary simplification (which is, to be precise, a profound spiritual insight in accord with early traditional typology, as in 1 Cor 10:1–12), the people mentioned in the gospel take on a universal relevance. Their attitudes matter for all time, because they illustrate the reactions of men when brought into close contact with Jesus, the Saviour not only of Israel but of the entire world.

The reader of the fourth gospel should therefore look upon the men in the story as personalities living today: unbelieving Jews and disciples gradually approaching belief are meant to be more than men who lived long ago. They represent us, who also have a part to play in the historical drama, for or against Christ.

Jesus first comes in contact with the Jews when he drives the merchants out of the Temple (2:13–22), and from that moment onwards he is presented as 'a sign that is opposed'. At that moment judgment begins, and those who listen to Jesus are divided into two camps by the basic dispositions of their hearts. Those who refuse to believe in him remain, or become, 'Jews', while those who accept his teaching become disciples, and then 'Christians'. The historical theme that one must make a choice for or against Jesus recurs on every page of the gospel: sometimes we read of the progressive hardening of hearts among the enemies of Jesus, and one has the impression that he is preaching to deaf ears, while at other times we see men being led towards the light. The point of the gospel is always that a man must make up his mind for or against Jesus.

Day by day throughout his public life Jesus seemed to be on trial, but in reality it was those who heard his preaching who were on trial before him; his earthly life ended with his trial, but again it was his accusers and his judges who were on trial before him. The Christian of today can see how the same historical process is ever being repeated, in that he, too, is challenged to make a decision for or against Jesus.

Nowadays we see clearly that a man must be for or against Jesus: in New Testament times, a man had to choose between Jesus and the Jews, where nowadays he must choose between Christianity and the world. For to be a Christian is to be in opposition to that world which condemned Jesus as a political agitator, and to affirm that Jesus is living with the Father. 'The world' has taken over from 'the Jews' the role of condemning a way of life which it cannot bear: formerly, 'the Jews' condemned Jesus, whereas nowadays it is 'the world' which condemns Christians. But it is still the same strange process at work, in which the one accused becomes the judge, and the judge is condemned. When Jesus was condemned by the Jews, he refuted their charges by showing that they could not convict him of sin (Jn 8:46); and when the Christian is in turn condemned by the world, he can rely on the Paraclete to prove the world wrong about sin, about righteousness and about judgment (Jn 16:8).

It is in this sense that the historical drama once played out in Palestine continues to be rehearsed today. The reader can always ask himself who is right—the world or Jesus; but the Spirit in his heart tells him that faith gives the right answer, and that if he is persecuted for his faith, he is already, along with Jesus, victorious over the world.

4. The Historical Value of the Fourth Gospel

The text of St John, both because it is a 'gospel' and because it is the work of a 'witness', confronts us at all times with the necessity of making (or renewing) a choice for or against

Jesus. But has it any historical value? It seems, more than any other gospel, to have historical detail so fused into its theology that it is scarcely possible to distinguish one from the other. The message of Jesus is stated in such a characteristically 'Johannine' manner that it is very hard indeed to find out which words Jesus himself uttered. It is not enough to say that the fourth gospel is historical simply because it contains certain details whose historicity cannot be doubted; when we consider the extent to which past events are projected into the present by the gospel itself, it becomes obvious that the problem of historicity is here very acute.

It is not easy to resolve this problem, and it is a delicate one; we shall therefore proceed step by step, showing first that the Gospel according to John deserves to be treated as trustworthy, and then that the different narratives in it need to be examined separately, to see whether other, non-historical, elements have not coloured the presentation of them.

(a) The Life of Jesus according to St John

One way of gaining a general certitude about the historical value of the fourth gospel is to compare its contents with those of the Synoptics. The reader will be sufficiently familiar with the Synoptics to follow the argument, even though we have not yet examined them in detail. In common with many modern scholars, we think that John was acquainted with the Synoptic tradition, but not with the written Synoptic gospels; that he may have known part of this tradition in writing; and that he often shows signs of having been closer to the Lucan tradition. John, in short, presupposes the Synoptic tradition, completes it and develops it in his own way; he reveals its limitations, but shows also where it ultimately leads to. This is the conclusion to which a close comparison of John with the Synoptics leads, whether we look at the places in which Jesus' ministry is exercised, or at the different episodes of that ministry, or at the content of his teaching, or at the portrait given by St John.

In describing the ministry of Jesus, John by no means excludes Galilee: he mentions it in 1:43; 4:3, 43; 6:1; 7:1; 2:1, but adds that Jesus went up to Jerusalem on the occasion of the various feasts (2:13; 5:1; 7:10). This last point is not really something new: Luke hints that Jesus made such journeys when he repeats, like a refrain, that Jesus 'was going up to Jerusalem' (Lk 9:51; 13:22; 17:11). Matthew also implies a number of visits to Jerusalem when he writes: 'Jerusalem, Jerusalem, how often have I wanted to gather together thy children' (Mt 23:37). Finally, all three Synoptics imply that Jesus had already been to the Holy City several times when they describe his triumphal entry into Jerusalem: he was evidently not unknown there.

But John also tells us that Jesus preached twice in Judea, once at the beginning of his public life, when the Baptist was still carrying on his ministry by the Jordan (Jn 3:22–23), and once at the end, just before the last week in Jerusalem (10:40; 11:54). Between these two periods in Judea, our Lord preached in Galilee; and here again John is the only evangelist to suggest a motive for his departure from Judea, and it is a highly probable motive, namely, the disquiet and jealousy of the Pharisees (4:1–3).

John also supplies most valuable information about the places in which certain events occurred. He tells us that there was a village called Bethany across the Jordan (1:28); that the Baptist preached at Aenon (3:23); that Jesus twice went to Cana in Galilee (2:11; 4:46), and once to 'a town called Ephraim, which lies on the edge of the desert' (11:54). He is helpful too on the dating of events: he mentions that the Temple had been under construction for 46 years (2:20), and that Jesus died on the 14th Nisan. He even gives the exact time at which Pilate condemned Jesus to death (19:14).

The background against which John describes the life of our Lord is therefore exactly the same as that in the Synoptics, and the fourth gospel has nothing in common with the fantasies of the apocryphal gospels. Jerusalem was the Holy City to which even Gentile converts went on pilgrimage (12:20); the Temple, not yet finished (2:20), was a haven for merchants (2:13–14); Galilee was ruled by a royal prince (4:46); it was despised in Judea (1:46; 7:41, 52) and was inclined to support revolutionary Messiahs (6:14–15). There was deep-rooted hatred between the Jews and the Samaritans (4:9; 8:48). Religious customs mentioned by John are no different from those mentioned in the other gospels: rites of purification (2:6; 3:25; 11:55), funeral customs (11:38, 44; 12:7; 19:31, 40) and religious prohibitions (18:28; 19:31). The sect of the Pharisees is described in exactly the same way as in the Synoptics, with the same stress on their formalism (5:16–18; 7:23; 9:16), on their contempt for the common people (7:49; 9:28–29, 34), and on their hatred for Jesus (5:16, 18; 7:1; 8:40, 59; 10:31).

Since the general background of John's Gospel is so closely related to that of the Synoptics, the reader may be puzzled to know why John does not relate the greater part of the episodes given by the Synoptics, or (conversely) why the Synoptics do not, as a general rule, relate the events described by John. A deeper understanding of John's way of writing may, however, modify this first impression. To begin with, we may note that the fourth gospel contains allusions to events which are more explicitly described in the Synoptic gospels: *e.g.* it *assumes* that Jesus' home was at Nazareth (Jn 1:45; 6:42; 7:41, 52; 19:19), that he had been baptized by John (1:31–34), that the Baptist was put in prison (3:24), that Jesus chose twelve disciples (6:70; 13:18; 15:16; 20:24), that Judas betrayed him (6:64; 12:4; 13:2, 27–29), that Jesus instituted the Eucharist (6:51), that he was put on trial by the Jews and their Sanhedrin (7–8), that he suffered an agony (12:27), instituted the practice of Christian baptism (3:5), and finally ascended into heaven (20:17). Above all, the Transfiguration, which is alluded to in 1:14 and 12:28–30, seems to command the whole earthly life of Jesus and to project its light and glory on to the least significant events of his life before the Resurrection.

Many details are mentioned, no doubt, because of their symbolism, but there was no symbolic reason for mentioning Philip (6:7) and Andrew (6:8), after the multiplication of the loaves, or for saying that Jesus ordered the disciples to collect what remained (6:12). The Passion story contains a multitude of tiny details which the historian must often recognize as having real value: *e.g.* the anointing at Bethany took place six days before the Passover (12:1); the story of the prophecy of Caiaphas (11:47–53) must have been handed down from a very early Jewish–Christian group which enjoyed close connections with the synagogue. It was Peter who struck at the servant named Malchus (18:10); Roman soldiers took part in the arrest of Jesus (18:3), and Jesus was first questioned before Annas (18:12). Jesus was interrogated by Pilate inside the governor's residence (18:33; 19:9), but the verdict of condemnation was pronounced outside (19:13), probably after the scourging (19:1–2, 16). The Jews tried to bring pressure on Pilate by threatening to appeal to Caesar: and Pilate perhaps had the honorary title of 'friend of Caesar' (19:12). John mentions, in his account of the crucifixion, the tunic woven without a seam (19:23); he tells us that the mother of Jesus stood by the cross (19:25–27), that the robbers were finally killed by having their legs broken, but that Jesus was pierced after death by a lance (19:32–34), and that he was buried by Nicodemus (19:39–40). All these details, and many others, are surely *a priori* 'probable', and if they were added simply to give colour to the story, then it is astounding that not one of them has ever been exploded by the findings of archaeology, or of the social history of the time.

If we now consider the style in which all these episodes are related, we cannot fail to see the Johannine stamp imprinted on the dialogues, the miracles and the controversies —but we must also acknowledge that there is a fundamental relationship with the Synoptics.

The dialogues are not, as in the Synoptics, bare outlines of conversations held by Jesus. It is true that we find in Luke the beginnings of more developed discourse couched in dialogue form (*e.g.* in the story about the disciples at Emmaus, Lk 24:13–35), and we find it also in Mark (*e.g.* in the story about the cure of the epileptic boy, Mk 9:14–29); but in

John the pattern is used far more widely and systematically. Those who put the questions are (as we have seen) 'types' of mankind, representing either the unbeliever who turns his back on Christ or the disciple moving gradually towards the light.

The miracles, too, are far less numerous in John than in the Synoptics. But if John made use of only a few miracle stories, he did so deliberately, knowing that there had been many more (Jn 2:23; 6:2; 7:3–4; 11:47; 20:30). He seems to have chosen seven particularly significant miracles because seven was a sacred number for the fullness of God's gifts. These seven miracles are, however, exactly the same kind of miracle as those recorded by the Synoptics (e.g. the cure of a paralytic, giving sight to a blind man, raising a dead man to life). The difference lies in John's treatment of them as 'signs' revealing the person of the Son of God, and they are therefore called 'works', i.e. works of the Father; they are no longer considered merely as manifestations of power (dunameis) which prove that he who worked them is the Messiah, or that he was a man of compassion, or that faith in him achieves wonders. John, though he uses the same materials as the Synoptics, brings out the inner meaning of the miracle, and transposes it into another key. Thus miracles reveal the glory of God (2:11; 11:4, 40) because they are works of the Father (10:25, 32, 37–38; 14:10–11; 15:24) accomplished by Jesus, who can initiate such works (cf. 4: 48). Their meaning is brought out by discourses which are appended to them (5; 6; 9; 11). This manner of interpretation had already been suggested by the Synoptics (e.g. in the controversy about the power to forgive sins which took place when Jesus cured the paralytic, Mt 9:1–8, and in the insertion of a series of events between the cures of two blind men, Mk 8:22–10:45).

Finally, the controversies in John are not about any and every topic (fasting, marriage, ritual cleanliness, etc.), but are all essentially concerned with the person of Jesus. We find nevertheless a concern for the sabbath, demands for a sign, and debates about who are the true children of Abraham.

The rabbinical style is still there, along with the appeal to
Scripture (3:14; 6:31; 10:32–36) and legal discussion about
the value of testimony (5:31–32; 8:13–18, 31–59). The controversies which follow the cure of the paralysed man and of
the man born blind call to mind similar controversies in the
Synoptics after the cure of the paralytic, and after the accusation that the disciples were gathering corn on the sabbath.
So often, both in John and in the Synoptics, the occasion of
the controversy is observance of the sabbath, and the episodes, though they are treated in very different ways, are
nevertheless exactly the same kind of episode in all four
gospels.

John gives us the message of Jesus principally in long discourses like the apologia in chapter 5 or the prayer in chapter
17. The statement that these speeches were composed by
the evangelist will come as a surprise only to those readers
who do not realize that the earlier gospels also contain similar
speeches put together by the writers on the basis of sayings
uttered by Jesus in varying circumstances: one need mention
only the sermon on the mount (Mt 5–7), the chapter of
parables (Mt 13) and the eschatological discourse (Mt 24–
25). We shall see later how in the Synoptic Gospels certain
sayings of our Lord were given a particular slant by the
primitive Church.

But in the fourth gospel the style of the writer seems to
be one with that of Jesus himself, though it is not always impossible to distinguish one from the other. Nevertheless, outside these great speeches (and sometimes even within them)
we come across lapidary sentences like those in the Synoptics (e.g. 'If the grain of wheat does not fall into the
ground . . .', Jn 12:24; 'The servant is not greater than his
master . . .', 13:16; cf. 15:20; 'A woman, when she is about
to give birth to a child . . . 16:21; 'Blessed are those who
have not seen . . .', 20:29). Such sayings, from the moment
they were embodied in the gospel, took on (by reason of
their context) a wider meaning, and become capable of
several interpretations, according to the dispositions of the
reader.

(b) The Historicity of the Fourth Gospel

If what has just been said about the *genre littéraire* of the fourth gospel is well-founded, certain conclusions must be admitted which make an appreciable difference to the way in which we assess the historicity of this gospel. We may begin by setting aside the wrong way of treating it: some writers begin by giving the prize for historicity to the Synoptics, and then try to show that John too is historical. This, however, is to assume (quite wrongly) that the Synoptic Gospels are works of a scientific kind. But we must distinguish in the gospel between the framework and the content, because the historian can reach a certainty about one which he cannot reach about the other.

The contribution of the fourth gospel to our knowledge of the framework of Jesus' life is of capital importance: without it, the historian would be compelled to rely on the Synoptic pattern alone, and this is notoriously over-simplified. One scholar has recently summed up the results of modern research on this point.[7] John is our primary source for historical information on six points of great importance: (1) two of Jesus' disciples were at first disciples of the Baptist; (2) Jesus exercised his ministry in Judea for a time before preaching in Galilee; (3) the multiplication of the loaves provoked an upsurge of enthusiasm for Jesus as a political Messiah; (4) Jesus worked for a time in the southern part of the country just before his Passion; (5) The Last Supper took place before the 15th Nisan; (6) Jesus appeared before Annas after his arrest. Further details could be added: for instance, it seems that Jesus had his disciples baptizing, and that Roman soldiers took part in his arrest.

Critical scholars are generally agreed about the framework of the gospel, but this unanimity breaks down as soon as we begin to discuss the historicity of particular episodes or of the

[7] A. M. Hunter, 'Recent Trends in Johannine Studies', *Expository Times* 71 (1960), pp. 219–222.

message. Here again, it is essential to beware of making statements which are too categorical or too general.

When an episode is related both by the Synoptics and by John (e.g. the cleansing of the Temple, the multiplication of loaves, the Passion), several elements in John will, as a rule, seem more authentic than those in the Synoptic tradition. And when the words of our Lord are presented as a development and a fulfilment of the Synoptic tradition, we have to ask how far John is really expounding the meaning of the Synoptic tradition. In both these questions detailed exegesis is called for.

It becomes harder to give an answer when the historian finds himself faced with passages or episodes which are not mentioned at all in the Synoptic tradition, but even so, the difficulty should not be exaggerated. John alone tells us, for example, about Cana, about the Samaritan woman, and about Lazarus; but we may equally well ask why the Synoptics say nothing about the ministry of our Lord in Jerusalem, which was of first importance. The real difficulty lies in the way John wrote his gospel: both the narratives and the speeches have been so thoroughly thought over that the historian who is looking for an unadorned account of the original event, or for the *ipsissima verba Jesu*, finds himself completely disconcerted. This, however, should lead him to wonder whether he himself is asking the right questions.

Two extremes are to be avoided: one must not refuse to accept an event or a speech as historical on the pretext that John alone relates it, and one must not uncritically accept an event or speech simply because it is related in the gospel. The historian who is trying to find out the truth about Jesus of Nazareth must make use of the fourth gospel, but he must see it as a prolongation of the Synoptic tradition. And if he is not limiting his work to this historical investigation, but wants *also* to study the reaction of the first Christians to Christ the Lord, then he will find the fourth gospel a light and a guide enabling him to discover the ultimate meaning of the gospel tradition.

Once the *genre littéraire* of the fourth gospel is recognized, one can see why those who limit their aim to knowing the historical Jesus find it of little use for their purpose. John wanted to be both a witness of Jesus of Nazareth (by telling what he remembered of him) and a witness of Christ the Lord (by trying to make us share his faith in Christ). John's gospel is therefore a challenge thrown down against the positivist idea of history, and positivist historians are only logical in refusing to accept that such a book can be historical. But John had a different idea in mind: he never considered a bald fact without looking at it in the light of the Spirit, to see its significance.

This consideration of events in the light of the Holy Spirit enabled him to see their full significance, and he thereby gave history a new dimension, which can be accepted only by faith. He never wanted to stay at the uncomprehending level of 'the Jews', for 'the flesh is of no avail—only the Spirit gives life'. For John, real facts had historical value, but they also showed him that God had intervened in history, and had thereby brought things to life by conferring on them a spiritual and symbolic value which could not be grasped by reason alone.

It is always necessary, therefore, to recall the facts by which God has left traces of his intervention in history, but the purpose of recalling these facts is, in the end, to invite everyone to make a judgment about Jesus. The events narrated in the gospels do not in themselves provide a ready-made answer dispensing men from faith, but are rather an appeal, summoning men to rediscover the One who lived these events at a given moment in our history. In this sense, the book of John is a real 'gospel', a book of good news, and an encounter with him who never ceases to put himself forward as the light of every man who comes into the world.

One cannot therefore dissociate in John the witness of the past and the witness of the present, any more than one can dissociate in Jesus of Nazareth the man and the Word: the earthly life of Jesus cannot be reduced to that of an ordinary man, because a dimension of eternity will always smash the mould into which men try to force that earthly life. Yet the

Gospel according to John is not just a theological meditation by a pious Christian living at the end of the first century; rather, it is a work in which the testimony of man and the testimony of the Spirit have been fused into one, to bring out the true meaning of Jesus' earthly life.

The Fathers of the Church often used the story of the miracle at Cana to illustrate how the New Testament fulfils the Old, and we may use it here for a similar purpose. Jesus did not create the wine out of nothing—he used the water already standing there to produce the 'best wine' of the feast. John the evangelist did not create the events in his gospel out of his own imagination; rather, he took the historical events themselves (which the historian can and must discover) and interpreted them. Historical research cannot exhaust the meaning of these events which it discovers, for the person whom the historian meets is Christ the Lord, whom the faith of John confesses in Jesus of Nazareth.

CHAPTER 5

The Gospel According to
Saint Matthew

1. Preliminary Remarks

The first three gospels are so similar in structure and sometimes even in wording that it is very instructive to look at
them side by side: for this reason, they are called the Synoptic
Gospels (from the Greek *syn-opsis* meaning 'looking at several
things with one glance'). Later on, we shall discuss these
similarities (and the differences) in some detail, for this will
enable us to discover the sources of these three gospels: indeed, during the past century scholars have concentrated
mainly on this task, trying to determine what written documents or oral sources lie behind Matthew, Mark and Luke.
During the last few years, however, the theological slant
proper to each of these three gospels has once more become
a focus of interest, and it is with this modern situation in
mind that we shall now examine each gospel on its own before passing on to consider the tradition common to them
all. The aim of the next three chapters, then, is to discover
the particular way in which each of the three Synoptics presents the historical facts about Jesus of Nazareth.

Even a general conspectus of each gospel, however, pre-
sumes that the writer has some theory about the way in
which the first three gospels are related to one another. For
instance, if he assumes that both Matthew and Luke used
Mark, it is sufficient to examine the way in which they used
him and their other sources, and he is at once able to appreciate their particular theological slant. This method looks
wonderfully clear, but is in fact too simple.

The reason is that each of the four gospels presents an interpretation of the facts about Jesus which derives ultimately (through the gospel writer) from a body of tradition handed down inside a particular Christian community. Behind the evangelist, therefore, we must look for the community to which he belonged, to see how it influenced his writing. This is particularly necessary with the Synoptic Gospels, for their authors, unlike St John, allowed their sources to shine through very clearly, keeping their own individual personalities in the background, and placing the emphasis on the faith of that community, the local Church, whose teaching they put into writing.

Moreover, in judging the relationship between the three Synoptic Gospels, the present writer works on a literary hypothesis which justifies him in examining each gospel separately before looking at their sources. It is assumed here that none of the three Synoptic Gospels is based directly on one of the others, and that the passages common to two or more of them come from *sources* which were common, but which were slightly modified in the communities to which the evangelists belonged before being incorporated into the gospels as we have them today.[1]

2. The Church to which Matthew belonged

Tradition tells us that the first of our four gospels was written by the apostle St Matthew. The earliest, and the main evidence for this tradition is a statement of Papias[2] recorded by Eusebius, who writes: 'Of Matthew he (Papias) has this to say: "Matthew compiled the *Sayings*[3] in the Aramaic language, and everyone translated them as well as he could." '[4] Many modern scholars think that the work to which Papias was referring was not what we now call the

---

[1] See below, pp. 170–175.

[2] See above, pp. 44–45.

[3] *i.e.* the 'Sayings of Jesus'.

[4] Cited in Eusebius, *HE* III, 39, 16 = *PG* 20:300 = Penguin Classics, p. 152.

Gospel according to Matthew, but simply a 'Collection of Sayings'; this view, though it is widely held, cannot be accepted, for all the ancient Christian writers like Eusebius who had read Papias' work (A *Commentary on the Words of the Lord*) take it for granted that he was speaking of a 'gospel'. Moreover, it would be astounding if a 'Collection of the Sayings of Jesus', written by one of the Twelve, had been allowed to disappear so completely that not a trace of it remained; and there is not a single reference to such a book in any early Christian writer. Papias' statement, then, must refer to a gospel, particularly as the same statement is made by all the great early Christian writers. Origen, for example, tells us that Matthew's gospel was written 'for believers who had come from Judaism',[5] and the same view is held by Irenaeus,[6] Clement of Alexandria[7] and Eusebius.[8]

Internal evidence does not formally contradict this ancient tradition, but it does lead us to accept it only with qualifications, for there is much evidence that the Greek version of the gospel—the only one we possess—has been thoroughly revised by its Greek editor. And it is this Greek version with which we are concerned. But even as we read the Greek version, we can see that we have before our eyes a thoroughly Palestinian gospel. This is evident from its vocabulary, from the customs it records, and from the theological tendencies it betrays. Whether or not Matthew the tax collector was its author, the first gospel was most certainly written for Jewish Christians resident in Palestine.

The author does not as a rule explain Aramaic expressions (contrast Mk 3:17; 5:41; 7:11, 34; 10:46; 14:36). He does so very occasionally (Mt 1:23; 27:33, 46), but more often he uses Jewish phrases without thinking (*e.g.* 'binding and loosing', Mt 16:19; 18:18, as a synonym for excommunication or for a decision about doctrine or law; 'the kingdom

[5] Cited *ibid.* VI, 25, 4 = PG 20:581 = Penguin Classics, p. 265.
[6] Cited *ibid.* V, 8, 2 = PG 20:449 = Penguin Classics, p. 210.
[7] Cited *ibid.* III, 24, 6 = PG 20:265 = Penguin Classics, p. 132.
[8] *ibid.*: see also PG 22:941 and 23:904.

of heaven', 'gehenna', 'the holy city', etc.). There are also certain phrases which are not just Jewish but typically Palestinian (*e.g.* 'flesh and blood have not revealed it to you', 16:17; the 'outer darkness and the gnashing of teeth', etc.). The only possible explanation of these phrases is that the author knew that his readers would understand them.

By contrast with Mark, Matthew assumes that his reader will be familiar with Jewish customs. Thus he does not comment on the custom of washing the hands before a meal (contrast Mt 15:2, 11, 18 with Mk 7:2–5), and simply mentions, without comment, 'the first day of Unleavened Bread' (26:17). All three Synoptic Gospels mention certain local customs such as wearing 'fringes' (Mt 9:20; *cf.* 14:36; 23:5), but there are several which are mentioned by Matthew alone (*e.g.* the sabbath-day customs of priests, Mt 12:5). He mentions also certain usages which were restricted to the Pharisees and to the teachers of the law, and in one sentence there may even be an echo of a celebrated controversy between two of the greatest Rabbis of the day, Hillel and Shammai, about the reasons for divorce (19:3). Again, there is but one possible explanation.

Lastly, there are many remarks which set the drama against the theological background of the time. Matthew alone mentions that Jesus was sent only to the people of Israel (Mt 10:5; 15:24; *cf.* 10:23); Jesus is presented as anxious to observe the Jewish law, and his language supports this. He commands men to obey the Law unreservedly (5:17–19; 12:5), and calls unfaithfulness to it 'lawlessness' (7:23; 13:41; 24:12; 23:28). He uses specifically Jewish expressions like 'sons of the kingdom' (8:12), 'scribes initiated into the kingdom of heaven' (13:52), and 'a feast with Abraham' (8:11); he even refers to the peril of flight on the sabbath day (24:20).

St Matthew's Gospel is thoroughly Palestinian in character, but it is also a thoroughly 'ecclesiastical' gospel. We can see the Church to which Matthew belonged at work in the very editing of the book, in its style and composition and in its theological slant.

3. A Catechetical Gospel

St Mark's Gospel contains many picturesque details which appeal to modern readers. He tells us for example that during a storm on the lake 'Jesus was asleep on a pillow in the stern' (Mk 4:38); that the woman with an issue of blood 'had suffered much from many doctors and spent all she had, and was none the better but rather the worse' for it (Mk 5:26). Details like these conjure up for the reader a vivid picture of Jesus, and the man who turns from Mark to Matthew may think that Matthew has simply summarized the rather longer accounts in Mark and missed out all the attractive details. In fact, however, Matthew's Gospel is of a very different kind: it is meant for solemn recitation and meditation, and therefore contains much symbolism and allegory.

The tendency to allegorize is strikingly evident in Matthew's treatment of the parables: thus a detailed exegesis of the parable of the tares is given in Mt 13:36-53, and even the short parable about the dragnet is carefully explained (13:47-50). Even the miracles in Matthew's Gospel sometimes seem to be phrased in order to carry a symbolic meaning which could be expounded by a preacher. For instance, the narrative of the cure of Peter's mother-in-law is, in Matthew (8:14-15), stripped of all adventitious detail, so that at first sight it looks like a mere abbreviation of Mark. Unlike Mark and Luke, Matthew speaks of 'Peter' (not Simon), i.e. the name by which this man was known as head of the Church. Andrew, James and John are not mentioned (as they are in Mark), and the disciples do not ask Jesus to heal the sick woman. Matthew simply says that Jesus faced her as she lay 'struck down' and in a fever and took hold of her hand; at this, the fever disappeared, the woman 'arose' (the same word is used of the Resurrection, and is not in Mark or Luke) and served 'him' (i.e. Jesus alone: Mark and Luke say she served them, i.e. the disciples). It is quite possible that the early Church interpreted this story as symbolic of the life of the Christian who, after having been 'struck down' by Satan is then 'raised up' by Jesus and 'serves' his Lord. A similar interpretation has been given of the story about the stilling of the storm (Mt 8:23–26).[9]

It is always instructive to compare parallel passages in Matthew and Mark, not because it enables us to say that one gospel is better written than the other, or that one is more trustworthy than the other, but because it reveals the originality of Matthew. We have just cited one or two examples of how Matthew explains parables and re-tells miracle-stories in order to bring out their application to the Christian community. Elsewhere, he re-arranges the teachings and narratives of our Lord's life into a catechetical framework; once more, his aim was to help the preacher.

Mnemonic arrangements, for example, are very popular in Oriental cultures, and they occur frequently in Matthew. Thus he classifies the ancestors of Jesus into three sets of fourteen each (1:17); he gives seven petitions in the Lord's Prayer (6:9–13), seven parables in 13:1–52, and seven 'Woes' against the Pharisees (23:1–36). Similar figures sometimes occur in Mark and Luke, and this may be an indication that these arrangements stem ultimately from the oral preaching of the Church, and even from Jesus himself; but it is Matthew who makes most use of them. He tells of three temptations (4:1–11), of the three good works—almsgiving, prayer and fasting (6:1–18), and of three prayers in Gethsemane (26:36–46). All these mnemonics are of great help to the catechist.

Another process he uses is sometimes called 'inclusion': it consists in repeating, at the end of a passage, a formula (sometimes stereotyped) which figures at the beginning of the text: thus the whole passage is, as it were, 'framed' as a unit. The Beatitudes, for example, are framed by the expression 'the kingdom of heaven', which occurs in the first and in the last (Mt 5:3, 10); the first four close with a reference to those who hunger and thirst after righteousness, the second

[9] See G. Bornkamm's essay in *Tradition and Interpretation in Matthew*, by G. Bornkamm and others, London, 1963, pp. 52–57.

four with a reference to those who are persecuted for righteousness (5:6, 10). Here, then, we have a double aid to the
memory. In Mt 7:16–20, the warning about false prophets
begins (v. 16) and ends (v. 20) with the statement 'You
will recognize them by their fruits'. Similar examples can be
found all over the gospel. This, then, is what we mean by
calling the Gospel according to St Matthew a catechetical
gospel. It was not meant primarily as a book to be read to
oneself in the quiet of a study, but as a lectionary to be
proclaimed aloud in church, commented on and interpreted.
And this is why from the earliest times it has always been
the liturgical gospel *par excellence*. It is the Gospel of Jesus
Christ composed for preaching in the Church, and this brings
us to the theme of St Matthew, which is rather different from
that of Mark or Luke.

4. The Double Theme: Christ and his Church

The theme of Matthew's work is revealed in the closing verses
of his gospel, in the last words of the Risen Christ to the
Eleven: 'All authority in heaven and on earth has been given
to me. Go on your way, then, and make disciples out of all
the nations, baptizing them in the name of the Father and
of the Son and of the Holy Spirit, and teaching them to observe everything I have commanded you. And I myself will be
with you through all the days to come, until the end of the
world' (Mt 28:18–20).

In these words a double theme may be discerned, concerning Christ and his Church. Jesus here presents himself as the
Son of Man foretold by the prophet Daniel to whom God
has given sovereignty over the entire world (Dan 7:13–14).
Thus Matthew states that for the future all who wish to acknowledge God as sovereign king must recognize the kingship
of Jesus Christ. This is his first idea.

Alongside it, there is another one, namely, that the Church
established on earth by Jesus is destined to fulfil the plans of
God, by achieving the task which had formerly been given to
Israel (Mt 21:43). This Church, unlike the earthly Israel,

would be catholic or universal, for Jesus charged the Eleven
to make disciples out of all nations by baptizing them and by
teaching them to observe all his commandments.

There are, then, two themes to be discussed—the kingdom
or reign of Christ, and the nature of the Church.

(a) The Kingdom or Reign of Christ

In St Matthew's Gospel we frequently come upon the words
'the kingdom of heaven'. The phrase probably goes back to
Jesus himself, but it is so rarely found in the New Testament
outside the Synoptic Gospels that it must have fallen into
disuse at a fairly early date. It was replaced by a number of
other words like 'the Church', 'eternal life' and 'heaven', each
of which expresses one aspect of 'the kingdom of heaven'.
'The kingdom' is, in Matthew, a rendering of the Aramaic
word *malkutha*, which has two meanings. Sometimes it denotes the exercise of sovereign power by a monarch or the
duration of his rule (*i.e.* his 'reign'); but at other times it denotes the territory or the population over which he rules (*i.e.*
his 'kingdom'). The phrase 'kingdom of heaven' oscillates
between these two ideas of 'reign' and 'kingdom', and both
elements are often present to the mind of the writer, with
the stress now on one, now on the other. When, therefore, the
phrase is used by Jesus, it can cover two concepts which were,
to the Jewish mind, distinct: it can stand both for the future
life (what the Jews called 'the kingdom of God') and for the
inauguration of that life here on earth by Jesus (what the
Jews thought of as 'the reign of the Messiah').

The kingdom is presented as something in the future when
it is called, for example, the kingdom of the Father (Mt
13:43; 25:34; 26:29), or when men are said to take possession of it (5:20; 7:21; 18:3; 19:23–24). Sometimes, however,
the kingdom is said to come to men, and then the reference
is to the reign of the Messiah, which comes about in three
stages: it is inaugurated by the coming of Jesus, developed
on earth after the resurrection of Jesus, and consummated
in glory at the end of time.

This is how Matthew presents the message. The kingdom of heaven is approaching, is near at hand, is here (Mt 3:2; 4:17; 10:7), and the exorcizing of devils is the proof of this (12:28). Everyone who hears Jesus preaching the Good News of the kingdom is faced with a decision which he cannot escape (4:23; 9:35; 10:7). Some enter the kingdom without difficulty (*e.g.* the poor and the persecuted, 5:3, 10), but everyone who enters must become like a little child (18:1; 19:14) and observe the least of the commandments (5:19). Jesus therefore preached that the kingdom already existed in some way during his lifetime, here on earth.

By preaching this message, Jesus was broadcasting God's invitation to all men to work in his vineyard (Mt 20:1), but not all were willing to accept the invitation. Tax-collectors and prostitutes entered the kingdom before the Pharisees (21:31), and many Pharisees, by barring access to the kingdom for others, showed themselves unworthy to enter it, because they lacked the right dispositions (23:13). Against this attitude, Jesus insisted that those who would not enter the kingdom here on earth would have no part in the heavenly kingdom at the end of time. Many Pharisees, who had waited so long for the kingdom of God, would eventually find themselves shut out from it; their places would be taken by those who joined Jesus and thus formed a 'people which would make the kingdom bear fruit' (21:43).

The kingdom, therefore, though not in all respects identical with the Church, certainly makes us think of the Church, especially when we consider its development. Jesus said that the kingdom would begin like a small grain of mustard seed and become a flourishing tree (13:31–32). In it, both wheat and weeds would be found growing together, *i.e.* both good men and bad (13:24–30, 36–43; 22:10), but at the end of time the Son of Man would send his angels to rid it of all evildoers (13:41). Then the kingdom of the Son would become the heavenly kingdom of the Father (25:34; 26:29).

This kingdom, therefore, although it does not belong exclusively to this world, takes shape on earth. It has laws demanding mutual service (18:12–14) and mutual pardon

(18:21–35). Peter is its key-bearer (16:19), and its disciples
are to be judges of the twelve tribes of Israel (19:28) when
the Son of Man claims his throne at his first coming (16:28).
Should we not recognize here a kind of 'constitution' for a
society which will endure?

Such is the kingdom which the disciples were summoned
to proclaim. After the Resurrection, it was no longer restricted to the race of Israel (contrast 10:23), but open to all
the nations of the world (24:14; 28:19; *cf.* 26:13). The kingdom of heaven, then, denotes a kind of society which takes
shape gradually as the true Israel of God, and develops into
the Church of Jesus Christ. But since the Church here on
earth will never have fully accomplished its mission (*i.e.* will
never have become the perfect realization of the kingdom)
until the end of time, it must pray throughout its history,
'Thy kingdom come!' (6:10).

(b) The Relation of the Kingdom to the
Earthly Life of Jesus

Since the Church is destined to become the kingdom of
heaven, its destiny (like that of the kingdom) is inseparably
bound up with the life of its founder, Jesus Christ, for in his
heavenly origin, earthly life and final glorification he pi-
oneered a road which the Church is summoned to follow.
This is the second theme implied in the words of the Risen
Lord at the end of the gospel: he promised to remain with
his disciples for ever, to guide them along the path ordained
by God.

The earthly life of Jesus, according to Matthew, contains a
most urgent message for the Church today, for it shows us
what is involved in the universality of the Church. Matthew
stresses that Jesus came to fulfil the Law, and that the history
of salvation which began with Abraham had to be extended
to the farthest ends of the earth, as the Old Testament
prophets had repeatedly foretold. At the time when Matthew was writing, the Church had already taken the first steps
to becoming the eschatological kingdom of God, by opening

its doors to men of all nations. But it had not been easy for those born and bred as Jews: the early Christian community had only gradually been able to detach itself, through the grace of God, from a too narrow and exclusively Jewish outlook (*cf.* Ac 10; 15), and this should warn us to beware of thinking that the Church of any later age has already achieved true catholicity, or even that it has already fulfilled all the necessary conditions to be truly universal. The Church is not yet fully transformed into the kingdom of heaven.

Twentieth-century Christians find it hard to appreciate Matthew's interest in catholicity, for they are no longer sensitive to their Jewish origins, and the problems which St Paul discussed in the Epistle to the Romans are very remote from them. In a general way, they think that the Church has simply taken over the place once occupied by Israel in the history of salvation. This, however, is too facile a view of history, so deceptive as to be positively dangerous: it represents as narrow a view of the Church as that which the Pharisees in our Lord's day entertained of their own race, Israel. St Paul reacted vigorously against this idea, and Matthew, too, is very concerned to show that the Christian Church is still linked with Israel.

Time and time again the author remarks that 'All this took place to fulfil the saying of the prophet . . .', after which he quotes a text of the Old Testament. The point of these remarks is to show how the events of the past fitted into the design of God. As the Acts of the Apostles show, the living Church reflected on past events in the light of the revelation formerly given to Israel. The life-story of Jesus as told in Matthew is not just a collection of memoirs, even personal memoirs; rather, it is an interpretation of what Jesus did, grounded on a very thorough understanding of the divine plan of salvation as revealed in the Bible.

Thus Matthew's Gospel took on the character of an apologia, as if his purpose was to clear Jesus of certain accusations made against him by the Jews. The evangelist never conceals this aim, but openly appeals to prophecy in order to justify (for example) the strange happenings in Jesus' infancy (his birth from a virgin mother, 1:22–23, at the insignificant little town of Bethlehem, 2:5–6, the flight into Egypt, 2:15, the Massacre of the Innocents, 2:17–18, and the upbringing of Jesus at Nazareth, 2:23). Matthew also uses the same method to justify the behaviour of Jesus, whenever it might seem surprising: Jesus went to live in Capernaum, not in Jerusalem, in order that the light might arise in Gentile-occupied Galilee (4:14–16); Jesus did not behave like the severe judge foretold by John the Baptist, because he wished to be like the Servant foretold by Isaiah, taking on himself our infirmities, healing our sicknesses (8:17), and refraining from debate in public places (12:17–21). And if his parables seemed obscure (13:35), if he entered Jerusalem in a modest way (21:4, 5), if he was arrested as a criminal (26:56) and was sold for thirty pieces of silver (27:9–10), it was always 'because the saying of the prophet had to be fulfilled'.

By this argument, Matthew was trying to show the Jews that they had been mistaken in refusing to accept Jesus as the Messiah. The life of Jesus, when seen in the light of prophecy interpreted by faith, was not just a series of past events which an historian might record; it was the great turning point in God's plan to save mankind. At the same time, Jesus' life had not only marked the time of fulfilment; it had also brought about a rupture with the Jewish people who failed to recognize him. Yet this rejection of Jesus by the Jews was the very occasion which allowed the message of the gospel to spread to the entire world. Thus Matthew (like John) presents, in his own way, an interpretation of history. It would be a mistake, therefore, to regard St Matthew's Gospel as merely a summary of the teaching of our Lord, with some examples of his actions to illustrate it. Matthew's principal concern was to publish the record of a life which had had far-reaching consequences for the whole of mankind, both Jew and Gentile.

In fact, the life of Jesus is presented as a drama. Some authors have claimed that the gospel is built up like a catechism, grouping the teachings of our Lord around his five great speeches, but there is no solid proof of this.[10] It seems rather that the gospel should be divided into two parts. First of all Jesus introduces himself, and then, by proclaiming that the Gentiles are to have a place in the kingdom of heaven, begins to demand of the Jews absolute faith in his own person; the Jews, however, as a body, refuse to believe in him (Mt 3–13). Thereupon Jesus follows the road which leads eventually to his passion and death, while laying the foundations of his Church (Chapters 14–28).

The prologue to Matthew's Gospel (the infancy narrative) gives a vivid illustration of the life of Jesus. Whereas Joseph, in the name of Israel and the house of David, welcomes the child conceived by Mary of the Holy Spirit, Jerusalem, Judea and Herod reject him, persecute him, and seek to kill him. They take this attitude because of the adoration of the Magi, who are types and representatives of the pagans, whom the gospel invites to salvation. But Jesus emerges unscathed, and goes to live in 'Galilee of the Gentiles', to which Judea must cede the throne.

5. The Content of St Matthew's Gospel

We have seen that St Matthew's Gospel was addressed to Palestinian Christians of Jewish origin, and we were able, by examining some of its literary characteristics, to conclude that it was written for catechetical use, that is, for preaching in the Church. Its broad theme is that Jesus Christ is Lord of the world, and that the destiny of Israel has passed to that small remnant of Jews who formed the nucleus of the Christian Church. Matthew sought to present this doctrine to Palestinian Christians, and therefore arranged his gospel in an orderly manner, taking care to give a very full statement of what Jesus had said and done. It will be convenient to

---

[10] This plan of St Matthew's Gospel, based on the five speeches, was put forward by the American scholar B. W. Bacon, in his *Studies in Matthew*, New York, 1930. It has been popularized in Catholic circles (especially in France) through *The Jerusalem Bible* and other works but it does not seem to stand up to a close scrutiny.

outline first his portrait of Jesus and secondly his account of Jesus' teaching for the Church.

Jesus is held up to the reader as the Messiah. Matthew calls him 'Jesus the Christ', the 'Son of David' and the 'Son of God'. Matthew, indeed, not infrequently omits attractive details and psychological observations in order to stress the dignity of Jesus, and to present his message in a solemn and liturgical style. The point can easily be illustrated by a rapid comparison with Mark.

In describing the feelings of Jesus, Matthew mentions his great compassion (Mt 9:36; 14:14; 15:32; 20:34) and his fury (23:1–6), but unlike Mark he never speaks of more subtle—what we may call more human—emotions, such as irritation (Mk 1:43; 8:12; 10:14) or tenderness (Mk 9:36; 10:16, 21). In Matthew, Jesus only twice asks a question like an ordinary man seeking information (Mt 16:15; 17:25), whereas such questions are frequent in Mark (Mk 5:9, 30; 6:38; 8:12; 9:12, 16, 21, 33; 10:3; 14:14); in Matthew, questions put by Jesus are usually meant as reproaches (Mt 8:26; 14:31; 16:8; 19:17; 22:20). In other words, Matthew stresses rather the dignity of Christ, and even qualifies certain rather bold statements. Mark, for example, tells us that Jesus could do no miracles among his own townsmen (Mk 6:5), whereas Matthew (13:58) says that he did not perform many. Perhaps, too, Jesus' reply to the rich young man in Mt 19:17 has been softened down from a more abrupt form, preserved in Mk 10:18.[11] In all these instances, Matthew is concerned to stress the dignity of Jesus.

The dignity of the apostles is also stressed, as it was in the early Church (*cf.* Ac 5:15; 19:12). Matthew does not, of course, pretend that they were equal to the teaching of the Master, but if we compare certain parallel passages in Mark,

[11] Compare also Mt 13:55 with Mk 6:3; Mt 15:33 with Mk 8:4; Mt 26:17–19 with Mk 14:12–16; Mt 26:39 with Mk 14:36; Mt 26:61 with Mk 14:58; Mt 27:58 with Mk 15:45. (In the last-mentioned example, Matthew calls the corpse of Jesus a *body*, though he had referred to the corpse of the Baptist as '*remains*'—a less dignified word which Mark employs on both occasions.)

we find that Matthew has toned down the lack of understanding displayed by the Twelve, much as the Chronicler passed over in silence the weaknesses of king David so faithfully described in the books of Samuel. To have related their shortcomings would have been, for Matthew, to detract from the more than human dignity with which these same apostles were endowed from the time of the Church's foundation.

Matthew's Gospel loses nothing of its historical value by omitting stories of the failings in the Twelve, for it shows us how revered they were in the Church of Palestine. It also enables us to perceive more clearly the pattern by which Jesus trained his disciples. Jesus, after the basic question about his own personality had been raised (8:27), grouped his disciples around him to strengthen their devotion (14:1–16:20), revealed to them the mystery of his Passion and taught them the law of brotherly service (16:21–20:28). When they saw Jesus walking on the water, they recognized that he was in truth the Son of God (14:33), and were saddened by his insistence that he had to suffer persecution and death (17:23); Matthew does not say (as Mark does) that they did not understand (Mk 9:32). The Church of which Matthew was the spokesman was just as anxious to tone down the familiarity of the disciples with the Master as to play down their imperfections: they were prophets, scribes of the New Law, wise men of Israel, sharing in the authority and even in the power of Jesus (9:8, 6).

Much of Matthew's Gospel is taken up with the teaching of Jesus, and here the evangelist shows himself a master of compilation. There are five long sermons by our Lord in Matthew, each of which is followed by the phrase, 'And it happened, when Jesus had finished these words' (Mt 7:28; 11:1; 13:53; 19:1; 26:1). These sermons are like five massive pillars on which the whole structure of our Lord's teaching rests: they are the Sermon on the Mount (Mt 5–7), the missionary charge to the disciples (10), the teaching in parables (13), the instruction on life in the Christian community (18) and the long discourse about the destruction of Jerusalem, the end of the Old Covenant and the end of the world (24–25).

In each of them sayings which Jesus must have pronounced on several different occasions are grouped together.

Thus in the Sermon on the Mount Jesus presents certain themes of the New Law by contrasting them with the precepts of the Old Law; and to some of these themes one or more sayings bearing on the same subjects are appended. Thus Jesus' teaching on murder ends in Mt 5:24, but the evangelist has added (vv. 25–26) another saying about the shrewdness of seeking reconciliation with one's enemies. (This second saying probably referred originally to the Last Judgment, as it does in the parallel text, Lk 12:58–59.) Similarly, Jesus' pronouncement about adultery ends in 5:28; but the mention of lustful looks (v. 28) calls to mind the word 'eye' (v. 29), and so a saying is added about giving scandal (vv. 29–30), which incidentally helps to complete Jesus' teaching about adultery. Thus because the interest throughout is catechetical, the author groups together several sayings pronounced at different times, but all applicable to the same topic.

Similarly, the missionary discourse in Mt 10 probably consisted originally of vv. 5–16, but in our gospel it has been given a preface (vv. 1–4) and followed up with other sayings which obviously apply to the time after the Resurrection rather than to that of the Galilean ministry. The discourse against the scribes and Pharisees (23) certainly gathers together passages of very disparate origin, and the great eschatological sermon in Chapter 24 is rounded off with the three parables of Chapter 25, in which its lessons are applied to the life of the individual Christian. These magnificent compositions, in which the doctrines of Jesus are grouped together, make St Matthew's Gospel an outstanding work of catechetics, and fully justify the preference which the Church showed to it in the early centuries.

Matthew is a past master of the art of compilation: not content with juxtaposing sayings and narratives, he often embodies a saying into a narrative. Thus in the story of the centurion's servant (Mt 8:5–13) he inserts a saying about the feasting in the kingdom of heaven which Luke reports not on the occasion of this miracle (Lk 7:1–10) but much later (Lk 13:28–29). Matthew, it would seem, placed the saying in an earlier passage because of the plan of his gospel and because of the close relationship of topics, and by so doing made this episode about the centurion into the paradigm example of pagans coming with faith to our Lord.

Thus a study of the theological interests of Matthew only confirms what has already been deduced from the style and structure of the gospel. The main centre of interest is everything related to 'the Church'. Matthew alone gives the text in which Jesus confers upon Peter the 'power of the keys' and calls him 'the foundation-rock of the Church' (Mt 16:18–19, cf. 18:18), and he alone relates two episodes showing the special place of Peter beside Jesus (walking on the water, 14:28–31; the payment of the Temple tax, 17:24–27). For Matthew, the divine plan for the kingdom of heaven, outlined above, was essentially destined to lead to the constitution of a Church, whose beginnings lay in the little community grouped around Jesus. This same community had its own way of presenting Christ, the apostles and the Christian life.

The first gospel, with its hieratic style, seems when compared with that of Mark to be less alive; though shot through with citations from the prophets, it seems to be denuded of all those charming touches which captivate the reader of Mark. But even if it does not appeal so much at first sight, closer examination reveals the deep faith of the author or authors who gave it shape.

6. The Historical Value of St Matthew's Gospel

The question which must by now be in the reader's mind is 'Granted that the Gospel according to Matthew presents a fine theology, what is its worth as history?' With all his concern for apologetics and for catechetics, does the author have a proper regard for historical exactitude? The question cannot be treated fully until we have examined the other two Synoptic Gospels, but we may perhaps try, by way of conclusion, to state the problem accurately.

It is quite clear that Matthew did not attempt to write a biography of Jesus of Nazareth as an impartial non-Christian observer might have written it. The reader he envisaged was the Christian who wanted to deepen his faith and to play his own part in the history of the divine covenant with God's people; Matthew therefore told his readers that in Jesus Christ, the Son of God, the history of Israel was summed up, and by so doing showed the reader how the events of the past had relevance in his own day, and for ever. The time of Jesus of Nazareth was not only a period in which the great hope of Israel was fulfilled, but also a privileged epoch in which future events in the life of the Church were foreshadowed.

St John the Evangelist was able, by the Holy Spirit, to bring the past to life, to such an extent that his reader feels himself to be a contemporary of Jesus, and knows that he must make a decision for or against this man who claimed to be the Son of God. Matthew too brings the past to life, though not so explicitly as St John: by the way in which he groups events and teachings, by the hieratic style of his narratives and by his adaptation of traditions to serve a catechetical purpose, he shows the meaning of Jesus' life on earth.

But if this is the type of writing in the first gospel, one may legitimately ask what its historical value is. To what extent can the historian discover the true Jesus of Nazareth by studying the testimony given by Matthew and his Church in the fullness of their faith? The question is not as difficult as it was for the fourth gospel, for not only does Matthew retain untouched a certain number of bald historical data in his setting of events, but it is often possible to work out the broad lines of what happened, and this for two reasons.

First, Matthew betrays a certain naivety in the way he groups and interprets the materials he used as sources, and it is often possible for the scholar to detect what actually happened before Easter Day; secondly, a comparison with the parallel passages in Mark and Luke enables the scholar to get a firmer grasp of the life-story of Jesus as an event in the past. This, however, cannot be done until the other two Synoptic Gospels have been examined, and it will form Part III of this book.

CHAPTER 6

The Gospel According to
Saint Mark

1. Authorship

Tradition affirms, without a dissentient voice, that the second of our four gospels was written by St Mark, and that it contains the memoirs of St Peter; hardly any modern scholar contests the authorship, though some are not so ready to admit its connection with St Peter.

The earliest witness of the tradition is Papias: writing shortly after A.D. 100, he tells what he had heard from an earlier generation. 'This, too, the presbyter used to say, "Mark, who had been Peter's interpreter, wrote down carefully, but not in order, all that he remembered of the Lord's sayings and doings. For he had not heard the Lord, or been one of his followers, but later, as I said, one of Peter's. Peter used to adapt his teaching to the occasion, without making a systematic arrangement of the Lord's sayings, so that Mark was quite justified in writing down some things just as he remembered them. For he had one purpose only—to leave out nothing that he had heard, and to make no mis-statement about it." '[1]

There is still some controversy among scholars over Mark's role as an interpreter of Peter, and about the lack of order in his gospel. We need not go into these matters, and can simply state that Papias' testimony shows that from the beginning of the second century Mark's Gospel was ascribed to an

[1] Eusebius, HE III, 39, 15 = PG 20:300 = Penguin Classics, p. 152. The translation is that given in the Penguin Classics.

author who had not seen the Lord—a rather surprising fact which would hardly have been invented, for it would only have lessened the authority of the work. This tradition was well known not only in Asia Minor, where Papias lived, but also in Egypt, Africa and Rome: witnesses from all these parts tell us that Mark's Gospel is dependent on the teaching of Peter, though there is some slight disagreement whether Mark wrote down his gospel before or after the death of Peter. For our purposes, it is not of great importance.

Internal evidence indicates that this gospel was written before A.D. 70, for there is not a single allusion to the destruction of Jerusalem (not even in Mk 13:10); most authors would date the book between A.D. 65 and 70. Mark, to whom the work is ascribed, is usually identified with that John Mark mentioned in the Acts of the Apostles: he was friendly with Peter (Ac 12:12; cf. 1 Pet 5:13, where there is a reference to 'Mark, my son'), and accompanied Paul in his first missionary journey (Ac 12:25; 13:5, 13). In spite of a temporary estrangement from Paul (Ac 15:37-39), he seems to have worked with him at a later date (Col 4:10; Phm 24; 2 Tim 4:11). This John Mark was therefore a close acquaintance of both Peter and Paul.

Internal evidence only confirms the early Christian tradition. We shall see later in this chapter that those passages in Mark which relate an event at which Peter was present bear all the traces of an account by an eyewitness; this strengthens the belief that Mark is recording Peter's memoirs. There is also some, though not much, evidence that the gospel was written at Rome. Tradition is not unanimous on this point: Clement, Jerome, Eusebius and Ephraem say he wrote at Rome, while Chrysostom says he wrote at Alexandria; and some modern authors suggest Antioch. Although Antioch, as a centre of Roman culture, can make some sort of claim to have been the cradle of this gospel, the weight of evidence lies on the whole in favour of Rome. We may perhaps detect the influence of a Roman environment in Mark's glossing of a Greek term by a Latin one ('two *lepta*'—a Greek coin—'*i.e.* a quarter of an *as*'—a Roman coin,

Mk 12:42; *cf.* 15:16); and there are also several constructions dependent on Latin syntax (*e.g.* Mk 2:23; 5:23).

Moreover, Mark seems to have written his gospel for Christians who were not of Jewish origin and who did not know Palestine well. He hardly mentions the relationship of the gospel to the Law of the Old Covenant, and only two or three times does he mention the fulfilment of prophecy (except when it is mentioned in his sources), *cf.* Mk 1:2–3; 14:49; 15:28 (?). He does take great care, though, to explain Jewish customs (Mk 7:3–4; 14:12; 15:42), to translate Aramaic words (3:17; 5:41; 7:11, 34; 10:46; 14:36; 15:22, 34), and to stress the significance of the gospel for the Gentile nations (7:27; 10:12; 11:17; 13:10). All this is readily accounted for if the gospel was written for the Christian Church in Rome.

2. The Sources of St Mark's Gospel

Two elements can still be traced in St Mark's Gospel: we find in it the record of what witnesses had actually seen, and the exposition of what a Christian community believed. These two elements, united in varying proportions, constitute the hall-mark of a gospel. In St John's Gospel, the testimony of an eye-witness and the faith of an official spokesman for the Church are fused into one; in St Matthew's Gospel, the word of the person who was a witness tends to disappear behind the preaching of the Church; in St Mark's Gospel, it is fairly easy to discern what comes from a witness and what reflects the faith or practice of the Church.

To separate the two elements which Mark combined is not to throw doubt on the value of his testimony. This matter will be treated more fully in Part III, but even at this point it will be useful to set down the findings of recent research on the sources of Mark's Gospel. Mark sometimes gives a short summary as an introduction to a section of his gospel (*e.g.* Mk 1:14–15; 3:7–12). Elsewhere he takes a number of stories which were loosely connected with one another and makes out of them a unified story (1:1–13; 3:13–19; 6:6–13; 9:30–10:52; 11:1–25). Sometimes he

makes one narrative out of several items which may have
come to him from different sources (1:21–38; 4:35–5:43;
6:30–56; 7:24–37; 8:1–26; 8:27–9:29); and sometimes he
simply narrates groups of stories as they had been used in
catechetical instruction (2:1–3:6; 3:20–35; 4:1–34; 7:1–23;
11:27–12:44; 13:1–37). The whole work reaches its climax
in the story of the Passion.[2] If we remember that St Mark's
Gospel is formed in this way, out of several different kinds
of sources, it is possible to distinguish three aspects of the
writer's work: we see him at work as a storyteller, as a catechist and as an evangelist.

3. Mark as a Storyteller

Turning from St Matthew's Gospel to that of St Mark is
rather like stepping out of a church and finding oneself
facing a glorious landscape. The parallel is not far-fetched,
for Mark is a very gifted story-teller, though his genius was
restricted by the raw material on which he worked (i.e. by
the vocabulary, the syntax and even the style of the sources
he used). However, precisely because of this genius, modern
historians, though they do not reject his testimony as worthless, feel the need to check carefully the value of Mark's
statements. The very vividness of pious stories like those of
Job and Judith led many generations of men in the past to
think that these narratives were true historical records; could
Mark's lively style also cover up a non-historical work? Semitic
peoples have a genius for telling stories, often wholly fictitious,
in the most lively way, and an historian will not readily concede that a narrative, because it is vivid, must be a record
of something which actually happened. Nevertheless, we are
led to the conclusion that Mark's Gospel is the work of a
witness (though the witness is not Mark, but Peter) because
of certain differences between the passages in which Peter
is mentioned and the rest.

A first clue to the presence of Peter behind the gospel

[2] See V. Taylor, The Gospel according to St Mark, London, 1952,
pp. 90–104.

lies in the vividness of the narratives where Peter is involved.
Here Mark hardly uses the past tense, the Greek aorist, which
is the classical tense for narratives. Instead, he uses the his-
toric present (*e.g.* Mk 1:21, 30; etc.), or the imperfect, which
fixes attention on an action which was going on at a certain
time (5:18; 12:41; etc.). Sometimes the author is carried
away by his story and mixes up the tenses as he pleases. 'And
he summons the twelve, and began to send them out in pairs,
and was giving them authority over the unclean spirits, and
he ordered them not to take anything for the journey except
only a staff—no bread, no knapsack, no coppers in their belt
—but wearing sandals and "don't wear two coats"' (6:7–9).
The story is certainly badly told, but one can almost hear
Jesus speaking.[3]

A second clue lies in the clumsy construction of many
narratives where Peter is present. Mark does not tell these
stories like an accomplished writer who dominates his subject; he is absorbed by what he sees, follows up a point wherever it may lead, and adds an explanation wherever he thinks
of it, even if it is not in the right place in the sentence or
story. We may note, too, how often his thought is swifter
than his pen, so that he breaks a clause apart by thrusting in
a parenthesis for explanation (2:15–16; 6:14–15; 7:18–19,
25–26; 13:10, 14; 14:36) or brings a clause to an abrupt
end without completing it (5:23; 6:8–9; 11:32; 12:40).

A third indication of Peter's presence behind certain stories
lies in the use of the 'impersonal plural', an Aramaic usage
exactly parallel to our English use of 'they': *e.g.* 'They' (we
are never told who) 'bring a deaf mute to him' (Mk 7:32).[4]
This use of the plural is all the more significant when the
next clause tells us that 'he' did something, without mentioning the name Jesus. In these instances the third person
plural can often be replaced by the first person ('we'), that
which would have been used in Peter's preaching as he told

[3] See also the following passages: Mk 1:29–31, 35–38; 2:13–14;
3:31–33.
[4] See also Mk 1:21, 22, 45; 2:3, 18; 3:32; 5:35; 6:14, 33, 43,
54; 8:22; 10:13; 49; 13:9, 11; 14:1, 12.

the story: thus 'we went into Capernaum, and he went into the synagogue and began to teach' (1:21), and the whole episode comes alive.[5]

A last clue lies in what are called 'Markan details' which are thrust in rather abruptly either during or at the end of a narrative. The age of Jairus' daughter is given right at the end of the story: the child got up and walked 'for she was twelve years old' (Mk 5:42; cf. 1:16; 3:31; 5:2-4, 7-8, 28; 6:14 etc.). These details add nothing whatever to the moral or apologetic lesson of a passage; they do not make a miracle seem more astounding, nor do they heighten the stature of Jesus' personality. Some of them may have been inserted to lend colour to the story: e.g. the mention of the Baptist's 'stooping down' to untie Jesus' sandals, Mk 1:7; 'the whole town gathered at the door', 1:33, etc. Other details may be attributed to an editor's desire to explain matters: e.g. 'so that Jesus could no longer go openly into the town', 1:45; the references to the seaside, the crowd and to teaching, 2:13, etc. But there are many other details which were very probably inserted into the gospel because they represent the evidence of an eyewitness: e.g. the mention of 'hired servants' in 1:20; the statement that the paralytic was carried by 'four men', 2:3; the description of the breaking up of the roof, 2:4; the 'little boat', 3:9; the 'other boats', 4:36; the 'cushion in the stern', 4:38. All these details, of which a long list could be made, are visual details, and there is no reason to deny that they come, as tradition asserts, from Peter.

Some narratives, then, may perhaps be due to Peter himself. Several scholars agree that we should count in this category the following episodes: the call of the disciples, the cure of Simon's mother-in-law, the sudden departure from Capernaum, the call of Levi, the true brothers of Jesus, the rejection at Nazareth, the confession of Peter, the Transfiguration, the story of the rich young man, the request of

[5] Texts in which 'they' is followed by 'he': 1:29-30; 5:1-2, 38; 6:53-54; 8:22; 9:14-15, 30, 33; 10:32, 46; 11:1, 12, 15, 19-21, 27; 14:18, 22, 26-27, 32.

the sons of Zebedee, the entry into Jerusalem, the purification of the Temple, the anointing at Bethany, Gethsemane, the arrest of Jesus, and the denials of Peter. All these episodes are quite different in style from many others, less highly coloured, which Mark may have had to edit or of which he may have had only a summary in tradition (e.g. 3:13–19, 21; 4:10, 12; 6:6–13; 9:9–13; 10:41–45; 14:1–2, 10–11).

Mark was a very gifted storyteller: he faithfully preserved the words of Peter, the eyewitness, and he could retell, skilfully and vividly, stories handed down inside the community. The historical value of his gospel cannot therefore be assessed as if the work were uniform. When Mark is recording the witness of Peter, the historian feels that here is firm ground; but when he records traditions which cannot be attributed directly to Peter, either because Peter was not present (e.g. the stories about the Baptist, of the Temptation, or of the trials before the Sanhedrin and before Pilate) or because the narrative lacks visual detail (e.g. the cure of the leper, the preparation of the Supper), then the historian must examine the value of witness given by the Christian community as a whole. This is far more complicated, and will be discussed in Part III. For the present, we may say that the Gospel according to Mark represents substantially the witness given by Peter and by a community. We must now turn our attention to the witness given by the community: it is most noticeable in the teachings of Jesus recorded by Mark.

4. Mark as a Catechist

Mark's genius for colourful narrative does not include a talent for presenting teaching: his accounts of Jesus' teaching are, by comparison with those in Matthew's Gospel, brief and colourless. Strictly speaking, there are only two speeches in Mark, the collection of parables (Mk 4:1–34) and the eschatological discourse (13). He has preserved only fragments of those long instructions given by Jesus to his apostles, e.g. only four verses on the apostolic ministry (Mk 6:8–9, 10–11) and only twelve or sixteen on the Church (9:33–37,

42–43, 47–50 and 38–41). The controversy about Beelzebub is equally brief (3:23–30), and so is the Philippic against the scribes and Pharisees (12:38–40—3 verses in Mk, by contrast with 36 in Mt and 19 in Lk).

Mark does relate some groups of sayings (e.g. Mk 4:21–25; 7:6–23; 8:34–9:1); but unlike Matthew, he seems scarcely interested in the content of Jesus' preaching. This, presumably, is why he keeps repeating the words 'he taught', 'he spoke the word' and so on, as if to make up for the omission of so much teaching.

The centre of interest in Mark's Gospel, then, is not the teaching of our Lord. Is it the story of his life? At the risk of surprising the reader, we must say 'no'. True, Mark's narratives seem at first sight to be rather long and detailed, but a closer look leads us to question this.

Some narratives are extremely short (e.g. the story of the Temptation, Mk 1:12–13; the call of the first disciples, 1:16–20; the last four controversies in Galilee, 2:13–3:5). On the other hand, five narratives are given at length: the cure of the paralytic, 2:1–12; the possessed man at Gerasa, 5:1–17; the raising of the daughter of Jairus, 5:21–43; the martyrdom of the Baptist, 6:17–29; the story of the epileptic boy, 9:14–29. But, for the most part, these stories have only a sprinkling of details taken from life. The story of the stilling of the storm is only three lines longer in Mark than in Matthew, and that of the multiplication of loaves only four lines longer. Sometimes Mark seems even to have condensed certain narratives, as he has summarized teaching into a few words.

Since Mark summarizes speeches and since his narratives are not as detailed as they appear at first reading, should he be called (to use the traditional term) an 'abbreviator'? If the term implies that he abbreviated a text longer than his own, the answer must be 'no'. But he does go straight to the point, like a good catechist anxious to inculcate in a few words the essential truths. One may, however, ask 'What is this point? Why did he write?' He is not content merely to set out the pattern of apostolic preaching, though this is perfectly recognizable in his work, because he adds to it geographical details, and explanations of Aramaic words or Jewish customs. It is true, too, that certain parts of his gospel seem to have been taken over from an earlier catechetical tradition (*e.g.* the five controversies in Galilee, 2:1–3:5; the parables, 4:1–34; the discussion about Pharisaic traditions, 7:1–23), and that elsewhere we find traces of mnemonic links between sayings (4:21–25; 8:34–9:1; 9:37–50; 11:23–25) or of a grouping of subject matter according to themes (10:1–31). The arrangement of these passages is due rather to men who preceded Mark himself; in other words, these sections stem ultimately from the infant Church, of which Mark is here the spokesman. That is precisely what we mean by a catechist; but Mark, though the spokesman of a Church, also makes a contribution of his own, and so the catechist becomes an evangelist.

5. Mark the Evangelist

Because of its shortcomings in catechetical teaching, Mark's gospel has always taken a subordinate place to those of Matthew and Luke. But even though his is the shortest gospel, he has succeeded perhaps more than Matthew or Luke in fixing the attention of his reader on the mystery of Jesus' Person.

The first words of St Mark are 'The beginning of the Gospel of Jesus Christ, Son of God' (Mk 1:1).[6] Mark is saying, in other words: 'This is how Jesus Christ showed that he was the Son of God, this is the Good News which I am going to tell you and which Jesus himself proclaimed to you.' The phrase 'Son of God' has, even at this early stage, the theological meaning given to it in Christian faith, and with a skill which is proof of the author's desire to teach his reader, the title is used very sparingly. It is used by devils in one story (5:7) and in a summary about exorcisms (3:11); but otherwise it is found only three times in the gospel—twice

[6] Some manuscripts omit the words 'Son of God', but most contain them, and they are accepted as authentic by many scholars.

from God himself at the Baptism and the Transfiguration (1:11; 9:7), and once on the lips of the centurion after the death of Jesus: on behalf of the pagan world, the centurion proclaims 'Truly, this man was the Son of God' (15:39). This was the purpose of Mark's Gospel—to reveal to the pagan world the Good News that Jesus was the Son of God.

This is the theological purpose, clearly stated, of Mark's Gospel, and from it two conclusions may be deduced. First, Mark intended to give a faithful account of what happened before Easter Day. This is particularly evident when we reflect how restrained he is in his ascription of titles to Jesus. As a rule, Jesus is called 'master': the titles 'Son of David' (10:47–48), 'prophet' (6:15; 8:28), and 'Lord' (11:3 (?); 7:28) are for Mark rather exceptional, and the term 'son of Mary' (6:3) is quite surprising. He usually speaks of 'Jesus' (81 times, never of 'Christ Jesus', and of 'Jesus Christ' only in the title (1:1) and in the deutero-canonical ending[7] (16:9). Jesus never refers to himself as 'Christ' except in 9:41 (which probably represents not his own words, but a rephrasing of the text by the Christian community), and insists that his Messianic dignity (*i.e.* the fact that he is the Christ) should be kept secret (8:30) until he himself solemnly affirms it before the Sanhedrin (14:61–62). The only title which Jesus claims for himself is 'Son of Man': he claimed that as Son of Man he would at the Last Judgment judge sinners (8:38), but as Son of Man he also offered them salvation and forgiveness in the present world (2:10), by inaugurating the Messianic era (2:28) and by becoming that Suffering Servant foretold in the book of Isaiah (8:31; 9:31; 10:33; 9:12; 10:45).

---

[7] The longer ending of Mark (Mk 16:9–20), for which there is good manuscript evidence, is considered as canonical and inspired. On the other hand, as Lagrange pointed out long ago (*Evangile selon s. Marc*, 1929 ed., pp. 456–466), several literary details suggest that these verses are not authentic (*i.e.* were not written by Mark himself), but were added by a disciple of the Lord whose authority was acknowledged. There is no good reason for denying that the passage dates back to apostolic times.

The second conclusion is this. According to Mark, Jesus called himself 'the Son' or 'the Son of Man', deliberately concealing his Messianic dignity until his trial; and it was only after his death that he was recognized as the Son of God. The distinctive character of Mark's Christology lies, therefore, in what is commonly called 'the Messianic secret', and this raises a serious problem for the historian. Did Mark himself invent this notion (that Jesus concealed his true identity) or does Mark here represent a very early tradition going back to Jesus himself? This question will have to be treated in the final part of the present book.[8]

For the moment, we shall content ourselves with understanding the teaching of St Mark, namely, that Jesus during his earthly life did not clearly proclaim who he was, but waited until he had shown by his death what his titles really meant. Jesus tried to lead his disciples step by step to a recognition of this truth, and Mark therefore shows how the faith of the disciples developed gradually, and heavily underlines their lack of understanding: in this, he was basing his teaching on the testimony of Peter.

The impetuous style of St Mark's narrative no doubt reflects the impulsive character of Peter; but in judging Mark's narrative we must remember also Peter's depth of vision. From seeing Jesus as a friend and companion, Peter gradually came to see him with the eyes of faith, and the reader of Mark learns how the disciples were led step by step to believe in Jesus as the Son of God. In this sense, Mark re-tells the gospel story as it was seen by the disciples before Easter.

But in another sense Mark can be called a gospel of Easter, for he is the only evangelist who systematically employs the term 'gospel'. His first line is 'The beginning of the Gospel of Jesus Christ', and it is essential to understand this term correctly. It was not until the second century that the word 'gospel' was applied to the four books we call gospels: the first certain instances of this usage occur in Marcion (about A.D. 140) and in St Justin, who mentions (about 150–155)

[8] See pp. 251–254.

'the memoirs of the apostles, which are called gospels',[9] and
the meaning did not become general until the third century.
During the first century, *i.e.* at the time when these four
books were written, the term 'gospel' denoted not 'one of
four books' but 'the Good News of salvation brought by
Christ and preached by the apostles'.

St Mark thought of himself as one of the heralds proclaiming the Good News. For him, the 'gospel' is not a book to be
appreciated or criticized, but an event to be broadcast to the
world. And the event is the arrival among men of the person of Jesus Christ, the Son of God. More accurately, the
event is the ultimate triumph of God through the earthly
life of Jesus.

For Mark does not attempt to write the biography of a
man, even of a God-Man: to a certain extent, this is what
Matthew tries to do, and it is much more true of Luke. Mark,
of course, knew well that Jesus was the 'son of Mary', that
he had 'brothers' and was by profession a 'carpenter' (Mk
6:3), but he is scarcely interested in the earthly background
of Jesus for its own sake: he tells us nothing about his birth
or boyhood or youth.

For Mark, the 'beginning' of the gospel lay not in the
birth of Jesus, but in the ministry of the Baptist, in the Baptism of Jesus and in the Temptation: this is Mark's prologue,
the first thirteen verses of his book. None of the events recorded there is concerned simply and solely with this earth:
Mark indicates their deepest meaning straightaway by intro-
ducing the actors who are going to take part in the drama,
the outcome of which will be salvation for all mankind. John
the Baptist only introduces the leading character, Jesus: the
other actors are the devil and his angels, the Holy Spirit who
reveals himself at the Baptism and drives Jesus to be tempted
in the desert, and God the Father, who speaks from heaven.
After this prologue, various events are narrated to show the
conflict between Jesus and the Strong Man armed: exorcisms,
controversies, disputes and teaching lead up to the Passion

---

[9] 1 *Apol.* 66:3 = PG 6:429 = ANCL Justin, p. 64.

and Resurrection, where Jesus finally emerges victorious. The Gospel of Mark is the Good News of the victory of Jesus over the forces of evil.

6. Mark as a Source for the Life of Jesus

Mark, a story-teller and a catechist, has given his gospel the appearance of a life of Jesus. He took over a certain number of traditions which had already been more or less grouped together by others, and arranged them around certain main centres of interest.

Three events dominate St Mark's presentation of the gospel: the Baptism of Jesus, the confession of Peter, and the Passion. His gospel therefore falls into two parts: (1) the mystery of the Messiah, *i.e.* all that precedes the confession of Peter at Caesarea (1:14–8:30); (2) the mystery of the Son of Man (8:31–16:8). The second period represents a deepening of insight into the knowledge of Jesus of Nazareth.

Inside these two divisions (leaving out the Passion story), the events are not, it would seem, arranged in chronological order. Rather, they are grouped around certain points of catechetical interest: Jesus and the people (1:14–3:6), Jesus and his own family and friends (3:7–6:6), Jesus and his disciples (6:6–8:30). Mark, however, took care to link these various collections of stories together by inserting summaries or connecting verses, and made his work look like the story of Jesus' life. In the Passion story, for example, we find chronological details which are not easily harmonized with one another (14:1, 12) and a reconstruction of the conspiracy against Jesus (does 14:1 depend on 11:18 or vice versa?).

The life of Jesus must have had a real chronological and topographical framework, but Mark's account of it is always subordinated to doctrinal interests, and even to catechetical themes. It is impossible, therefore, to use St Mark's Gospel for a reconstruction of the life of Jesus without taking into account all the re-arrangement which has taken place for doctrinal or catechetical reasons. In other words, literary criticism of Mark is indispensable for anyone who wants to make a sound historical judgment about the work. But in order to assess the historical value of the second gospel, it is not sufficient to study Mark alone: all three Synoptics must be studied together, and along with them, the fourth gospel too. For the moment, we shall have to be content with putting down certain questions, which we shall endeavour to answer at the end of the book. Does Mark's account of the progress of the gospel preaching reflect what really happened? Is the division of Jesus' self-revelation into two periods truly characteristic of the way in which Jesus taught during his ministry? Did Jesus deliberately conceal the fact that he was the Messiah? Can we have complete confidence in Mark's version of events?

And if Mark can on the whole be said to have written a true history, can we say that the details of his work are also historically reliable? Only after his work has been compared with those of Matthew and of Luke will it be possible to outline an answer to this question.

CHAPTER 7

The Gospel According to Saint Luke

1. Authorship

According to tradition, the third gospel was written by a man called Luke, a physician from Antioch in Syria, and a travelling companion of St Paul. This tradition, which goes back to the second century, was never questioned in the early Church, and can safely be accepted by the historian, particularly since it is confirmed at several points by internal evidence.

Everyone agrees that the Acts of the Apostles and the third gospel were written by the same author, for the language and style of each work is the same, and they have a common plan. They are, in fact, two volumes of one work, both addressed to a certain Theophilus (*cf.* Lk 1:3 and Ac 1:1). From internal evidence we know that the author of the Acts was a companion of St Paul, because in certain passages the author suddenly switches into the first person plural (*e.g.* 'We sailed direct to Samothrace': the passages are Ac 16:10–17; 20:5–21:18; 27:1–28:16). And among the companions of St Paul, only Luke would appear to have possessed the breadth of mind and culture to write this great work. We need not delay on this topic, however, since the Lucan authorship of the third gospel and Acts is not contested.

Luke's close relationship with Paul will no doubt make his witness as an evangelist suspect in the eyes of some people. His vocabulary, his style and even the traditions he records (*e.g.* his account of the institution of the Holy Eucharist, Lk 22:19–20) bear marks of Pauline influence; and for some, this will be enough to raise doubts about his version of events. But though the influence of Paul was very real and very deep, it must be clearly said that Luke, unlike Paul, does not present a systematized theology about Christ. Rather, as he tells us in the prologue to the gospel (Lk 1:1-4), his aim was to give a truthful account of the public life of Jesus.

Luke's Gospel is very different from those of Matthew and Mark. The Gospel according to Matthew was, as we have seen, strongly influenced by the needs of the community for which it was written; that according to Mark was cast along the lines of St Peter's preaching. Luke, however, set out to write a 'book' about 'all that Jesus did and taught from the beginning until the day when, having given instructions to the apostles whom he had chosen by the Holy Spirit, he was taken up to heaven' (Ac 1:1-2). He prefaced his gospel with an assertion that he had made careful and exhaustive inquiries in order to provide a solid basis of evidence for the Christian faith. His opening lines run as follows: 'Since many have undertaken to compose a narrative of the events which have taken place among us, just as they have been handed down to us by those who were from the beginning eyewitnesses and servants of the Word, I too have decided, after having informed myself carefully about everything from the beginning, to write the following orderly account for you, most excellent Theophilus, so that you may be fully informed how solidly based is the teaching you have received' (Lk 1:1-4).

It is evident from this sentence that Luke intended his work to be taken as a severely accurate account of events, but in the middle of the sentence he refers to the eyewitnesses whose evidence he cites as 'servants of the Word'. By this phrase we recognize that Luke did not consider them merely as eyewitnesses, as a secular historian might have done; to Luke, they were also preachers, men qualified to narrate and to give the true interpretation of events in the past—*i.e.* they were both witnesses and interpreters. Luke, who recorded their views, is therefore to be considered both an historian and an evangelist.

2. Luke as a Man of Tradition

Every historian endeavours to base his writings on sources which are as close as possible to the events about which he is writing: to have the evidence of a truthful and observant eyewitness is the ideal. Luke claims to have set down the evidence of eyewitnesses, but his manner of dealing with his sources differs from that of most historians in that the traditions which he set down in writing already possessed (in his eyes) a certain authority before he wrote his gospel. Luke did not consider it necessary to check the truth of what those eyewitnesses had said, nor did he seek to provide, by his gospel, an historical justification for a doctrine which was devoid of historical basis. His sole concern was to demonstrate that the current teaching of the Church was in complete accord with apostolic tradition.

Luke wrote his gospel, in fact, at a time when the infant Church was disturbed by nascent heresies. St Paul had to warn the Elders of the Church of Ephesus against certain 'dangerous wolves' who were threatening the Church (Ac 20:29-30); and in the Pastoral Epistles he repeatedly urges Timothy and Titus to hold fast to the doctrine they have received (1 Tim 1:3-7; 4:1-3; 6:3-4; Tit 1:10-11; 3:9-10; 2 Tim 2:14-16, 18; 3:1, 8; 4:3). The activities of some of these men are mentioned in the Acts of the Apostles (e.g. Simon the magician in Ac 8:9-13, 18-24; Elymas, in Ac 13:8-12, etc.).

Like St Paul, Luke was anxious to put Christians on their guard against these false teachers, and though he had not himself been a disciple of the Lord, he was determined to show that the official teaching of the Church and the traditions handed down from the apostles were in full agreement with each other. In other words, he wanted to give Theophilus (to whom his work is addressed) solid evidence that what he had learnt from the Church was what Jesus himself had taught. Hence Luke did not, like Mark, content himself with proclaiming the 'Good News', the 'Gospel'; rather, he com-

posed a book about the teaching of the Church concerning
the life of Jesus.

Since the book was intended to be a kind of 'companion'
to the catechetical teaching of the Church, something must
be said about that teaching. In early days, the pattern of
apostolic preaching consisted of an outline of the main events
in the life of Jesus, together with a summary of his preaching,
in which certain particularly striking 'Sayings of the Lord'
were central. Some of these sayings may have been preserved
in the Pastoral Epistles, where Paul says 'The word is reliable' (*e.g.* 1 Tim 1:15; 3:1; 4:9; 2 Tim 2:11; Tit 3:8), but
the majority, of course, are to be found in the gospels. We
should probably think of the 'essays' (*diegeseis*) mentioned
by Luke in his prologue (1:1) as outlines of the ministry and
summaries of the teachings of Jesus.

St Peter's discourse to the centurion Cornelius would seem
to give a perfect example of this primitive teaching (Ac
10:37–43). It relates the story of Jesus' life from his baptism
to the Resurrection, and this is the framework around which
the third gospel is built. Though it has recently been suggested that Luke himself may have thought up this framework, all the evidence points the other way, and we can safely
say that it must have been taken over by him from the
catechetical teaching of the Church. Luke merely stresses
certain major points in the plan.

To show Theophilus that the teaching he had heard was
no different from what the apostles preached, Luke decided
to read several accounts of what Jesus had said and done, and
then to compose his own book. He insists on the care he has
taken over his research, and (unlike so many other ancient
historians) he does not begin by denigrating his predecessors.
On the contrary, he gladly admits that they had had one
great advantage over him, namely, that they had themselves
been 'eyewitnesses of the Word', while he was writing at
second hand. It is generally admitted that St Luke's Gospel
was written towards the end of the apostolic generation, but
in some ways this was an advantage, which Luke exploited

fully, for he was thus able to examine several accounts of the life of Jesus before setting out to give, in his own version, an 'orderly account'.

This brings us to a most critical point: how did Luke handle his many sources? His command of the Greek language has been admired by all who read the book of Acts (*e.g.* the description of the storm in Ac 27), and yet his gospel offers the strangest mixture of elegant prose and almost barbaric expressions. If we compare Luke's gospel with that of Mark, we find that Luke sometimes writes, instead of a rather crude Markan phrase, a more refined expression; but the next moment we find him writing something which is evidently a bald and literal translation from the Hebrew or Aramaic, while Mark has a thoroughly Greek word. One example will illustrate the point. In the story of the Transfiguration, Mark (9:2) says that Jesus 'brought the disciples up to a high mountain privately alone' whereas Luke (9:28) says that Jesus 'took along with him Peter and James and John to pray'. Yet in the very next verse Mark employs a genuinely Greek term, saying that Jesus was 'transfigured' (*metemorphôthê*) before them, while Luke has the far weaker phrase that 'the aspect of his face became other', as if he had translated it straight from Aramaic or Hebrew. Hundreds of comparisons can be made between Luke and Mark along these lines, and it is not true that Luke's Greek is always more elegant than that of Mark. What is disconcerting is the lack of consistency displayed by Luke in his choice of words, ranging from pure Attic Greek to thoroughgoing Semitic phrases.

The same problem arises when one considers Luke's syntax. Mark, as we have seen, wrote very simple Greek, with a strong preference for co-ordinate rather than subordinate clauses. Luke, in general, prefers subordination, makes full use of the optative mood, and is quite careful in his use of connective particles, as any writer of literary Greek would be. Yet the reader is occasionally astounded to find that where Mark has, for once, a good Greek phrase (*e.g.* Mk 9:18),

Luke puts down a thoroughly Semitic expression which is second-rate Greek (Lk 9:39).

What made Luke so inconsistent in his use of a language in which he was a master? In the prologue to the gospel (Lk 1:1–4) and in the Acts, he writes with a grace rarely found in the New Testament writers. If he had a copy of Mark's Gospel before his eyes, why did he not always polish the literary style as he rewrote each episode? And if he was deliberately using Semitic turns of phrase in order to convey to the reader a 'Palestinian atmosphere', why did he not do so continually and consistently? The simplest, and the only truly satisfactory answer, is to say that Luke did not have a copy of Mark's Gospel to hand when he was writing, and that in his scrupulous regard for detail he made a point of reproducing verbatim whatever sources he did have before him. In other words, Luke was more concerned to reproduce his sources than to write a gospel in literary Greek.

This fidelity to his sources is evident not only in his copying of their words, but also in his arrangement of the narrative. Here it is especially interesting to compare Luke with Matthew. Matthew really 'composed' his gospel in the true sense of the word: he never hesitated to insert a saying of Jesus in a context where he judged it would be appropriate, even though it might have been pronounced on a very different occasion. The Lord's Prayer, for example, was in all probability not taught during the Sermon on the Mount, where Matthew places it (Mt 6:9–13), and Luke may have preserved for us the true context (Lk 11:1–4). Similarly, the saying about the entry of the Gentiles into the kingdom is placed by Matthew in the story about the centurion's son (Mt 8:11–12), where it suits the context admirably; but Luke, though he related this miracle-story (Lk 7:1–10), gives the saying in a totally different place (Lk 13:28–29). Unlike Matthew, Luke did not 'compile' the sayings of Jesus.

Luke's respect for his sources can be deduced from his vocabulary, from his syntax and from one or two isolated texts; and the same respect for sources is evident even in the

verall plan of the gospel. Luke must have had before him a
ource very similar to the Gospel according to Mark, for he
ollows the Markan order closely, and does not intrude non-
Markan material into what we may call 'Markan groupings
f events'. Twice, however, he departs from the order of Mark
nd inserts sections which are found (as such) only in his
ospel. The following plan will make this clear.

	LUKE	MARK
rologue	1: 1– 2:52	
. In Galilee	3: 1– 9:50	1: 1– 9:50
a)	3: 1– 6:19	= 1: 1– 3:19
b)	6:20– 8: 3	
c)		(3:20–35)
d)	8: 4– 9:50	4: 1– 9:50
		(except 6:45– 8:26)
. The Journey to Jerusalem	9:51–18:14	
	18:15–19:27	= 10:13–52
. In Jerusalem	19:28–24:53	= 11: 1–16: 8

Luke made two major insertions into the story of Jesus' life
s recounted by Mark, Lk 6:20–8:3 and 9:51–18:14. The
assages about Beelzebub and the true brothers of Jesus
Mk 3:20–35) do not occur in the Markan order: Luke gives
he former in 11:14–23 and 12:10, and relates the episode
bout the brothers in 8:19–21. Mark 6:45–8:26 is virtually
mitted by Luke, though he has some parallel sentences here
nd there. In short, Luke generally retains the Markan order;
wice he interrupts it to insert a section of his own, but only
nce (Mk 3:20–35) does he change it.

Whatever hypothesis is accepted about the sources of Luke
did he have a copy of Mark before him?), he certainly seems
o have handled them with a respect for traditional order
mounting almost to scrupulosity. Thus, although (as he tells
s) his information was gathered at second-hand, he can be
aid to have handed down faithfully the traditions he had re-
eived.

3. Luke as a Writer of the Theology of History

The historian, though he must be faithful to his sources, ought not to be a slave of them; rather, after examining them, he must arrange and present them according to his understanding of history. This he can do largely because he is able to stand back from the events and see them in perspective. And Luke, because he first examined his sources most carefully and then presented his book as a well-organized narrative, certainly deserves to rank as the evangelist who expounded the history of God's redemptive plan.

Most historians are scrupulous in giving the dates and places of the events they record. Luke does not always succeed in doing so, partly because he did not always have the relevant information, and partly because he was more anxious to present a theological interpretation of events than to write a chronological biography of Jesus. Sometimes, however, he gives extraordinarily detailed information (*e.g.* 2:1–3, on the birth of Jesus, and 3:1–2, on the date when the Baptist began to preach). At other times, he tones down details, apparently because he thought them too precise: thus Matthew and Mark say that the Transfiguration took place 'six days after' the confession of Peter, but Luke writes '*about* eight days afterwards' (Lk 9:28). Elsewhere he inserts the word 'around' in order to qualify a statement (1:56; 3:23; 9:14; 22:59; 23:44).

We have just seen that Luke, in general, follows the same plan as Mark, but not always. For example, when he found a more detailed tradition about the call of the first disciples (Lk 5:1–11), he gave that, but not the story in Mk 1:16–20.[1] As a rule, too, he never gives two stories when they are similar in content: thus he omits the feeding of the four thousand,

---

[1] Here is a list of events reported by Mark which Luke also reports, but in another context: Mk 3:22–30 = Lk 11:14–23; Mk 4:30–32 = Lk 13:18–19; Mk 6:1–6 = Lk 4:16–30; Mk 8:11–13 = Lk 11:16, 29; Mk 9:49–50 = Lk 14:34–35; Mk 10:41–45 = Lk 22:24–27; Mk 12:28–34 = Lk 10:25–28.

because he has related the feeding of the five thousand, and the story about the cursing of the fig tree, because he has already given a parable about the barren fig tree (Lk 13:6–9). He misses out the walking on the water, because he has related the stilling of the storm (8:23–25), and the anointing at Bethany, because he has included the story about the woman who was a sinner (Lk 7:36–50), and so on.

Luke sometimes gives positive details which are lacking in Matthew and Mark. Thus he tells us that the stilling of the storm took place not on the day when Jesus taught in parables, but on another day (Lk 8:22), and he clearly implies that the Transfiguration took place during the night when Jesus, as was his custom, had retired to a hillside to pray (Lk 9:32–37; cf. 6:12; 22:39–40). (This would explain why the disciples were 'overcome with sleep', 9:32.) There are several other examples.

Luke's habit of qualifying statements which are found without qualification in the other evangelists is a blessing to the historian who wants to write a 'Life of Jesus', because he feels justified in subjecting the other gospels to a closer criticism. Unfortunately, it is not absolutely certain that Luke wanted to relate everything in strict chronological order. Some exegetes, for example, have argued that Luke's three statements that 'Jesus went up to Jerusalem' (Lk 9:51–53; 13:22; 17:11) refer to the three journeys mentioned in Jn 7:1,13; 10:22 and 11:54, but this interpretation is now commonly rejected. Luke (in the texts mentioned) is simply reminding the reader that Jesus was on the way to his Passion and Resurrection.

In fact, Luke is so interested in presenting a religious message that he frequently omits chronological data given in Mark. In 5:17 and 9:46, Luke omits all mention of Capernaum (contrast Mk 2:1; 9:33), and in 8:39 he does not mention the Decapolis (contrast Mk 5:20). He does not mention Caesarea Philippi (Lk 9:18) where Mark does (Mk 8:27), or that Jesus' agony took place in Gethsemane (Mk 14:32; Lk 22:40). Once more, these are only a few examples among many. Now in the second half of the book of Acts

(Ac 14–28), which is much more carefully written than th
first, Luke shows an extraordinary liking for detailed plac
names. Why, then, are there so many details missing fron
his gospel? Either they were deliberately omitted because o
some theological reason, or Luke did not read these detail
in his sources; to the present writer, the latter explanatio
seems the more probable.

In fact, certain texts seem to indicate that Luke was no
himself very familiar with Palestine: for example, Palestin
ian houses were not built as he describes in 5:19 and 6:47–4c
in 6:29; 7:14 and 8:5, 6 he refers to customs which were no
prevalent in Palestine, and he is not always accurate on cl
mate or topography (4:29; 9:10; 21:29). The author of th
third gospel evidently lived in a different world from tha
of Palestine, and since he admits that he had not been a wi
ness of the events recorded, his work must be examined ver
critically before it may be used as a source for the life o
Jesus.

This critical assessment of Luke's writing is all the mor
necessary since Luke was not just writing a straightforwar
biography of Jesus, but expounding a theological theme. Whe
we read his gospel, and especially when we compare it witl
those of Matthew and Mark, we discover that Luke (like th
others) is not primarily concerned to give the chronologica
sequence of events, but rather to present, in literary form,
profound insight into the redemptive plan of God. This i
principally evident from his handling of place-names.

The entire gospel is centred on Jerusalem. It opens in th
Temple at Jerusalem, with the appearance of the angel t
Zachary (Lk 1:5–25), and the infancy gospel ends with tw
journeys to Jerusalem, one for the presentation of Jesus ii
the Temple, and one when he was twelve years old (L
2:22–38; 2:41–50). Then, in the introduction to the pub
lic life, the temptations of Jesus reach their climax not (a
in Matthew) on the high mountain, but in Jerusalem (L
4:9–12). After that, Jesus never sets foot in Jerusalem unti
his Passion is at hand (cf. Lk 4:14).

Jesus begins his public ministry in Nazareth, where he i

mmediately rejected by his fellow citizens (Lk 4:16–30), o that he goes to live in Capernaum, a town in Galilee (4:31). From this point onwards, until 9:50, the whole ministry of the Lord takes place in Galilee: the first great omission from the Markan narrative (Mk 6:45–8:26) deals partly with a journey Jesus made outside Galilee, in the neighbourhood of Tyre and Sidon. Luke only takes up the Markan narrative when Jesus returns to Caesarea Philippi (Lk 9:18), but he carefully refrains from mentioning the name, which would have alerted his Gentile readers to the fact that Jesus was not in a Jewish region. In short, the first half of our Lord's ministry is firmly restricted to Galilee (Lk 4:31–9:50).

The second, and longer, insertion made by Luke into the Markan narrative runs from 9:51 to 18:14, and is cast in the form of a journey to Jerusalem. In these chapters, all precise details about place-names are noticeably absent. We read of 'places he had to visit' (10:1) and of Jesus' entering 'a certain village' (10:38), but no names are ever given. Similar vague references occur in Lk 11:1; 13:22; 13:31 etc. Three times in this section the reader is reminded that 'Jesus was going up to Jerusalem' (9:51–53; 13:22, cf. vv. 33–35; 17:11), and when the thread of the Markan narrative is taken up again, the sense of climax is heightened by the repetition that Jesus was nearing Jerusalem (18:31), and even entering Jericho (19:1, cf. 18:35). When they left Jericho, 'Jesus spoke a parable to them, because he was near Jerusalem, and they thought that the kingdom of God was going to start at that very moment' (19:11). Luke concludes the journey with a solemn description of the Lord's entry into the Holy City: he mentions the approach to Bethany (19:28–29), the descent from the Mount of Olives (19:37), the first glimpse of the City, at which Jesus wept (19:41), and finally his entry into the Temple (19:45).

Luke presents much, if not most, of our Lord's teaching in these chapters, and they could rightly be entitled 'The Following of Christ'. The first story in the section is about a man who said to Jesus 'I will follow you wherever you go' (9:57), the second about a man to whom Jesus said 'Follow

me' (9:59), the third about another man who said he would
follow Jesus (9:61). Soon afterwards, a scribe asked Jesus
what he had to do to gain eternal life (10:25), and so the
story continues, with Jesus challenging one man to more de
cisive action, cautioning another by asking had he really
counted the cost, and always teaching crowds and his dis
ciples what following him would mean. In addition to the
three accounts of vocations just mentioned (9:57–62), there
are three sayings about the privileges of discipleship
(10:18–24), three instructions about prayer (11:1–13), three
parables about God's mercy to sinners (15:1–32), three say
ings about the Law (16:16–18) and so on. The lack of pre
cise chronological detail implies that these sayings of Jesus
may have been pronounced on very different occasions, but
as in Matthew's Gospel, they are gathered together by themes
Once more, this creates difficulties for the historian today.

Eventually, the story ends in Jerusalem, with the trial
death and Resurrection of the Lord. In the final chapter o
the gospel (Lk 24), all the scenes (except that on the road
to Emmaus) are set inside Jerusalem, from which Jesus as
cends in glory: there is no mention of any appearances in
Galilee. Thus the story of man's salvation, which had begun
in the Temple, is achieved in the Holy City, and in Acts 1:8
we read that from there the Good News will pass to al
Judea, to Samaria, and to the ends of the earth. The Book
of Acts ends, significantly, in Rome.

The Gospel according to Luke, therefore, is no more a
scientific biography than the Gospels according to Matthew
and Mark. Rather, it is the story of what happened before
Easter told and interpreted in the light of Easter Day. In
deed, the theological interpretation is even more consciously
developed in Luke, in that half of the gospel is devoted to
the theme that it is only by the Passion and Cross that man
can reach the glory of the Resurrection (cf. Lk 24:25–26
45–46). And yet, in pursuing this theme, Luke has (as we
have seen) treated his sources with scrupulous respect. We
may conclude this chapter by trying to penetrate more deeply
into his understanding of the divine plan.

4. Luke as an Evangelist of the Holy Spirit

We must now consider the work of St Luke as a whole (*i.e.* both the Gospel and the Acts) in relation to the first two gospels. Mark simply proclaims the Good News that Jesus Christ, the Son of God, has come to save mankind from sin and death, by means of his own death and Resurrection. The story of Jesus as told by Mark was meant to shock men out of their complacency and to induce them to live in the Church in accordance with the Good News. Mark, however, does not dwell on the consequences which ought to follow from hearing the gospel message; he leaves this out because it is not part of the Good News as such.

Matthew, by contrast, undertook to develop this theme of living in the Church, and therefore composed a systematic gospel in which the major themes of how to live in the Church are systematically expounded.

Luke's aim was different again: his purpose was to trace the history of God's plan from the coming of Jesus until the time when the gospel was preached to the ends of the earth, and therefore he wrote to a particular plan. In Luke, the events of Easter time dominate not only everything which precedes them, but also everything which follows them. Mark, for example, began his gospel with the preaching of the Baptist that 'the kingdom of God was at hand', and ended it with the Resurrection, for on that day the eternal reign of Jesus was truly inaugurated.

Luke retains the basic idea of prophecy and fulfilment, but he alters slightly the Markan details. The 'beginning' is no longer the preaching of the Baptist, and the end is not on Easter Day. 'Until John, there was the Law, and the Prophets; from that time onwards, the kingdom of God is proclaimed' (Lk 16:16). Luke tells the story of Jesus' baptism, but carefully places before it the statement that the Baptist had been thrown into prison by Herod (Lk 3:19–22). Thus the time of fulfilment begins, for Luke, not with the preaching of John, but with the Baptism of Jesus, who is

filled by the Spirit (3:22; 4:1), comes to Galilee with all the
power of the Spirit (4:14), and opens his preaching at Nazareth with the words of the prophet: 'The Spirit of the Lord
is upon me, therefore he has anointed me and sent me to
preach the Good News' (4:21). As the prologue to the Acts
reminds us, the era of fulfilment ran from the beginning
of Jesus' ministry until the day when he was taken up into
heaven (Ac 1:1–2).

The earthly ministry of Jesus, and all the events before his
Ascension, were therefore regarded by Luke as the turning-
point of history. But the Book of Acts tells of a second era
of fulfilment, beginning on the day of Pentecost. Unlike
Matthew and Mark, who thought of history as divided into
two periods, one of promise and the other of fulfilment,
Luke envisaged history as divided into three periods: the time
of Israel, the time of Jesus and the time of the Church.

But in fact the Holy Spirit did not start a new period,
for he had been at work already, during the lifetime of Jesus,
as the texts cited above show. Luke, however, stresses more
than Matthew or Mark the role of the Spirit, and by so doing shows forth the inner unity of history.

CHAPTER 8

What is a Gospel?

In Part I we saw that the gospels enshrine a body of tradition about an historical event. This tradition, handed down by the apostles to the Church and continuously preached in the Church, is presupposed by the epistles in the New Testament, some of which were written before any of the four gospels. There was, then, a common tradition preached and accepted in the Church before any of the New Testament books was written, and it is this tradition which is related by the evangelists in four different ways.

In the second half of this work we shall try to answer the question whether the evangelists give a true picture of Jesus of Nazareth. Do they relate events as they really happened, or have they altered the facts in any way? To answer this question, it is necessary to know what kind of a book each evangelist was trying to write, and how he handled the sources of information which he used.

What, then, were the evangelists trying to write? We can find this out both by comparing the four gospels with one another, and by comparing them with other forms of literature.

Forty or fifty years ago, many authors refused to accept that the gospels were in any way a distinct type of literature, but this position is now virtually abandoned. Today, nearly all scholars admit that they present us with an utterly unique kind of writing, to which there is no exact parallel in any other literature, before or afterwards. Conservative exegetes used to think of the gospels as edifying biographies, and the adherents of that school of thought known as Form Criticism treated them as something rather like scrapbooks compiled from earlier sources, written or oral. The advent of *Redaktionsgeschichte* has brought about a return to a more balanced view, in which the part played by the individual evangelist in the composition and arrangement of his book is seen as something very real and effective. This should be clear from the last four chapters.

Moreover, once a person appreciates the different angles from which the four evangelists wrote their books, he should not easily fall into the error of dismissing the fourth gospel as unhistorical. The Synoptics do not make clear (as the fourth gospel does) that their concern is to arouse and to strengthen the faith of the reader. Some theologians in the past concluded from this that the Synoptics were 'more historical' than John, and either accepted only those data in the fourth gospel which harmonized with the Synoptics or else neglected the fourth gospel completely. But as we have seen, John contains many valuable historical data not recorded in the first three gospels; and one may legitimately ask whether it is possible to understand Matthew, Mark and Luke if they are regarded simply as reporters and not as theologians.

All four gospels claim to be reporting events, and yet all of them are also interpretations. Should we therefore say that they are works of apologetic? Here it is apposite to remember what was said about the apocryphal gospels, which were certainly written to glorify Jesus or a particular apostle, and to show the unbeliever his error in not assenting to the faith. All the apocryphal gospels without exception parade under a well-known name (*e.g.* the Gospel of Peter). In our discussion of the canonical gospels, it was often hard to point to hard-and-fast evidence about the authorship. Indeed, the canonical writers seem to have been almost over-anxious to let their private personalities fade into the background so that they might simply give expression to the faith of the Church.

This point is worth pursuing. Even in early days, the prestige of the apostles became yearly more marked. Luke tells us that in the earliest days, before the martyrdom of Stephen, the Christians in Jerusalem 'used to carry their sick into the streets, putting them in beds or on stretchers, so that when Peter was coming at least his shadow might fall upon one of them' (Ac 5:15). St Paul, in his letter to the Galatians about A.D. 56, calls James, Cephas and John 'these pillars' of the Church (Gal 2:9). It is hard for us to appreciate the extraordinary veneration with which those who had known the Lord were surrounded—St Paul was compelled to denounce some Jewish Christians who attacked his teaching on the ground that they had known Jesus in his earthly life. Yet in the four gospels these same men are presented as foolish, ambitious, cowardly, unwilling to believe; they discussed incessantly the coming of an earthly, Jewish kingdom, and in the hour of trial, all abandoned their Master. Is not the picture of the Twelve given in the gospels a sound guarantee that the evangelists were recording what really happened, and not just projecting on to the past the attitudes of the Church in which they lived twenty or thirty years later?

A similar, and even more cogent argument may be advanced concerning the gospel portrait of Jesus. At the time the gospels were written, Jesus was adored by the entire Christian world as Lord and Christ, as the co-eternal Son of God who would return in glory to judge the world. Yet in the canonical gospels there are hardly any texts spoken by Jesus in which he claimed this role: at the most, there are a handful of allusions which would probably have been incomprehensible to his hearers. He frequently claimed to be the 'Son of Man', but what precisely would this have implied to those who listened to him? And why do the gospels place such stress on this title, when it is conspicuously absent from the epistles of the New Testament? Moreover, why do the gospels not eliminate certain sayings of Jesus which raise immense difficulties about his divinity: *e.g.* his statement that 'the Father is greater than I' (Jn 14:28), his prayer in Gethsemane, his cry on the cross 'My God, my God, why hast

thou abandoned me?' If the evangelists were really writing
naked apologetic, they made a poor success of it, stressing as
they do the sufferings, the weakness, and the disappoint-
ments of Jesus. St Paul has summed up the reaction of men
who read the gospels without faith: 'to the Jews, it is a
stumbling-block, and to the Greeks, plain folly' (1 Cor 1:23).

It is even more obvious that the four gospels are not works
of speculative theology: there is no need to labour the truth.
They are less concerned with doctrine than with a person,
and they see the answer to everything not in rational argument or mystical contemplation, but in listening to Christ
Jesus. They must, therefore, of necessity have claimed to
record what he did and said, because this is all-important for
the Christian. At the same time, a minimum of interpretation was demanded, to guard against possible or actual misunderstandings. Thus we can define the gospel as we did at
the beginning of this second part: it is a written work of
witness and interpretation by an author expounding the
preaching of the Church about the public life, death and
exaltation of Jesus.

PART III

THE PRE-SYNOPTIC
TRADITION

A pious Christian might be content to read and to study the
four gospels simply in order to deepen his own faith by observing the different lessons which the four gospels teach. But
such faith would not be reasonable unless the facts related
by the evangelists (in four different ways) were real facts;
consequently, thinking Christians naturally want to determine
what historical facts lie behind the fourfold gospel tradition.

The title of this third part, however, is 'The *Pre-Synoptic*
Tradition'. Of set intention, the fourth gospel will not be
systematically discussed in this part: it represents (as we have
seen) a prolongation and development of the Synoptic Tradition, and it is also a witness of a tradition parallel to, but
independent of, the pre-synoptic tradition. Our immediate
concern, however, is with the sources which lie behind the
Synoptic Tradition; in other words, we are now going to try
to discover what written documents or oral traditions are
embodied in the Synoptic Gospels as we know them. Once
we have discovered these sources, we shall then try to go one
step further back to the first source from which they orig-
inate, Jesus Christ himself.

CHAPTER 9

The Formation of the Gospel Tradition

i: The Synoptic Problem

There are many striking resemblances, and several equally striking differences, between the first three gospels, and it is not easy to classify them. This raises two questions: why are the gospel accounts often almost word for word the same, and what explanation is there for the surprising divergences? Did the three evangelists make use of earlier written documents, so that the verbal similarities in the gospels are due to the fact that the gospel writers drew on a common source or sources? And if that is so, were these earlier documents long accounts, or were they perhaps just short stories? We shall answer these questions later on, but before we can attempt to do so, we must make clear how complicated the problem is. To appreciate it properly, the reader needs to study the text in an edition which sets out Matthew, Mark and Luke side by side, such as the *Gospel Parallels* edited by B. H. Throckmorton,[1] or A *Synopsis of the Gospels* edited by H. F. D. Sparks.[2] By looking at the way in which verses, and even words, are spaced, it is possible to see at a glance how the gospels agree or differ, even in the smallest details.

[1] New York and Edinburgh, 1957 (Revised Standard Version).
[2] Oxford, 1964 (Revised Version).

1. The Facts

The broad lines of the first three gospels are very much alike: they record more or less the same miracles, the same parables and the same controversies. In short, they present the same picture of the main events in the life of Jesus. The fact is particularly obvious when their narratives are compared with that given by St John's Gospel.

Some modern writers have examined these literary similarities with mathematical methods (*e.g.* by drawing up statistics of word-frequency). Unfortunately, this approach makes no provision for the influence of oral tradition, and takes no account of textual criticism, so that the statistics vary somewhat from author to author, depending on the text he has used. Thus Mt 17:21 is omitted in some editions of the Greek New Testament, put into a footnote by others, and accepted as authentic in others. And it is by no means the only example (*cf.* Mt 18:11; 21:44; 23:13; Mk 16:9–20; 7:16; 9:44–46; 11:26; 15:28; Lk 17:36; 23:17 etc.). Again, if two gospels relate the same story, and one of them contains more detail than the other, should we conclude that the author of the more detailed account had access to supplementary information, or are we to say that he invented it? These are questions which cannot be answered by amassing statistics, and they are not rare in the gospels. In the story of the epileptic boy, for example, Mark (9:15–16, 20–26) gives several details not recorded in Matthew (17: 14–21), and Luke (9:38) tells us that he was an only son. In this instance, statistics can tell us nothing about the truth of the details in Mark and Luke.

But that does not mean that all statistics may be written off as worthless. Statistics can supply figures which give a broadly accurate picture. Thus, 330 verses are common to Matthew, Mark and Luke. This represents about half of Mark (330 out of 661 verses), about one third of Matthew (330 out of 1068 verses), and almost one third of Luke (330 out of 1150 verses). Mark contains only 50 verses or so which are found neither in Matthew nor in Luke: they are the parable of the seed growing secretly (Mk 4:26–29), two verses about the relatives of Jesus (Mk 3:20–21), the healing of the deaf mute (Mk 7:31–37) and of the blind man at Bethsaida (8:22–26), and a few scattered sayings of Jesus. At first sight, then, it looks as if Mark represents the highest common factor of the Synoptic tradition; but this does not explain why Mark contains these episodes which are absent both from Matthew and from Luke, or why Mark omits so much else which is found both in Matthew and in Luke.

If we next consider those passages which are common to Matthew and Luke and have no parallel in Mark, we find that they represent about one-fifth of these two gospels, *i.e.* between 230 and 240 verses. These passages comprise the stories of the infancy, eight parables, a number of stories about Jesus and many sayings of the Lord. Luke has in addition between 500 and 600 verses to which there is no parallel either in Matthew or in Mark. It would seem, then, that Matthew and Luke both drew on a common source, and that each had access, in addition, to a different source (or sources) with which the other Synoptics were not acquainted, or which they purposely did not use.

A detailed comparison of the parallel texts, however, raises real problems. Why are the two versions of the Lord's Prayer (Mt 6:9–13 and Lk 11:2–4) so different in detail? Why do we read in Mt 10:10 and in Lk 9:3 = 10:4 that Jesus forbade his disciples to carry anything at all on their journeys ('not even a staff'), when Mk 6:8–9 says that he expressly allowed them to take a staff?

These are most certainly parallel and related texts. If no one of them was based on any other, how can we ever explain the close verbal similarities? And if any one text represents a rewriting of another, why did the writer make such tantalizing changes in the wording? The 'Synoptic Problem' lies in this: how are we to explain these verbal similarities and discrepancies?

And it is not only in verbal expressions that similarities and discrepancies are found: they occur also in the very order of events in the gospel story. Broadly speaking, the three Synoptic Gospels all begin with the preparation for the public ministry, then tell the story of the ministry in Galilee, then relate the story of his journey to Jerusalem, and conclude with an account of the Passion and Resurrection of our Lord. The broad plan is the same in all three, and it differs widely from the plan followed by St John.

But once again, as soon as we consider this plan in detail, astonishing divergencies come to light. For example, the events related in Mk 1:21–5:43 are all recorded in Matthew; but Matthew presents them in a different order, as the following table shows:

(1)	Mk 1:21–45	=	Mt 7:28–8:15	(1)
(2)	2:1–22	=	9:1–17	(3)
(3)	2:23–3:6	=	12:1–14	(6)
(4)	3:7–12	=	12:15–16	(7)
(5)	3:13–19	=	10:1–4	(5)
(6)	3:22–4:34	=	12:22–13:34	(8)
(7)	4:35–5:20	=	8:18–34	(2)
(8)	5:21–43	=	9:18–26	(4)

Matthew's order is utterly different from Mark's.

Similar remarks could be made about St Luke's Gospel. As a rule, he follows the same order as Mark (much more than Matthew does), but on occasion he has a different one. Thus Mark says that Jesus called his first disciples to follow him before he began preaching in Capernaum (Mk 1:16–20), whereas Luke places this episode afterwards (Lk 5:1–11). Mark records the rejection of Jesus at Nazareth about half-way through the Galilean ministry (Mk 6:1–6), whereas Luke places it at the very beginning (Lk 4:16–30). Other examples may be found by consulting the table of contents in a Synopsis of the Gospels.

The reader can find all these details for himself, and sometimes he will wonder why two gospels differ on an apparently minor point. Why are the second and third temptations of Jesus given in a different order in Matthew and in Luke (Mt 4:5–10 and Lk 4:5–12)? Why, in the parable of the sower, does Matthew say (13:8) that the seed gave harvest a hundredfold, sixtyfold and thirtyfold, and Mark (4:8) that it produced thirty-, sixty- and a hundredfold (in ascending order)? Is it all pure accident? The more closely one compares the Synoptic Gospels with one another, the more astonishing their differences of expression and the variations in the sequence of events become. Is there any hypothesis which will account for all these facts?

2. Various Solutions of the Synoptic Problem

It is generally agreed that the close similarities between the Synoptic Gospels prove that they must be based upon common sources (written or oral), or else, to some extent, upon one another. There is no such general agreement, however, when scholars try to explain the discrepancies which are there. Some authors think that all the discrepancies are due either to the stylistic preferences of the individual evangelist, or to his overall literary plan, or to his particular theological interests. Others, however, while readily admitting these factors, consider that they do not provide a complete explanation of all the facts: they believe that the differences sometimes represent alternative translations of a text originally written in Aramaic, and at other times reflect different versions of an event which were current in the oral preaching of the Church.

During the last two centuries, three main solutions of the Synoptic Problem have been put forward. The first one we may label 'the theory of oral tradition'. According to this theory, the early preaching of the Church rapidly assumed a stereotyped form, partly because of the limited vocabulary available in Aramaic and partly as a result of constant repetition. This alone is said to be sufficient to account for all the resemblances between the Synoptics, and the discrepancies are due (it is claimed) to the different circumstances in which the gospel was preached. Hardly anyone accepts this theory nowadays, for the texts are often so similar and the differences so slight, that there must be some connection between the written *Greek* texts, or at least between our gospels and Greek texts which existed before, and were incorporated into, the gospels.

A second theory is that the gospels are to some extent interdependent. The almost universally accepted form of this theory is that Mark was the first gospel written down, and that Matthew and Luke wrote with a copy of Mark before their eyes. (It is generally agreed that neither Matthew nor Luke had access to the work of the other.) The present writer must here state that he cannot accept the theory that Matthew and Luke wrote with a copy of Mark in front of them: the theory leaves too many facts unexplained (especially in the Passion story), and the arguments put forward in its favour prove only that Matthew and Luke had access, to some extent, to the *sources* incorporated in Mark.[3]

A third theory is that all the resemblances and discrepancies can be explained by positing the existence of written documents which are no longer extant. Some have argued that everything can be explained if we posit that *all three* Synoptic Gospels as we possess them are based on the now lost Aramaic Gospel according to St Matthew. Others posit that Matthew and Luke wrote with a copy of Mark and a written collection of 'Sayings of Jesus' in front of them. The flaw in both these theories is that neither explains *all* the facts, as their supporters, when pressed, admit. It is practically impossible to reconstruct the lost Aramaic Gospel of Matthew; and the 'Collection of Sayings' (often referred to as 'Q') would seem to have been a very bizarre document, lacking any proper order.

Hence scholars are more and more coming to support the view that our three evangelists had access not to any long or well-constructed work, but to various collections of stories and sayings. The idea was originally put forward by Schleiermacher in 1817, a hundred years before Form Criticism was

[3] On the sources used by Mark, see above, pp. 137–138.

heard of. According to this theory, short accounts of Jesus' deeds and words were put together in the very early days of the Church, as a help to catechists: thus there came into being short collections of miracle-stories or of parables, an outline of the Passion story, of the appearances of the Risen Christ, and so on, which the evangelists made use of when writing their gospels. This theory is very widely accepted nowadays as the most satisfactory explanation of the Synoptic Problem.

3. The Documents used in the Synoptic Gospels

The reader should here be warned against an obvious temptation. It might appear from the last paragraph that the evangelists merely collected stories about Jesus which were current in the Church, much as a local historian might collect the folklore and legends of his native town. The pioneers of Form Criticism often treated the gospels as if they had been compiled in this way, without much regard for historical truth. This attitude, however, overlooks the scrupulous regard for fact which was almost a passion in the early Church, as we shall see in the following chapter. At the moment, however, our concern is to demonstrate that small collections of stories did in fact exist before the Synoptic Gospels were composed.

The first piece of evidence lies in the connecting links by which a story is tied to what precedes it. Thus in Mt 8:1 we read that 'when Jesus came down from the mountain, great crowds followed him, and lo! a leper came and fell down before him, saying . . .' It is most unlikely that a leper came to Jesus among 'great crowds'; and if Jesus healed him on the spot, it was rather pointless to enjoin him not to tell anyone about it! Consequently, the first words about Jesus' coming down, with great crowds following, must be just a way of changing the scene after the Sermon on the Mount: in short, they are a literary link, without chronological or topographical significance. The miracle-story may well have been told without any particular context, and Matthew has put it in here. This seems almost certain when we compare the parallel passage in Mk 1:40–45, in which the same story again has no connection either with what precedes or with what follows it. There are many similar examples.

The different passages in the gospels can be classified in various ways. The most obvious distinction is between those which tell a story and those which consist of sayings of the Lord. Often enough, though, his words form part of a story, and a story about him may include some very pointed saying, like 'The son of man is Lord even of the sabbath' (Mk 2:28). Modern scholars try to classify the different kinds of passages by looking for the main point of the episode, on which the writer wishes to fix attention.

Pronouncement stories are passages whose point lies in a saying of Jesus to which all else is subordinated. For example, if the story is about a miracle, then the miracle itself will not be described in detail. Thus in the healing of the man with a paralysed hand (Mk 3:1–5), no details are given about the paralysis and (in contrast with other stories) the amazement of the bystanders is not mentioned. On the other hand, the opening words tell us that the enemies of Jesus were trying to catch him out (Mk 3:2), and the whole issue between Jesus and the Pharisees is summed up in our Lord's saying 'Is it lawful to do good on sabbath days?' (Mk 3:4). This is what is meant by a pronouncement story.

Akin to this type is the *controversy story*, in which everything centres round a short, incisive dialogue between Jesus and his opponents. (The example just quoted would have been a controversy story if the Pharisees had engaged in dispute with our Lord.) Examples of controversy stories can be found in the dialogues with the Pharisees and Herodians over tribute to Caesar (Mt 22:15–22), and with the Sadducees over the resurrection of the dead (Mt 22:23–33). Here all the attention is fixed on the dispute, which leads inexorably to a saying of Jesus whereby his opponents are silenced.

Other passages are known simply as 'Stories about Jesus' —for example, the story about Jesus' blessing of little children (Mt 19:13–15).

There are also *miracle stories*, which nearly always follow a regular pattern. First the circumstances are described, then the miracle, then the effect produced. The style is stark in its simplicity: apart from Mk 7:31–37 and 8:22–26, there is no long description of Jesus' touching anyone or speaking at length (as is generally the case in non-Christian miracle stories). Where there is detail, it is all directed to showing that Jesus was fulfilling his messianic mission. Thus in Mk 1:23–27 the reader's attention is gripped not by the brief saying of Jesus ('Be silent, and go out of him', Mk 1:25), but by the reply of the possessed man: 'I know who you are: the Holy One of God' (Mk 1:24), and by the cries of the crowd: 'What is this? A new teaching, with authority!' (Mk 1:27). The stress is on Jesus as Messiah.

Finally, certain passages in the gospels are simply *summaries* of what follows (*e.g.* Mk 3:7–12). And there is no need to add that the above labels are used merely for convenience: the same episode may be a miracle story and a controversy story and a pronouncement story (*e.g.* the healing of the paralysed man in Mk 2:1–12). The labels are not meant to indicate hard and fast divisions. Rather, they are a help in evaluating the gospels when we see, for example, that Matthew groups several miracles together (Mt 8:1–9:34) or that Mark has a whole series of controversy stories one after the other (Mk 2:1–3:6). Could it be that the evangelists found these groups of stories together, and inserted them as they were into their gospels? If so, then we cannot say that they all took place one after the other, for the evangelists would not have intended to imply that.

One fact, however, is certain: that whatever kind of narrative they were dealing with, the evangelists grouped them all around the person of Jesus. Each of them composed his gospel with the aim of throwing light upon the person of Jesus of Nazareth, and of summoning men to answer his call.

CHAPTER 10

The Formation of
the Gospel Tradition

ii: The Background—The Life of the Church

Since all the short passages underlying the Synoptic Gospels centre round Jesus, it might be thought that if they were arranged in some sort of order, we could at once begin to outline his life. The flaw in this proposal is that it does not make sufficient allowance for the influence of a cultural background on a man's writing: to appreciate accurately any kind of literature, a person must be thoroughly familiar with the culture from which it comes. Hence, before we begin to discuss how the pre-Synoptic traditions can be used to work out a life of Jesus, we must examine the social, cultural and religious background against which those traditions took shape. In other words, we must describe the life and the mentality of the infant Church between A.D. 30 and A.D. 60. We must examine in particular the role played by the Church in the formation and editing of those collections of parables, miracle-stories etc., mentioned at the end of the last chapter.

In the present chapter the influence of the Christian community on the formation of the gospel tradition may seem to some readers to be unduly emphasized. It is well to remark, therefore, at the outset that the author has no desire to underestimate the contributions made by the individual evangelists. In all kinds of writing there is a double element, social and personal; and the really great writer is the man who can give a genuinely personal interpretation of what is commonly known or felt—perhaps only vaguely or obscurely —within the community in which he lives.

What ideas or attitudes, then, did the gospel writers take over from the communities in which they lived? To answer this question, we must ask another: what did the early Christians think of Jesus Christ their Lord? Here much depends on whether we begin by studying the early Christian Church, or by examining first the life of Jesus Christ. The school of thought known as Form Criticism (of which the leading exponents were Bultmann and Dibelius) concentrated all its attention on the early Church, to such an extent that the life of Jesus portrayed in the gospels was regarded as being almost entirely the creation of the early Christian believers.

Their theory is that the early Christians were dazzled by the doctrine of the Resurrection. They were on the whole simple, unsophisticated souls, full of good will and religious enthusiasm, craving for a super-human hero to imitate. Hence they quickly began to idealize Jesus, improving on the original stories about his life until he became a legendary figure of divine stature. This theory, though it is more and more abandoned by scholars, is still widely accepted by others, and is often taken for granted in more popular works even today. The fatal weakness of the theory is that it rests on a false conception of the attitude of the early Christians towards Jesus; and if this presupposition is false, then the whole theory falls.

1. The Church and the Witnesses of the Living Christ

The Church did not begin its life—as a modern society or modern state might—by drawing up a constitution and enacting a code of laws to define its ideals and the conditions of membership for all to see. It began as a group of people sharing a common life, stirred to a religious fervour because some of their number had been privileged to enjoy an unparalleled experience. The earliest examples of Christian preaching sum up the faith of those early believers in words like these: 'Christ died for our sins, in accordance with the scriptures; he was buried, and on the third day was raised to life; he appeared to Cephas, then to the Twelve' (1 Cor 15:3–5). All the earliest texts used in preaching or in worship concentrate on these facts: that a man called Jesus, who was a well-known preacher, had been publicly executed by crucifixion, had been buried, and had afterwards appeared to several of his friends, alive.

It is an undeniable fact that the early Christians believed this story to be true. But they were not content simply to state it as a fact: they also preached everywhere that it had been foretold by God in the Jewish Scriptures, and that by these events salvation was offered to all men. The bald material facts were never stated alone: always and everywhere their significance for mankind was proclaimed, and the happenings themselves were alleged to mark the culmination of God's plans for the whole human race.

These facts can help us to interpret the longer and more developed versions of the early catechesis which we find in the Acts of the Apostles. Indeed, they also supply valuable information about the early years of the Church which is not immediately evident from the Book of Acts. St Luke's work is not a 'History of the Primitive Church', of the type written later by Eusebius of Caesarea; it is far too incomplete. It contains nothing about the foundation of the Church of Rome whose faith, according to St Paul, was renowned throughout the world (Rom 1:8); it tells us nothing about St Peter's life after his release from prison (Ac 12:17), nothing about St Paul after the first Roman captivity, and gives no clear picture of the organization and structure of the early Christian communities.

These lacunae are proof that Luke was not attempting to write an exhaustive account of the life of the primitive Church. Nor is his work a history of the Church's missionary activity, for the work concentrates on three men alone—Stephen, Peter and Paul. All three—and no one else—are called 'witnesses', and Professor P. H. Menoud has even suggested that a more apposite title for the book might be

'The Acts of the Witnesses of the Risen Lord', for these
three witnesses proclaim the Good News first to the Jews,
then to the Samaritans (whom we may call half-Jews) and
finally to the pagan world.

Luke's theme, therefore, was that the Christian community
throughout the world came into being by men's acceptance
of this 'witness'. To write a book with this theme could have
been his own idea; but the theme itself was accepted as a
fact in the Christian Church. Jesus had warned his disciples
that they would be called upon to 'bear witness' about him
in courts of law (Mk 13:9; Mt 10:18; Lk 21:12–14), and before the Gentiles (Mt 24:14; Mk 13:10). St John, too, has
the idea of witness embedded in his theology. Clearly, it was
an accepted notion in the early Church.

(a) Who were the Witnesses?

To qualify as a 'witness' of Christ, it was not sufficient to
have been an eyewitness of his earthly life. The word is sometimes used in the New Testament with this sense (for instance, with reference to the witnesses at the trial of Jesus,
Mt 26:59–61; Mk 14:56–59, or of Stephen, Ac 6:13), but it
then denotes a merely human testimony, based on a purely
human conviction. When, however, certain men are said to
be witnesses (*martureis*) of the Risen Christ, the implication
is not merely that they can give evidence about the Resurrection of Jesus, but also that they have been summoned by
God to explain the religious import of this fact.

This is clearly shown in Luke's account of the election of
Matthias. One hundred and twenty persons were gathered in
the Upper Room when the Eleven met to choose a successor
to Judas. Peter explained that they wanted someone who had
been a witness of the Lord's life from the Baptism to the
Resurrection (Ac 1:21–22), and two disciples were put forward who fulfilled all the conditions. Yet this was not sufficient to make them 'witnesses': God was asked to show, by
the drawing of lots, which of the two was to succeed to the
'ministry and apostolate' left vacant by the death of Judas.

The scene is parallel to that in which the Risen Christ charges the Eleven 'to be his witnesses' (Lk 24:48; Ac 1:8). The witnesses are divinely appointed to proclaim the Good News of salvation. This is the first lesson to be drawn from the text.

We may note secondly that by the preaching of the apostles men are brought into contact, here and now, with the living and risen Lord. St John teaches this doctrine openly (*cf.* Jn 14:26; 15:26–27; 16:13), but it is contained implicitly in St Luke's narrative. When Jesus charged the Eleven 'to be witnesses', he added: 'I will send you the one promised by the Father' (Lk 24:49), or 'You will receive power, that of the Holy Spirit, coming down upon you' (Ac 1:8). So Matthias, after his election, at once receives the gift of the Holy Spirit at Pentecost (Ac 2). When the apostles bear witness, then, the Holy Spirit also bears witness, either directly, by astounding manifestations of power (as at Pentecost, Ac 2:4; *cf.* 2:32), or by giving the apostles an absolute certainty of their mission (Ac 4:31; *cf.* 5:32). It is this conviction of a divine mission, produced by the Spirit, which makes the testimony of the apostles unique, and totally different from merely human testimony about what they had seen and heard.

Thirdly, we see in the story of Matthias that the Church thought of the Twelve as a body of witnesses, specially chosen by God for this task. It is true that Stephen also is called a witness (in Ac 22:20), presumably because he had had a vision of Christ 'standing at the right hand of God' (Ac 7:55). The fact that Christ is said to have been 'standing' (and not, as is more usual, 'sitting') may perhaps imply that he is thought of as 'bearing witness' at Stephen's trial against the false witnesses for the prosecution (Ac 6:9, 11, 13; 7:58). Thus Jesus bears witness that the words spoken by Stephen, through the power of the Holy Spirit (Ac 6:5, 10), are true; and Stephen, therefore, is also a witness, at the hour of his trial.

The only other person to whom Luke gives the name 'witness' is St Paul, presumably because of the mission he had received direct from the Lord (Ac 26:16). Paul was entrusted with a mission by the same Lord who had commissioned the Eleven, and therefore had the same title to be called a witness, but his mission had a different purpose. He had not known Jesus during his earthly life, and therefore could not 'bear witness' that the Christ who had appeared to him in glory was the same person as Jesus of Nazareth who had been crucified. Only the Twelve could do this. They made up the apostolic body of witnesses, and were therefore the foundation of the new Israel, as the twelve patriarchs were of the old (cf. Mt 19:28 = Lk 22:30). As a text in the Apocalypse states, 'the rampart of the City stands on twelve foundations, each one of which bears the name of one of the twelve apostles of the Lamb' (Apoc 21:14).

(b) The Place of these Witnesses in the Church

Though the Book of Acts is not a complete History of the Primitive Church, it does seize hold of the essentials in the infant Church. The early Christian community was not a democracy in which everyone had an equal voice; on the contrary, it was genuinely hierarchical, and its centre was the body of the Twelve Witnesses. The disciples soon became a firmly established community, and the Twelve still retained their unique position. They instructed newly converted Jews (Ac 2:42); when men sold property, they gave the proceeds to the Twelve to administer (4:34–37); to lie to them was to lie to the Holy Spirit (5:3). Their authority was beyond questioning.

Among them, Peter had a special place. He spoke on behalf of them all (Ac 1:15; 2:14; 37–38; 3:4, 6, 12; 4:8; 5:2–3, 29), and such was his prestige that in Jerusalem they would 'carry the sick into the streets and put them down there on beds and stretchers, so that when Peter passed by, at least his shadow might fall upon one of them' (5:15). Later on, the same story is told about Paul (19:12), and it might in fact have been true of other apostles as well, but at least it shows the extraordinary veneration with which they were surrounded. Small wonder that they eventually found it necessary to hand over the administration of money and of relief to others (6:6) in order to devote themselves to prayer and the service of the Word (6:2–4). In these circumstances, the traditions of the tightly-knit community were almost bound to have been immune to outside influences: the danger was rather that they might be stifled in a ghetto of their own making. Closed groups of religious enthusiasts are notoriously prone to creating legends.

The infant Church was saved from turning in on itself by the outbreak of persecution. Stephen was martyred (Ac 6–7), Peter imprisoned (Ac 12), the Greek-speaking disciples compelled to leave Jerusalem (8:1). As a result, the infant community was scattered, but each group carried with it from Jerusalem the memory of what had been taught there in the early years. With the passage of time, their memories of that early preaching would naturally become blurred, at least in details, but it was always possible in the first years after the exodus to check against one another the accounts preserved in the different churches of the new diaspora, as St Luke claims to have done (Lk 1:1–4). It is worth considering these events in some detail.

The first stage was the spreading of the gospel throughout Palestine. After the persecution in which Stephen was put to death, Philip, one of the seven deacons, took refuge in Samaria and began to preach there (Ac 8:1–5). 'On hearing that Samaria had received the word of God, the apostles who were in Jerusalem sent Peter and John' there (8:14) because they alone could set the seal on these new conversions by calling down the Holy Spirit on those whom Philip had instructed and baptized (8:15–16). The Twelve, then, seem to have reserved to themselves, at first, control over the expansion of the community: it is fair to assume that they exercized equal control over what was taught in the name of the community. In the following pages of the Book of Acts, we read that Peter and John preached in several Samaritan villages during their journey back to Jerusalem (8:25), that Philip worked his way down to the coast at Caesarea, preach-

ing everywhere (8:40), and that communities of disciples
were established in Judea, in Galilee and in Samaria (9:31).
Peter visited them all in person (9:32), and when he was
visiting Lydda (the modern Lod, Ac 9:32–35), he received
an urgent request to visit the disciples in Joppa (the modern
Jaffa) too (Ac 9:38).

Peter stayed some time at Joppa, and while he was there
he was called to Caesarea, where he received into the Church
the centurion Cornelius and his friends (Ac 10:1–48). At
first, this action was not well received by the community in
Jerusalem: Peter's stay with the uncircumcised seemed to
them an unwarranted flouting of the Mosaic Law (Ac 11:3;
cf. 10:28, 48). When Peter explained that God had bestowed
on these Gentiles the Holy Spirit, the first step was taken, by
the Jerusalem community, towards accepting the possibility
of a non-Jewish Church.

The second stage in the expansion of the new faith saw
the spreading of the gospel through the neighbouring lands,
Phœnicia, Tyre, Sidon, Beirut, Cyprus and Antioch. During
this period, the disciples seem to have been mainly of Jewish
origin: four out of the five leading teachers at Antioch,
for example, had Jewish names (Ac 13:1). It was at Antioch
that the Church came of age: there they were first recognized
as a group distinct from the Jews—'in Antioch the disciples
were first called Christians' (11:26).

It was in the same city, the cosmopolitan capital of Syria,
that serious tensions within the community began to develop. One group of Christians, of Jewish origin and strictly
conservative, wanted all converts to be bound by the Mosaic
Law: the baptism of Cornelius, after all, had been rather a
special case, in which Peter had been instructed by a divine
command. They regarded it as an exception, not a precedent.
Another group of Christians, however, had their eyes on the
need to preach the gospel to all nations, and perceived that
if the infant Church continued to be bound by the Mosaic
Law, the conversion of the pagan world was no more than a
dream. The story of the controversy between these two
groups, and of St Paul's part in it, is among the best-known

in the New Testament. A group in Jerusalem endeavoured to impose on new converts at least the practice of circumcision (Ac 15:1), but the Twelve as a body refused to accept their plea: the decision of 'The Council of Jerusalem' (Ac 15:23–29) marks the end of the second stage in the expansion of Christianity, and the definitive separation between the Church and the synagogue. Soon afterwards (if not before) the Twelve left Jerusalem to spread the gospel throughout the world, leaving James, the brother of the Lord, in charge of the community in the Holy City. From that moment, the Church of Jerusalem was no longer the focal centre of all Christian believers: it was honoured, of course, as the mother Church of all, and it remained a place of pilgrimage, but it was no longer *the* Church, the sole and unquestioned keeper of the gospel tradition. This was henceforward to be found also in Antioch, in Ephesus, in Rome and in the many churches throughout the world. The Christian Church had become catholic in fact.

During the years which followed, the unity of traditional teaching was secured by the frequent contacts between the various communities. St Paul was not exceptional in the range of his travelling: we know that Peter visited Antioch (Gal 2:11), that some Christians at Corinth claimed him as leader of their faction (1 Cor 1:12), and (as tradition firmly states) that he died a martyr in Rome. There were, of course, quarrels and dissensions, between Paul and Barnabas (Ac 15:36–40; *cf.* Gal 2:13) and even between Peter and Paul (Gal 2:11, 14); but in spite of the strong words spoken, and the clash between different temperaments, one and the same traditional teaching about Jesus continued throughout the world.

Thus from the beginning the Church was built up by the chosen witnesses and apostles, who guided its destinies at each major turning-point and controlled its teaching until the age in which the gospels were committed to writing. Some German scholars have recently suggested that this picture of the Church as given by Luke in the Acts of the Apostles is not accurate: they say that when the early Christians began to feel that Christ's second coming was being delayed longer than they had expected, Luke put forward a new version of events, presenting the Church as a society organized for a long existence. But is it not antecedently probable that the first Christians would have grouped themselves round the Twelve, and accepted them as their natural leaders? Moreover, the account given by Luke in the Book of Acts harmonizes with everything else we know from the New Testament: Jesus continued to speak to his disciples through the Twelve whom he had chosen precisely for this task, and through them to guide and inspire his Church, by the gift of the Holy Spirit.

2. The Gospel before the Gospels

In spite of this rapid expansion, the Twelve do not seem to have contemplated writing a 'definitive biography' of their Master which might have stood as a monument to his memory for all future ages. He had never told them to write his biography, but he had commanded them to preach about himself to all nations. This they did.

(a) The Proclamation of the Gospel

Modern Christians, brought up in an age of almost universal literacy, often wonder that Jesus did not write a book—even a book of sayings, for example, like the *Meditations* of Marcus Aurelius. The early Church had no such worries, and for thirty years or so was content to hear the story of Jesus' life, and the content of his teaching, passed on by word of mouth. With our modern habit of reading, we are inclined to look upon the four gospels as being rather like biographies; but to see them as their authors did, we must make a mental adjustment and try to hear in them the echo of that apostolic preaching which they are concerned to set forth.

The proclamation of the Resurrection was certainly something without precedent, but even the fact of the Resurrection is presented in the New Testament as one event—the central event, of course—in a broad historical design. In the earliest text of the New Testament, written around A.D. 50, St Paul describes how the people of Thessalonica had come to know about Jesus. 'Our preaching of the gospel to you did not consist in words alone; it also had a power, and a Holy Spirit, and was full of confidence . . . (All) are telling the story about us, about the welcome we received from you, and of how you turned away from idolatry to God, to become servants of the living and true God, and to await his Son from heaven, Jesus, the one whom he raised from the dead and who will rescue you from the wrath that is coming' (1 Thess 1:5, 9–10).

In this text, St Paul mentions, along with the Resurrection, two other facts which are closely related to it, the bestowal of the Holy Spirit, and the return of Christ in glory. In his theology, the miracles which accompanied the establishment of the Church (cf. Gal 3:2–5; Ac 10:44), and the joy felt by Christians even under persecution (1 Thess 1:6; cf. Ac 5:41 and 1 Pet 4:13) were proofs of the presence of the Spirit and of the fact of the Resurrection; and they were at the same time guarantees that Jesus would one day return in glory.

These three elements (the experience of the Holy Spirit, faith in the Resurrection, hope in the coming of the Lord) are always and everywhere essential to the preaching of the gospel, but stress will be laid on one or another at different times. The first Christians, for example, were so conscious of the gift of the Spirit and so convinced of the fact of the Resurrection that their main interest turned towards the future, as they eagerly awaited Christ's return in glory. At Thessalonica in particular, this expectation became at one period so intense that it led some of the community to pity those who had died, because they would not witness the Second Coming (1 Thess 4:13–18), and even to give up their ordinary work in the world (2 Thess 3:10–13). It was necessary to correct extreme opinions of this kind by placing the emphasis where our written gospels place it—on the fact of the Resurrection.

St Luke took up the threefold theme of the Resurrection,

Pentecost and the Second Coming, and built around it the various speeches in Acts, in which great care is taken to present not just the naked facts, but also their religious significance.

For instance, he records the story of Pentecost, at which men from every nation in the Roman world heard the apostles speaking in their own tongues (Ac 2:4, 11). Peter explained that this was the fulfilment of a passage in the book of Joel (3:1–5), that young men and old would give utterance to prophecy 'in the latter days', in the final epoch of time. Later, when the Jews were astounded to see a man crippled from birth walking and leaping around, Peter explained that this healing had been performed by the invocation of the name of Jesus of Nazareth (Ac 3:6, 12), and immediately seized the chance to assert that the death of Jesus had been foretold in the Jewish Scriptures, and was part of God's design (3:18). The presence of the Holy Spirit and the miracles performed by the apostles were set forth as so many proofs that Jesus, who had been crucified, was alive again, and at work through his Spirit and his disciples (Ac 2:22–24, 36; 3:13–15; 4:10; 5:30–31; 10:39–40; 13:27–30). Indeed, the apostles repeatedly claimed to have seen him (2:32; 3:15; 10:39, 41; 13:31 etc).

In their certainty about the Resurrection, the Twelve could not but proclaim it. They believed that the same Jesus would one day return to judge all mankind (Ac 10:42), and that all men were therefore confronted with the alternatives of accepting or rejecting their claim that Jesus was alive. This was the theme of their preaching: that Jesus was again alive, summoning all men to repent of their sins and to accept the gift of eternal life. Thus the Book of Acts is really just a further development of the theme stated in the first Epistle to the Thessalonians, showing forth more clearly the connections between the Resurrection, the gift of the Spirit and the Second Coming in glory.

The more closely we look at the speeches in the Acts of the Apostles, the more clearly we perceive that the new religion is not presented as the creation of a religious genius, but as the final flowering of the Jewish faith. Jesus himself had claimed that he had come to fulfil the Mosaic Law, not to destroy it (Mt 5:17), and Paul made the same claim before the Roman governor of Judea (Ac 24:14). Luke never ceases to stress this point. The apostles, according to Acts, always dwelt at length upon the plans of God for sending salvation to all mankind, and then explained that these plans had come to maturity in the death and Resurrection of Jesus, both of which had been prophesied in the Jewish Scriptures. Following the example of Jesus (*cf.* Lk 24:25–38), they insisted everywhere that he was the expected Messiah (Ac 18:5, 28), of whom Moses and the prophets had spoken (3:21; 9:22; 10:43; 13:15; 17:2, 11; 26:22, 27; 28:23).

And the apostles did not refer to the Scriptures only in a vague or general way. Peter explained the miracle of Pentecost by citing a very precise text from Joel (3:1–5) about 'the end of time' (Ac 2:17–21). Before the Sanhedrin, he and John argued that even the conspiracy against Jesus had only fulfilled the prediction of Ps 2, that the kings of the earth—Herod and Pilate—would conspire together against the Lord and his Messiah (Ac 4:25–26). The death and ultimate triumph of the Servant of the Lord had been unforgettably described in Is 53, and the early Christians never tired of stressing how exactly this text fitted in with the passion and exaltation of their Lord. Is 53:7–8 are cited in Ac 8:32–33, but elsewhere Jesus is called 'God's holy son' (3:13, 26; 4:27, 30), 'the Righteous One' (3:14; 22:14; *cf.* Is 53:11), who was 'handed over' to sinners (3:13; *cf.* Is 53:12). His rising from the tomb (the apostles claimed) had been foretold in the 16th psalm (vv. 8–11): 'Thou wilt not permit Thy Holy One to see corruption' (Ac 2:25–28; 13:35). Jesus, by commanding his disciples to preach to all the Gentiles, had even fulfilled one of the oldest prophecies in the Bible: God had promised Abraham that all the nations of the world would be blessed in his offspring (Gen 22:18), and in Jesus, a true son of Abraham, God's word had been fulfilled (Ac 3:25–26). The prophecies cited, like the stained glass in Chartres Cathedral or the frescoes in the Sistine

Chapel, are a continuous reminder that God's plans reach across history and envelop all things in their scope. The apostles did not cite these various texts to 'prove' things by rigorous logic (as a modern reader might hope); rather, they used the Bible to explain and interpret to the Jews the inner unity and harmony of God's designs.

In fact, it would seem that quite early on Christians began to put together *florilegia*, or 'selections' of Old Testament texts which were obviously apposite to the life of our Lord. We know for certain that such collections were available by A.D. 200, but by examining which Old Testament texts are most frequently cited in the New Testament, we can see at once what themes and passages commanded most interest. C. H. Dodd, in his remarkable book *According to the Scriptures* (London, 1953), groups what he calls 'the Bible of the primitive Church' under four heads.

The first set of texts concerns the 'end of time', 'the latter days', *i.e.* that 'final epoch' in the history of salvation when God's plans would reach maturity. The texts used were principally Joel 2–4, Zechariah 9–14, Daniel 7 and 12, and Malachi 3:1–5. A second series spoke of the 'new Israel' which the Church saw foretold in Hosea (principally in 2:1, 25), in Isaiah 6:1–9:7; 11:1–10; 29:9–14; 40:11, in Jeremiah 31:10–34; 7:1–15 and Habakkuk 1–2. The third and fourth series concerned the person and the work of Jesus: here the main texts were Is 42; 52–53, the psalms about the sufferings of the Righteous (Pss 69; 22; 31; 34; 118; 41–43; 80) and the Messianic psalms (Pss 2; 8; 110). From these texts it is possible to reconstruct the outlines of the earliest Christian theology.

Peter expressed the conviction of the early Christians that they were living in the final epoch of history when he inserted into the text of Joel one word: 'in those days', said Joel, but Peter quoted the text as 'in the *last* days' (Ac 2:17; *cf.* Joel 3:1). He made this insertion because he believed that the promise in Joel had been fulfilled by Jesus' sending out his Spirit upon all mankind. According to Joel, God had said that he himself would bestow his Spirit on all mankind; according to Acts, Jesus, enthroned at the right hand of God, had done this. The burden of the gospel preaching, therefore, was that 'Jesus was Lord'. This was a staggering message to preach to Jews, and therefore the apostles were at pains to stress that his ignominious treatment had been foreseen and ordained by God (Ac 2:23; *cf.* 4:28), and predicted by the prophets. In support of this contention, the apostles interpreted the Old Testament texts mentioned in the last paragraph by applying them to Jesus (*e.g.* Ps 16:8–11 = Ac 2:25–31; 13:34–37; Ps 110:1 = Ac 2:34–36; Ps 132: 11 = Ac 2:30; Ps 2 = Ac 4:25–27). Jesus had brought salvation to all the races of the world. 'Those who stood far off' were now invited to come and sit with the children of Abraham at the Messianic feast in the new kingdom (Is 57:19 = Ac 2:39; 22:21). All that was required of them was 'to call upon the name of the Lord' (Joel 3:5 = Ac 2:21) and to obey the age-old injunction of Moses (Lev 23:29 = Ac 3:23) by repenting of their sins and turning to the Risen Christ (Is 59:20 = Ac 3:26).

This, then, was the content of the gospel, deeply rooted in the ancient traditions and beliefs of the Jews, but at the same time firmly orientated to the future, when Christ would return in glory. How was it presented? To this question we must now turn.

(b) The Contexts in which the Gospel Tradition was formed

There are three principal contexts (what German scholars call the *Sitz im Leben*) in which the gospel tradition was formed. Each of them contributed something to the style of presentation: the gospel was taught through divine worship, by catechetical instructions, and in missionary discourses. In other words, the gospel story was recounted in a slightly different way according to the background. Our main sources of information are the epistles in the New Testament and the Acts of the Apostles. Three times in Acts St Luke makes statements about the life of the early Christians (Ac 2:42–

47; 4:32–35; 5:12–16). Two verses sum up his description:
'They were firmly attached to the teaching of the apostles,
to fellowship, to the breaking of bread and to prayer' (2:42);
'with great power, the apostles bore witness to the resurrection of the Lord Jesus, and they were all held in high esteem'
(4:33). Worship, teaching, and preaching backed by miracles
were the characteristics of the apostolic ministry. We must
discuss each in turn.

The distinctive act of *Christian worship* was the ceremony
referred to as 'the breaking of bread' (Ac 2:42), which along
with 'the Supper of the Lord' was a standard term for the
celebration of the Holy Eucharist. St Paul was probably
familiar with both terms (*cf.* 1 Cor 10:16; 11:23–25), and
the slight verbal discrepancies between his account of the
rite in the second text mentioned and that given in Matthew
and Mark show that there was at that time no firmly fixed
form of words. Indeed, there was probably a real difference
of rite from place to place.

Apart from the eucharistic rite, the disciples met for common prayer (Ac 2:42), over which the apostles presided
(4:24–30). The ceremonies of baptism were apparently performed with great solemnity (Ac 2:41; 8:36–39; 9:18; 10:
47–48; 19:5; 22:16). From other evidence in the New
Testament, it would seem that during the ceremony of baptism suitable hymns were sung (*e.g.* Eph 5:14; 1 Tim 3:16;
1 Pet 1:3–5; 2:22–25; 3:18–22; 5:5–9). The eucharist and
baptism were the essential and central acts of worship, but
elsewhere we read of the 'laying on of hands' to confer on
the baptized the Holy Spirit (Ac 8:17), or to commission the
seven deacons for their new office (6:6), or to prepare
Barnabas and Saul for their missionary work (13:2–3). (The
last text shows that fasting and prayer were associated with
worship, and that 'revelations' took place in the course of it.
We may note also that divine worship at Corinth seems to
have been at times a very disorderly and unedifying spectacle,
to judge from St Paul's reactions in 1 Cor 12:3; 14:1–40.)
It would have been surprising if the regular worship of the
Church had not had deep influence on the presentation of

the gospel. The importance of this influence is today acknowledged by all scholars.

The story of the Last Supper, for example, as it is given in the gospels, probably reflects the liturgical formulas used in the eucharist at Jerusalem (Mt, Mk) and Antioch (Lk, 1 Cor 11) in an age when these formulas were more or less fixed, without having attained a hard-and-fast form. Indeed, the same eucharistic formulas seem to have influenced the wording of the miracle story in which Jesus, to feed the five thousand, 'broke bread, and gave it to his disciples' (Mt 14: 19 and parallels; *cf.* 26:26 and parallels). In the eyes of the early Christians, this miracle foreshadowed the gift of the Holy Eucharist—an idea which John developed at length (Jn 6). Great care is needed, of course, in assessing the degree to which liturgical formulas have affected the expression of a story in the gospels, and one must not exaggerate its influence. But neither must one neglect it.

Much more influential than liturgy, however, was the *catechesis,* or the regular *instruction* given by the Church. Luke tells us that from the first days, the faithful were 'strongly attached to the teaching (*didache*) of the apostles' (Ac 2:42). New disciples had to be taught the principal facts about the Lord Jesus, and about the meaning of the Jewish Scriptures. Philip's instruction to the Ethiopian provides a clear example of the method used (Ac 8:26–40); it is modelled upon the discourse of Jesus on the road to Emmaus (Lk 24:25–27), and is exactly the same kind of explanation as Jesus had given in the synagogue at Nazareth (Lk 4:17–21). Where the apostles, in their preaching to non-Christians, usually began with Pentecost and the Resurrection, and then went on to show how these events had been foretold in the Scriptures, Philip began (as seems to have been the custom when preaching to believers) by taking an Old Testament text and then going on to explain the Good News about Jesus (Ac 8:35).

In this teaching, the main stress fell on the assertion that Jesus was Lord, the Son of God and the Messiah or Christ. And the evangelists often changed slightly (but significantly) the wording of a story to bring home to their hearers these truths. For instance, in the story about the stilling of the storm, Mark (4:38) and Luke (8:24) record that the disciples in their panic awoke him with the word 'Master', but Matthew (8:25) says they addressed him as 'Lord' (*Kurios*), a title given to Jesus only after the Resurrection. And in the story about Jesus' walking on the water, Mark (6:51) says the disciples were overcome with amazement, while Matthew writes (14:33) that they cried out 'Truly, you are the Son of God'. In these two examples Matthew is telling the story rather freely, using language which is (strictly speaking) anachronistic, in order to teach the faithful who already believed in Jesus about the devotion of the disciples. In doing so, he has no scruples about placing on the lips of the disciples terms and phrases like 'Lord' and 'Son of God', even though these had not been applied to Jesus before the Resurrection. It would be pedantic to criticize him for this: we should not despise a journalist who wrote that 'Pope John XXIII was born at Sotto il Monte' on the ground that he ought to have written 'Angelo Giuseppe Roncalli . . .' Matthew has only taken the process one step further, for a didactic purpose, and without any thought of misleading the reader.

The Synoptic Gospels, especially Matthew and Luke, are shot through with this 'theological' language. When the disciples abandoned Jesus at his arrest and took to flight, one might attribute it to simple cowardice; but the gospels insist that they had been 'scandalized' (*i.e.* had found his arrest a stumbling block to their faith, Mt 26:31, 33), and that the event itself fulfilled the prophecy of Zechariah (13:7). The material, historical fact was thus presented with a theological and biblical interpretation.

It would seem that when the preachers were eye-witnesses, the teachings and sayings of Jesus were related with considerable details of time and place (as in Mk 1:21–39). This was practicable as long as the closest disciples were recounting their own, firsthand, experiences. But as the number of disciples increased and the new religion spread geographically, more and more catechists were needed, and they had not all enjoyed the same close intimacy with the Lord. It was presumably for their convenience that short summaries of Jesus' teaching were drawn up, without any precise historical context, for the catechists' main work was answering the questions put to them, applying the gospel to problems of the day and so on, to show how the Christian message ought to inform their lives. So we read stories which are evidently meant to illustrate Jesus' teaching on fasting (Mt 9:14–17 and parallels), on divorce (Mt 19:1–12), on paying dues to the Temple (Mt 17:24–27) and taxes to the imperial government (Mt 22:15–22). Some of the most burning questions concerned the end of the world and the Return of Christ: when would he come (Mt 24:4–8)? How (Lk 17: 20)? Why did he delay his coming (Lk 12:45; Mt 25:5)?

Almost every page of the Synoptic Gospels bears some trace of the influence of catechetical instruction, and there is no need to labour the point. It is, however, essential to grasp the full implications of admitting the influence of catechetical instruction on the style and general presentation of the gospel message. The gospels may relate an event in widely different contexts; or there may be significant verbal discrepancies between their narratives (as in the story of the stilling of the storm). This does not necessarily mean that one gospel has set the story in its correct historical context, and that the others have put it in a false context either by mistake or by deliberate falsification. It does mean that we have to ask 'Why did *this* evangelist place it *here*?' Perhaps (like Mark in 2:1–3:6) he was simply setting down a collection of controversy stories to show our Lord's mind on various disputed issues, or to show the attitude a Christian should take to the Jewish law. And even when Matthew shows the disciples addressing Jesus as 'Lord' and 'Son of God' before the Resurrection (Mt 8:25; 17:4, 15; 14:33), he does not intend to trick his readers into believing that the disciples had acknowledged the divinity of Jesus even before his death: Matthew is merely telling Christians that amid the storms of life they should cry out 'Lord, save us! We are lost', as the apostles had done on the lake of Galilee (Mt 8:25), and as Peter had done when he felt himself sinking into the water as a result of his doubting the Lord (Mt 14:30). For (as the apostles recognized) one who could save them from such disaster was truly the Son of God (Mt 14:33).

The third great influence on the formation of the gospel tradition was the need for *missionary preaching*, i.e. preaching to those outside the community. Here, alongside ordinary preaching, controversy and apologetic played a large part.

Its influence, naturally enough, was first and foremost on the miracle stories, for these formed the foundation of Christian apologetics to the world. Peter appealed to the Jews to remember the 'mighty works, wonders and signs' which Jesus had performed among them (Ac 2:22): surely these were evidence that 'the finger of God was there' and that 'the kingdom of God had arrived' (cf. Lk 11:20). Moreover, as Peter elsewhere explained, these miracles were themselves evidence that God's time for redeeming Israel had come: Jesus had done good everywhere, healing all those who were under the control of the devil (Ac 10:38). His healings were visible signs of the Messianic age, as he himself had told the disciples of the Baptist (Lk 7:18–23).

To the missionaries, the miracles of Jesus were obviously of first importance, but the most remarkable feature of the gospels is the relatively small number of miracles recorded. John informs us that Jesus performed many other miracles in the presence of his disciples (Jn 20:30), and similar remarks are found here and there in the Synoptic narrative (e.g. Mk 1:39). It would seem that the early Christian preachers selected only one or two examples of each kind of miracle (e.g. of giving sight to the blind, enabling cripples to walk, etc.) and so the stories became standardized accounts. It is interesting to observe how they do not stress the extraordinary—i.e. the strictly miraculous—side of the occurrences, but the faith or astonishment of those who witnessed the event: the evangelists were concerned not primarily with the material fact, but with the response it provoked, in the hope of eliciting a similar response from their hearers. This is especially evident in St Matthew's narratives of the storm on the lake (8:23–27) and the walking on the water (14:24–33). The first led the disciples to ask 'What kind of man is this?', and the second led them to answer 'Truly, you are the Son of God!'

In certain groups of miracle stories, a theological intention can be perceived. For example, Mt 8:1–17 seems to be a collection of miracle stories placed side by side to show Jesus as the Redeemer 'who took upon himself our infirmities and shouldered the burden of our sins' (Is 53:4, cited in Mt 8: 17). We read there of the healing of a Jew, of the servant of a pagan centurion, and of Peter's mother-in-law. By placing these three stories together, Matthew teaches us that Jesus had come to take upon himself the burdens and sufferings of all mankind—of Jews, Gentiles and Christians alike. There is no reason to think the events are set in chronological order.

The influence of missionary preaching is seen in the controversy stories also, which illustrate how Jesus so often silenced those who made accusations against him. These passages provided the disciples with guide-lines in their debates (sometimes bitter ones) with Jews. Almost any series of controversy stories would illustrate this point, but perhaps the clearest group is that in Mt 22:15–46, in which Jesus reduces to silence each of the main schools of Jewish thought one after another. Indeed, Jewish hostility to the infant Church led the disciples to say clearly that the leaders of the people had committed an appalling crime by plotting the death of Jesus (Ac 2:33; 3:13; 7:60; 10:39), though it must not be forgotten that the same texts assert that they acted through ignorance (Ac 3:17; 7:60) 'without realizing' what they were doing (13:27). The apostles did not want to make Christians hostile to the Jews; how could they, being Jews themselves? But equally they were determined to preach to the people of God that the Scriptures, the eternal plans of God (Ac 2:23; 3:18), had reached fulfilment, and that Israel was summoned to 'listen to his voice, today'. In this, they were but echoing the appeals of the great prophets of old—Amos, Isaiah, Micah and the rest.

Worship, catechetical instruction and missionary preaching each had its influence on the way the gospel stories were expressed, or on the way in which they were grouped together. The early preachers were anxious to stress the relevance of our Lord's life and teaching (*e.g.* in his attitude to the Mosaic Law), and its universal appeal to men of all nations. Thus, when the time came to set down in writing the life of the Lord, there was no danger that it would be written as a cold, rationally ordered list of facts and speeches. The whole Church had been thinking about it for thirty years, from A.D. 30 to 60, and the written version of his life and teaching was bound to be an 'existential' writing, showing forth the significance for men of all that he had done or said.

3. The Writing of the Gospels

The various collections of records of Jesus (parables, miracle stories etc.) which underlie our gospels were given a central theme and an existential interpretation by their use in the preaching of the Church. It would seem, too, that soon afterwards these same records began to be arranged on a biographical plan roughly similar to that found in the Synoptic Gospels. This last point has been contested, and some scholars argue that the arrangement of the stories into a kind of 'Life of Jesus' came much later on, so that its historical value is low, if not negligible.

Dibelius and Bultmann, for example, have argued that the earliest records about Jesus consisted of short sayings, pronouncement stories etc., on the ground that the simplest forms of the gospel literature must have been the oldest. They conclude (logically enough) that the more complex 'Stories about Jesus' must have been composed at a later date, and that the arrangement of all the different types of literature into a chronological framework must have been the last step of all.

But why must we assume that the simplest forms are necessarily the earliest? There are no parallels in other literature to provide an argument by analogy. In the opinion of the present writer, the various forms of literature found in the gospel arose quite naturally from what we may label the 'theological' and 'historical' preoccupations of the Church. (In speaking of 'historical preoccupations' we do not imply that the early Christians were interested in, say, the archaeology of the Holy Places. They did turn their attention to the past, but not in order to study it as an 'objective fact'; rather, they sought to find in it guidance about the way in which they themselves ought to respond to the teaching of their Master. In modern language, we should say that they had an existentialist, rather than a positivist, attitude to history.)

In the first years after the Resurrection, Christians developed insights of their faith in worship, in catechetical instructions and in missionary preaching, all centred round the person of our Lord Jesus Christ. This inevitably created a demand for some kind of 'biography' of Jesus, and so the chronological and geographical framework of his life became part of the customary preaching. It is an over-simplification, however, to say (with Dibelius and Bultmann) that the earliest strata of the gospel tradition are necessarily to be found in the least complex passages. The more 'biographical' details are supplied, the more probable it is that the passage represents preaching given to people who had never known (even by hearsay) about Jesus. By and large, these would have been people outside Palestine; and therefore it is generally true that the more biographical passages will belong to a later date, when the Gospel was being preached to the Gentiles. At the same time, it must not be forgotten that these biographical details do not occur everywhere, and are usually found in those parts of the gospels where there is good evidence to think that the other details betray an eye-witness. (The fourth gospel, though it was the last to be set down in writing, contains many details which had passed unmentioned in the earlier gospels: *e.g.* John alone mentions that it was Judas who protested against the anointing at Bethany, Jn 12:4, and that the two parties to the scuffle in Gethsemane were Peter and a man named Malchus, Jn 18:10.)

The historian must assess the value of these details. The first point to be noted about them is their comparative rarity. Form critics have dwelt eloquently on the 'creative imagination' of the early Christian community, claiming that the early disciples made up many of these stories, or else refurbished the true history of Jesus with a wealth of newly created doctrinal truths. If that were true, why did the early Christians not make up more convincing stories, especially about those problems which exercised their minds, such as the mission to the Gentiles, the necessity of circumcision, the order of charisms in the community, and the external organization of the Church? They could easily have invented directives from Jesus on these issues, yet (as Vincent Taylor has pointed out[1]) the number of episodes connected with these problems *diminishes* as time passes: there are twenty in Mark, seven or nine in Luke, four or five in the source common to Matthew and Luke, one in Matthew and none at all in John. Moreover, if the early communities were inventing their own versions of our Lord's life, why did they retain so many stories about his controversies with the Jews, which—though of interest to Jewish Christians—would have been rather perplexing and pointless to Gentiles? Is it not more reasonable to think that the early Christians were genuinely interested in the earthly life of their Lord, and wanted to know the historical facts about him? In short, a close *literary* analysis of the gospel tradition leads us to conclude that it records trustworthy historical fact, precisely because the early Christians were interested in the life of their Master.

The same conclusion is forced upon us if we reflect on the *social background* to the expansion of Christianity. The first converts, in Palestine, would certainly have known about the life and teaching of Jesus, at least from hearsay; and, as Jews, they believed that the God of Israel would one day send redemption to his people, to bring them forgiveness of

[1] *The Formation of the Gospel Tradition*, London, 1933.

sins. They, therefore, could quite legitimately concentrate their attention on Christ in glory, because the earthly life of Jesus was known to them. This is precisely the presentation we find in the Gospel according to Matthew.

Once the gospel began to be preached to pagans, such as those in Asia Minor or in Philippi or Corinth or Rome, it was not enough to speak about the Risen Christ, for the hearers would automatically have thought that Christianity was just another mystery religion about a demi-god. The Greek-speaking world was full of mythological cults of this type, and St Paul found that he was misunderstood in precisely this way at Athens (Ac 17:18). The only safeguard against such misunderstanding lay in emphasizing, to pagans, the concrete details of his life. There is a good example of this type of preaching in St Peter's address to the centurion Cornelius, in Ac 10:37–41. So the earthly life of Jesus was described in its four principal stages: (1) the preparation for the ministry, at the time the Baptist was preaching; (2) the public ministry of Jesus in Galilee; (3) his journey to Jerusalem; (4) the Passion, death and Resurrection in Jerusalem. Into this catechetical framework the stories and sayings of the gospel were fitted, rather freely, and without any great concern for chronological sequence.

Any attempt to trace the stages by which the raw material of the gospel story was arranged within this fourfold framework must be largely hypothetical. Several sayings of Jesus seem to have been quoted frequently in the early Church without any context, and eventually to have been incorporated into stories where they would be apposite. E.g. the saying 'You are the salt of the earth' is inserted by Matthew into the Sermon on the Mount (5:13), but placed in another context, and given a different meaning, by Luke (14:34–35) and Mark (9:50). Similarly, the metaphor about the light of the world is applied to the disciples in Mt 5:15, to the gospel in Mk 4:21 = Lk 8:16, and to Jesus himself in Lk 11:33. In these cases, there is often no way of knowing which (if any) was the original context.

The various stories, however, were soon grouped into collections, and stray sayings found a home in a definite context (sometimes in a story, sometimes in a discourse). We have already drawn attention to the group of miracles in Mt 8:1–17, in which Jesus heals a member of a Gentile household, of a Jewish one and of a Christian one. There is another group of miracle stories in Mk 4:35–5:43. We have mentioned also the group of controversy stories in Mk 2:1–3:6; there is another group in Mt 22:15–46. This last group was very probably put together to show how Jesus silenced Jewish adversaries of every kind,[2] but the pattern may be drawn from rabbinical customs: it was common for inquirers to put to a rabbi three questions or cases to be solved, after answering which the rabbi would himself question his disciples. This is exactly the pattern followed in Mt 22.[3]

For catechetical purposes, it was convenient also to group together events which took place in one locality. The miracles which happened around the Lake of Galilee (Mk 4:35–5:43), or the events which took place at Jericho and Jerusalem provide a good illustration. Or again, the stories about the Baptist would be best understood if they were presented *en bloc*. All these various collections of related stories thus became, as it were, ready-made blocks of tradition which could easily be set into the broad chronological framework of our Lord's life.

There are, however, good reasons for thinking that after some stories had been grouped into collections, and before these collections were used by the evangelists, certain sections of the gospel were put together.

The story of the Passion provides a fair example. Many scholars think that there was a brief narrative of the main events, into which more details were inserted at a later date. The short account would be represented by Mk 14:43–52, 55–65; 15:1–47; later, this account would have been filled out by an introduction (Mk 14:1–25) recounting the events

[2] See above, p. 199.

[3] D. Daube, *The New Testament and Rabbinic Judaism*, London, 1956, pp. 158–169.

which preceded the Last Supper, and by the insertion of several details remembered by Peter (Mk 14:26–42, 53–54). Similarly, groups of stories about Jesus' ministry in Galilee were perhaps put together as a little work which could be called 'The Galilean Ministry', at a time before the earliest gospel was written.

What is absolutely certain is that the formation of the tradition expressed in the Synoptic Gospels was a slow process. The final outcome was a kind of biography of Jesus which answered well the needs of an ever-expanding community. During the years when a common, 'traditional', way of presenting his life was slowly taking shape, all kinds of factors were at work. The Church was preaching the gospel by word of mouth to Jews who were familiar with the Old Testament, and to Gentiles who were not; stories about Jesus, and sayings of his, were also being written down, and some were not. Some of the stories and sayings written down were being grouped into collections, and some were left unattached to any group. Finally, some of the 'collected stories and sayings' were gathered into essays which told about a certain part of the Lord's life, such as the Galilean ministry or the Passion. This was the material on which the Synoptic writers worked.

If (as the present writer believes) the above account of the formation of the gospel tradition is substantially true, then the theory of 'Two Sources' (Mark and 'Q') must be regarded as a hypothesis which served a very useful purpose in its day, but which ought to be consigned to an honourable grave. None of the three Synoptics can be taken as a yardstick by which to judge the historical value of the other two, or of St John. Matthew in particular should not be regarded as the poor relation; this attitude has been too widespread for too long. Instead, all the details of each gospel should be respected and compared, when a man is trying to discover, without prejudice, which account represents the earliest tradition. All of them have something to offer.

But in order to find the earliest tradition, it is essential to see the different accounts against the background from which they emerged, and to perceive the various influences which affected the telling of the story (*e.g.* the scruples of Jewish Christians about the sabbath; the question in every Gentile mind—'Why did he not come to us?' etc.). The age when scholars argued interminably whether Matthew or Mark wrote first ought to be considered as over: it did not, in any case, contribute much of spiritual value to the ordinary Christian. But the modern endeavour to read the parallel texts against the background of the living Church—worshipping, catechizing, and preaching to all nations—should bring the story to life for the scholar, the priest and the student. Then, and only then, will they be able to bring it alive for others.

CHAPTER 11

The Ultimate Source
of the Gospel Tradition—
Jesus of Nazareth

We are now in a position to resolve one of the most obvious difficulties felt by every reader of the Synoptic Gospels, namely, the problem of the apparent contradictions between them. As long as the reader compares only the final statements of the gospel tradition (*i.e.* the three texts of Matthew, Mark and Luke), he will naturally be puzzled and even perturbed by the discrepancies. But if, when he reads these texts, he keeps in mind the life of the Church during the first century (as outlined in the last chapter), he will see that he is faced with *one* tradition, expressed, interpreted, contemplated and explained from several different angles. The primitive Church, which was mainly responsible for the wealth of interpretation in our gospels, did not try to produce a logically coherent system of thought—a *summa* of dogmatic and moral theology —or to take every possible precaution to ensure that Christians were everywhere given only one version of an event. On the contrary, the early Christians were eager to tell the gospel story to all men, from every possible angle, because they were exuberant with life.

This attitude of theirs had many advantages, and it has enabled successive generations to discover ever new insights into the mystery of the Word made flesh. If the early Church had issued only one 'officially authorized' and definitive 'Life of Jesus', the rationalist historian would perhaps have felt happier, but the ordinary disciple of Christ would never have realized what Jesus meant to his followers. The world, certainly, would have been spiritually poorer. Furthermore, the differences between the four accounts should not be exaggerated: fundamentally, all four gospels relate exactly the same story, as the early Church recognized by speaking of the one gospel which has come to us in fourfold form, according to Matthew, Mark, Luke and John.

Scholars of all creeds and none are agreed that the four gospels revolve round the idea that Jesus of Nazareth is Lord of the world since his Resurrection. But there the unanimity ends, and there is today considerable disagreement on two major issues.

The first concerns the part played by the early Christians in the formation of the gospel tradition. To what extent did they embellish, alter or even distort the story of Jesus' life? The last chapter set out the basic principles of a solution, by showing that they were not indifferent to historical truth. The first two chapters of Part IV will discuss this matter in detail, and will take up a clear stand on this issue.

The second point of disagreement is, however, even more basic. Bultmann and some of his followers (the 'Form Critics') have repeatedly asserted that it is impossible to know the real truth about Jesus of Nazareth because all the evidence we possess (in the gospels and elsewhere) comes from people who looked at him with the eyes of faith, and saw him as the victor over death. In modern terminology, we are presented with a portrait of the 'Christ of faith' (*i.e.* as seen by the evangelists and the primitive Church), and the Form Critics think it is impossible to reconstruct from this an accurate picture of 'the historical Jesus' (*i.e.* as he can be known, without faith, through historical research). Bultmann goes so far as to say that 'we can no longer know anything about the life and personality of Jesus',[1] and con-

---

[1] 'I do indeed think that we can now know almost nothing concerning the life and personality of Jesus, since the early Christian sources show no interest in either, are moreover fragmentary and often legendary; and other sources do not exist' (*Jesus and the Word*, London and New York, 1935, Introduction). Later in the same in-

cludes that the historian must be content to know what ideas the early Christians had about him.

Before we can discuss the first question, therefore, we must at least show that it is not impossible to ascertain some facts about the historical Jesus. We shall begin by asking whether the Synoptic Gospels do not contain a stream of tradition which goes back, ultimately, to Jesus himself. Then, by employing the literary methods of Form Criticism, we shall try to sketch out the living environment of the disciples in the years before the Resurrection, before the establishment of the Church, when Jesus of Nazareth was alive, surrounded by the Twelve.

1. The Reliability of Traditions about Jesus

For many years past, even the most critical scholars have conceded that the early Christians, like their Jewish contemporaries, were very conservative in outlook. Most of the teaching was done by word of mouth, and in such an environment, the human memory regularly performs feats which to us Western Europeans seem almost unbelievable. The author once knew an Indian whose mother, though unable to read or write, could recite perfectly, by heart, a Hindu prayer about as long as the present book! Similar feats of memory are not unknown, or indeed uncommon, when men have to rely on memory alone, without the aid of the printed word. It was in such an environment that the apostles lived.

Moreover, many of the sayings of Jesus are—even in English —quite unforgettable: it is difficult not to remember them in their exact wording. We realize this particularly when using modern versions of the Bible: the Authorized Version will keep intruding into our minds. Examples are beyond counting, *e.g.*

'Blessed are the poor in spirit: for theirs is the kingdom of heaven' (Mt 5:3).

---

troduction, however, Bultmann affirms that he thinks it highly probable, though not certain, that we can find out something about Jesus' *teaching* from the gospels.

'Consider the lilies of the field, how they grow; they toil not, neither do they spin: and yet I say unto you, that even Solomon in all his glory was not arrayed like one of these'(Mt 6:28–29).

'Come unto me, all ye that labour and are heavy laden, and I will give you rest. Take my yoke upon you, and learn of me; for I am meek and lowly in heart: and ye shall find rest unto your souls. For my yoke is easy, and my burden is light' (Mt 11:28–30).

Sentences like these are indisputably of Palestinian origin; and if we ask who coined these phrases, why should anyone suggest that they were thought up by Greek-speaking Christians in the early Church? Why not attribute them all to the same person, Jesus, whose homeland was Palestine and whose mother tongue was Aramaic?

In fact, there is ample evidence that many of the sayings attributed to Jesus in the gospels were originally pronounced not in Greek but in Aramaic.[2] That is not to say that every single word attributed to our Lord in the gospels is quite evidently 'translation-Greek'; much of it is certainly not. But all over the gospels we find sentences which, when translated into Aramaic, yield a double meaning, or a clearer sense, or a hidden assonance between words. These are questions for the specialist, of course; we may simply note that modern scholars (of all creeds) are generally agreed that behind the Greek text of the gospels there is a substantial quantity of Aramaic sayings.

It should not be forgotten, either, that in the early years after the Resurrection there were many disciples of the Lord in Jerusalem whose native tongue was Greek. They must have made up a large part of the community, to judge from Ac 6:1, and we know that Greek-speaking Jews had their own synagogues in Jerusalem (Ac 6:9). In all probability, then, these men, once they had become Christians, would

[2] There is an excellent work on this topic: *An Aramaic Approach to the Gospels and Acts*, by M. Black, Oxford, 2nd ed., 1954; 3rd ed., 1967.

continue to talk about Jesus, and to preach about him in their synagogues, in their native language, Greek. Thus the gospel would have been preached in Greek from the earliest years.

These, then, are certain general considerations which must be kept in mind when assessing the reliability of oral traditions about Jesus: (1) we are dealing with a world in which memories were far more exact than in our own; (2) even in English, many of the Lord's sayings are unforgettable; (3) many of the sayings which we possess only in Greek are evidently translations from Aramaic; (4) from the beginning, the gospel was preached both in Greek and in Aramaic. These four arguments all favour the essential reliability of oral traditions about Jesus, and they apply with particular force to traditions about his teaching. Their relevance has been well brought out in some recent studies by Swedish theologians of the University of Uppsala.

At a Congress held in Oxford, in 1957, Professor H. Riesenfeld of Uppsala read a paper entitled 'The Gospel Tradition and its Beginnings. A Study in the Limits of *Formgeschichte*.'[3] His thesis was that too many exponents of Form Criticism (including its early practitioners) had adopted an attitude of general scepticism towards the gospels because they had concerned themselves exclusively with the catechetical activity of the early Church. They had more or less presumed that the early disciples would have arranged (or altered) all the facts to suit their own catechetical aims. The pioneers of the method in particular had judged it almost impossible to distinguish in the apostolic tradition how much went back to Jesus.

Riesenfeld argued that the gospel tradition took shape inside a community whose lives were dominated by worship rather than instruction. He pointed out, too, that (though the parallel was not absolutely perfect) there were analogies

[3] Printed in *Studia Evangelica, Texte und Untersuchungen* 73, Berlin, 1959, pp. 43–65; also published separately in London, in 1957.

to be found in the origins of the Mishnah, especially in the section entitled 'The Tradition of the Fathers' (*Pirke Aboth*), in which the teaching given orally by rabbis is presented as having been handed down by God himself on Mount Sinai. In much the same way the disciples of Jesus 'handed down' his words in what may be termed an 'official' version, and their veneration for him would have ensured that his teaching was passed on substantially unchanged.

In fact, we know that the 'teaching of the apostles' (Ac 5:42) was given at the service known as 'the breaking of bread'. In this liturgical ceremony, it would have been only natural for the preacher to relate not merely the sayings but also the deeds of the Lord. Thus the 'Gospel of Jesus Christ' which was preached there would have included the Good News about him, as well as the Good News which stemmed from him in person.

Riesenfeld's paper struck at the very heart of one of the main assumptions of Form Criticism, but a more detailed exposition of his arguments was required, if his thesis was to carry the day. This came in a dissertation published at Uppsala in 1961: its author was a young Swedish exegete, B. Gerhardsson, and its title *Memory and Manuscript: Oral Tradition and Written Transmission in Rabbinic Judaism and Early Christianity*.

The author first surveys all the documents we possess about the way in which the written Law and the oral Law were handed down among the Jews. The latter is of more particular concern to us, for oral tradition supplied the interpretation of the 'Holy Scriptures' or 'Holy Writings'. Now until A.D. 150 or thereabouts, 'Holy Scripture' meant—even for Christians—the Old Testament, and that alone, while the gospels were known as the 'Holy Word'. There is, then, a striking parallel between the formation of the gospels and of the Mishnah and Talmud: both took shape gradually as oral teaching, both were based on the Old Testament, and both were set down in writing, in a definitive form, only after many years.

There were in Palestine schools called *beth hammidrash*

where the pupils were taught how to interpret Scripture by the aid of oral traditions: each generation of rabbis added its own contribution, and from this there grew up that body of traditional teaching which was given definitive form in the Mishnah and the Talmud. The training given in these schools was of a type widespread in the ancient world, however deplorable in the eyes of the modern educationalist. The pupil first learnt the biblical text by heart, section by section; he then had to learn all kinds of mnemonics (*e.g.* alphabetical links, repetition of words etc.) to make sure that he would not forget it; and finally he was allowed to make written notes in case his memory should after all need a reminder. In short, every possible step was taken to ensure that the original text, and the authentic interpretations of the rabbis, were passed on to succeeding generations as accurately as was humanly possible. Is it not highly probable that the apostles, and even Jesus himself, taught in the same way—the one which was taken for granted among their own people? Can we perhaps still see a trace of it in the interpretations which follow some of the parables in the gospels?

Gerhardsson does not maintain, of course, that the teaching of Jesus consisted of a commentary on passages of the Old Testament memorized by the disciples. Jesus spoke rather about himself as the fulfilment of the Law, and to this extent the parallel between the teaching of Jesus and that of the rabbinical schools is not exact. The content of the instruction was certainly different; but there is every reason to suppose that the 'educational methods' used in Palestine would have been adopted by the disciples. The words of Jesus would then have been repeated over and over again, and St Luke may have had this method in mind when he wrote that preaching was 'the service of the Word' (Ac 6:4), reserved at first to the Twelve, because they were both 'witnesses' and 'servants of the Word' (Lk 1:2).

Such is Gerhardsson's thesis, and the broad lines of it are both true and valuable; but a word of caution must be inserted. The argument as stated would prove only that the early Church was meticulously careful to preserve the actual words spoken by Jesus, or those used by the apostles in recounting his life. It takes no account of those various interpretations and applications of his doctrine which (as we saw in Part II) occupy such a prominent place in the gospels. This is a genuine weakness in the argument, for it presupposes that Christians were—like the pupils of a rabbi—concerned only with remembering teaching; and the history of the early Church (as seen in the last chapter) shows that they were at least as deeply concerned to understand and to apply the spirit of the Lord's teaching.

Ultimately, the flaw lies in this: that the Swedish writers accept too readily the distinction between a 'gospel about Christ' and a 'gospel from Christ'. Bultmann claims that nowadays we possess only the former; the Swedish theologians are trying to prove that we possess the latter also. In this, they are right, but they should add that the distinction between the *evangelium de Christo* and the *evangelium Christi* was thought out at the beginning of this century, not in apostolic times. The early disciples knew only one doctrine about Jesus, that taught by him in person, and faithfully developed and interpreted after the Resurrection by those who had been witnesses of his life.

2. Jesus of Nazareth and the Twelve

Some Form Critics, when they say we can know nothing about the events which preceded the death of Jesus, overlook the one indisputable fact which is of decisive importance, namely, that twelve men grouped themselves round Jesus before his death, and (except for one) became devoted disciples. It is the very existence of such a group that enables the historian to go further back than the community of Christian believers. Consequently the difficulty raised by certain Form Critics with regard to the isolation of the new Church from the events that preceded Easter can be solved. But it is not just a question of simply trusting in the first Christian community and thereafter drawing historical conclusions from that trust; we must also, on the grounds of literary criticism, test its evangelical tradition. Is its tradition earlier than it-self? Does it go back to the community which Jesus estab-lished and which we call the 'pre-paschal' community? If this is the case, the evangelical tradition takes its origin in the earthly, pre-paschal life of Jesus of Nazareth. The critics them-selves agree that a group of men formed a community around Jesus—a community whose faith held them together as a group and whose pre-paschal apostolate animated it.

From the first—and this before Easter—there was a group of men who believed in the fulfilment of God's promise. Their faith is an anticipation of the Christian faith in this sense that it is prior to it in time; its object, however, is the same. The pre-paschal commitment of the disciples to Jesus of Nazareth derived from a real, if as yet undetermined, faith that he was already the true fulfilment of the purpose of God even in his pre-paschal life.

It was with unique authority that he called men to follow him. His summons has an astonishing ring about it: every-thing here below, be it family (Mt 12, 46–50), reputa-tion (Lk 11, 27–28) or duties within the home—all must cede to this event; for the event was God's Word in our midst. And this Word not only commanded obedience; it also had to be transmitted in a strict 'tradition'. For his word, as such, possesses a unique value, quite apart from any use to which we may put it. No rabbi of his time could have made such a claim. Therefore it was on faith in his mission—and on that alone—that Jesus established his community. There is strict continuity between the loyalty given to the man Jesus by the disciples whom he called and the faith by which they con-fessed that the same Jesus, risen from the dead, was the Christ, the Son of God.

The demands that he makes on all who are ready to follow him are, seemingly, exorbitant: total loyalty, without reserve, to one who has nowhere to lay his head (Lk 9, 57–62); the acceptance of a wanderer's life, completely dedicated to him, and to the will of his Father. The disciple cannot retrace his path: 'Let the dead bury their dead' and 'No man who puts his hand to the plough and looks back' is worthy of him. His words are intransigent: 'If anyone comes to me and does not hate his father and mother, wife and children, brothers and sisters, even his own life, he cannot be a disciple of mine' (Lk 14, 26–27). Men are told to weigh carefully the cost of following him. Is it possible to imagine that it was the apostolic community that invented such demands? On the contrary, we have reason to believe that the tendency of the community was to tone down some of his demands in the interests of practical organization.

Nor was the community that was formed by Jesus an esoteric côterie; it was a group of men whose only care was to spread the Good Tidings that he gave. We know—even from the critics—that they were sent out preaching . . . they were 'servants of the Word'. The sacred trust of handing on the words of Jesus was begun before Easter by the group of disciples who followed him. After Easter it was continued, substantially the same, in the light of the Resurrection.

We know that after the Resurrection the apostolic preaching took as its theme the Risen Christ; before, the theme was the kingdom of heaven. The Sermon on the Mount is not about the Risen Christ, but about the conditions for entry into the kingdom. Jesus, too, explained that his exorcisms were solid proof that the kingdom of God had come (Lk 11:20; cf. Mt 12:29). It is therefore antecedently probable that several miracle stories and perhaps certain 'stories about Jesus' are authentic versions of happenings before the Resurrection, because they have little to do with the Risen Christ and are concerned only with the coming of the kingdom. They reflect, in short, the interests of the disciples *before* the Resurrection.

Many other examples could be cited to illustrate the essential continuity of doctrine before and after Easter Day, and modern scholars are more and more disposed to admit that we can know a great deal about the life of Jesus before Easter. To do so, it is of course necessary to study the gospels in minute detail, with all the techniques of literary analysis, but without any non-literary prejudices (*e.g.* without assuming that whatever is not capable of a natural explanation is impossible). So far, this book has concentrated almost exclusively on the literary analysis of the gospels, and the conclusion must be that, in general and in their broad outlines, they give a faithful account of the life of Jesus, while at the same time interpreting that life for the Church.

It now remains for us to see whether these documents about the life of Jesus—our four gospels—are historically trustworthy in the details they record.

PART IV

PROLEGOMENA TO A
LIFE OF JESUS

After this long examination of the gospels as literature, it is possible to attempt an outline of the life of Jesus. His life, however, could be written in two ways, and in this final part of the book we shall endeavour to set down the broad lines which these versions might take.

A historian would synthesize the material gathered from the gospels through the kind of literary analysis which has just been described; and some historians might then consider that their task was over. But there remains a further question: what made the early Christians acknowledge 'the historical Jesus' as Lord and Son of God? It is legitimate to press this question on anyone who writes about the earthly life of Jesus of Nazareth.

In this fourth Part, therefore, we shall first try to outline the earthly life of Jesus, and then ask what led the early Church to proclaim that he was Lord and Son of God.

CHAPTER 12

The Quest of
the Historical Jesus

i: The Value of the Gospel Traditions

Since the aim of this chapter is to reconstruct, as accurately as possible, the events in the earthly life of Jesus, it will not be out of place to explain what principles will be used in reconstructing the pattern of his life. The simplest and clearest way of explaining them will be to give a few illustrations and examples.

A hundred years ago, Strauss rejected as myths all the events related in the gospels which are presented as fulfilments of Old Testament prophecy. Since that time, however, the essential credibility of many such events has been confirmed by the findings of secular historians. Thus we now know that it was customary for the executioners to share out the clothes of those crucified, to offer them a drink in order to dull the pain, and even to break their legs.[1] Moreover, there are many occasions when the evangelists could have cited an Old Testament verse in support of an assertion, and did not: *e.g.* they could have said that Jesus was nailed to the cross, and then have quoted Ps 22:17—a psalm very familiar to the early Christians. Matthew cites verse 9 of the psalm (Mt 27:43); verse 8 is cited by both Matthew and Mark (Mt 27:39; Mk 15:29). If Strauss's principle is correct, why did none of the evangelists see a rather obvious reference to the nailing in verse 17: 'They have pierced my hands and

[1] *Cf.* J. Blinzler, *The Trial of Jesus*, Cork, 1959, pp. 250–255.

my feet'? Something similar could be said about the piercing of Jesus' side with a spear: why did none of the Synoptics mention it, when it could so easily have been presented as a fulfilment of Is 53:5, 'He was wounded for our transgressions'? In short, if (as Strauss claimed) the gospel writers or their predecessors made up several stories to prove that Jesus had fulfilled ancient prophecies, why did they not make up more, and better, stories?

In fact, several episodes recorded in the gospels seem, from internal evidence, to come from an eyewitness of the particular event. For example, Mark mentions a young man who ran away from Gethsemane after the arrest of Jesus (Mk 14:50–52); many think that this young man was Mark himself. Even if this is not true, it may perhaps be a hint that Mark had heard the story of the arrest from this person. Or, to take another example, the mentioning of Simon of Cyrene as the father of Alexander and Rufus may imply that this family could vouch for the details about the carrying of the cross and the crucifixion, for we know that Rufus and his mother later lived in Rome, where Mark's gospel was written (Rom 16:13). We have already mentioned, too, the numerous passages in Mark which seem to be based on Peter's testimony.[2] There are, then, a number of episodes recorded in the gospels for which a certain degree of eyewitness evidence can reasonably be claimed.

Unfortunately, this kind of internal evidence does not extend to the whole of the gospel record, and what is needed is some rather general criterion which will enable us to assert that more or less the whole of the gospel tradition is historically reliable. Can such a criterion be found?

An excellent way of checking the value of traditions about Jesus is to compare them with what we know about the attitudes of the early Church. Whenever we find that the gospels attribute to Jesus an attitude which is the opposite of that which obtained in the early Church, there is every reason to think that the gospels are relating historical fact. For instance,

[2] See above, pp. 138–141.

Jesus is said to have instructed his disciples not to preach to pagans or Samaritans (Mt 10); would the early Christians have made up a discourse so completely contradictory of their own policy and practice? Here, if anywhere, there is an absolutely reliable criterion.

But, it may be argued, it is dangerously double-edged. Is there not good reason for saying that those sayings of Jesus which are in harmony with the practice of the early Church may well have been invented, or re-phrased, to justify that practice? Here a second criterion must be taken into consideration: those sayings which are in harmony with the practice of the Apostolic Church must be compared with parallel texts whose authenticity cannot be denied. An example will illustrate this point. According to some modern scholars, it was because the Apostolic Church attached great importance to the fulfilment of prophecy that the evangelists attributed to Jesus the words of Zechariah, 'I will strike the shepherd, and the sheep of the flock will be scattered' (Mt 26:31; cf. Zech. 13:7). We shall say more about this text later on, and do not wish to claim here that Jesus pronounced these very words; but we do assert that Jesus several times spoke of himself as 'the Shepherd', and of the disciples as a 'little flock' (Lk 12:32) or as 'sheep among wolves' (Mt 10:16), in texts whose authenticity cannot (because of the first criterion) be doubted. One must remember also what has often been stressed earlier in the book, namely, that the evangelists are far more concerned with the tenor and the substance of Jesus' words than with the precise phrases; so that even if Jesus did not utter the words from Zechariah which are ascribed to him, those prophetical words nevertheless express his thoughts as he forecast that his disciples would flee in terror when he, their shepherd, was attacked. We may now develop this argument in some detail.

1. The Sayings of Jesus

There are so many widespread misconceptions about this topic that it will be well to make clear at the outset what is meant by saying that the gospels contain the words or sayings of Jesus. First, even those who accept that the Bible is divinely inspired are not obliged to hold that all the words attributed to Jesus in the gospels were spoken by him in that form during his earthly life: otherwise, one would have to admit that he taught the disciples two different forms of the Lord's Prayer, and pronounced the words instituting the eucharist in four different ways. All that the believer need hold (by virtue of his acceptance of inspiration) is that the words of the gospel truly record the teaching of Jesus.

Secondly, even those who do not accept the Bible as divinely inspired must agree that in the ancient world (and not only in Palestine) it was customary for an author (e.g. Thucydides) to place upon the lips of his characters speeches written by himself, in order to set forth the man's thoughts: a modern historian would never dare do this, but would explain the ideas in some other way. The evangelists were men of their own age, not of ours, and therefore we should not expect from them a report such as would have been recorded there and then by a shorthand writer, or by the use of a tape-recorder. This does not imply that the gospel accounts are 'less objective' than a tape-recording would have been, for an intelligent presentation of a man's ideas may render them more faithfully than a bald and literal version. With these provisos, we may now examine the sayings ascribed to Jesus in the gospels.

There are in the gospels certain short phrases which we can be absolutely sure were spoken by our Lord: e.g. that he addressed his heavenly Father as 'Abba!' ('Father!'), that he used the phrase 'Amen, Amen I say to you'; that he once said *'Talitha qum!'* (Mk 5:41) etc. Elsewhere the vividness of the gospel phrasing sometimes seems explicable only if the phrases go back to Jesus himself (e.g. the astonishing anacoluthon in Mk 6:9, translated literally on p. 139). It must be admitted, however, that these phrases are not numerous, and are rarely of importance.

Moreover, even where we might most expect to find the very words used by Jesus, we do not always find them. In the narrative of the Last Supper, all four accounts state that Jesus said, 'This is my body', but modern scholars have demonstrated that the word 'body' could not be used in this sense in Aramaic; Jesus must have said (in Aramaic), 'This is my *flesh*', which the Synoptics, St Paul and the early Church rendered into Greek as 'This is my *body*'. Paradoxically, it would appear that St John has in all probability kept closest to the words spoken at the first eucharist (Jn 6:51).[3]

Similarly, it is highly probable that the original form of the first beatitude was 'Happy are you that are poor!' (Lk 6:20), and not 'Happy are the poor in spirit', as we read in Mt 5:3. St Luke's text is a reminder that Jesus calls men to forgo earthly wealth, and invites the rich to give practical expression to their detachment from worldly goods. This could easily be misunderstood, however, as if the gospel sought to produce economic equality between all men—an absolutely equal standard of living for all, for example. Hence St Matthew's version is also important: he reminds us that it is the 'poor in spirit' who will inherit the kingdom. It is possible to have no money at all, and to be gripped by lust for wealth: such a person is hardly 'poor in spirit'. Equally, it is possible for a man possessed of great riches to be genuinely unattached to them; but he must put his detachment into practice. Matthew and Luke teach complementary aspects of the truth Jesus proclaimed in Galilee, and thus give the full meaning of his message.

The historian, therefore, when he wishes to discover the original message of Jesus, must take into account all the various versions of a saying which may be recorded in the gospels. This is far more important (and much more useful) than seeking out the actual phrases used. When the high priest asked Jesus, in the presence of the Sanhedrin, 'Are you the Messiah, the Son of the Blessed One?', Jesus replied, ac-

[3] For a full discussion of this text, see J. Bonsirven, 'Hoc est corpus meum. Recherches sur l'original araméen', in *Biblica* 29 (1948), pp. 205–219, and J. Jeremias, *The Eucharistic Words of Jesus*, new edition, London, 1966, pp. 107–108, 178 and especially 198–201.

cording to Mark (16:52), 'I am.' Matthew, however, implies that he avoided giving a direct answer, by replying 'That is what you are saying.' Which is nearer to the original, historical, saying—Matthew or Mark?

In this case, St Matthew's version seems more likely to represent the actual phrase used, because Jesus would then have begun by refusing to answer a deliberately ambiguous question. The high priest had asked, 'Are you the Messiah?' Jesus replied: 'It is you who are saying that, not me. But I do tell you that I am the Son of Man, the judge foretold by Daniel, as you will see for yourselves very shortly.' Jesus, in other words, refuses to discuss whether he is the Messiah as long as the term is understood in the way the high priest understands it, and asserts instead that he is the Son of Man. This saying could never have been invented by the primitive Church, for the early Christians held that the risen Christ could be known only by those who had faith, and Matthew here implies (in the second part) that his victory over death would be evident to the Sanhedrin.

If Matthew, then, is here closer to the original event, what is the value of Mark? Mark gives essentially the same message as Matthew ('I am indeed the Messiah, but not the type of Messiah you are thinking of'), but he has couched it in more direct terms ('I am') to show that Jesus' revelation of his own personality reached its culmination at the moment of his condemnation. Luke has made the issues still clearer, by separating two questions: 'If you are the Messiah, tell us' (Lk 22:67), and 'Are you, then, the Son of God?' (v. 70). Jesus refused to answer the first question, but claimed instead to be the Son of Man (vv. 67–69); he refused to answer the second also, except by the words 'It is you who are saying that I am.' All three Synoptics, then, tell substantially the same story.

Many other examples could be cited, especially from the parables, to show how the early Church took over the words of the Lord and adapted them to its own situation. In the parable about the labourers in the vineyard, for example, Jesus was trying to show the Jews that the sinners and outcasts and even the Gentiles would have the same reward as the faithful Jews, because God's generosity is beyond measuring. According to Matthew, however (19:23), Jesus addressed the parable to his own disciples: they were now the chosen ones, but they too needed to be reminded that God was free to give the same reward to others who had not at that time entered the kingdom. The lesson is in each case the same: election to the kingdom gives no man the right to criticize God for calling others to share it.

Rational criticism of the gospels, then, is indispensable in order to grasp the religious teaching of Jesus. We have already referred to the alleged citation of Zechariah in Mt 26:31, and we may end this section with a remark about it. In Jn 16:32 we read substantially the same message: 'The hour is approaching when you will be scattered, each to his own home, and will leave me alone.' Is it not possible that there were men in the early Church who remembered that Jesus had said something like this, but did not know the actual words? They could then have searched in the Old Testament for a verse which would perfectly recapture the thought, and have found the text cited, in the book of Zechariah. A similar example occurs in the story of the cleansing of the temple. According to John (2:16), Jesus said to the traders 'Stop turning the house of my Father into a house of trade!' Early Christians who remembered the event but not the words may therefore have expressed the sense of this saying by combining two prophetical sayings, one from Is 57:6 and the other from Jer 7:11: 'My house shall be called a house of prayer; but you are making it a hideout of robbers.'

The historian, then, and indeed any Christian, must approach the gospels with the right attitude of mind. It is less important to discover the actual words used by Jesus than to understand what he meant to convey by those words, by tracing the history of its interpretation throughout the apostolic age. For what he meant to convey can, as a general rule, be best discerned by seeing how his disciples interpreted and applied his teaching after his death.

2. Events in the Life of Jesus

Slightly different versions of one and the same event are frequently found in the gospels, and most readers are content to think that each of the evangelists has set down a substantially true account of what happened, without troubling much over the minor details. Though there is a certain measure of truth in this, there is also a danger that it may lead a person to overlook, or even deliberately to neglect, the details in the gospels, because he judges them to be of small importance.

Before giving examples of details which are highly significant, we may here recall certain general principles which have often been stressed in this book. There are in the gospels certain stories which may reasonably be thought to have acquired a fairly fixed pattern during the life-time of our Lord: some of them may even owe this fixed form to Jesus himself (*e.g.* the account of his Temptations). More often, however, the basic pattern of a gospel story seems to have been developed and then fixed through the teaching of the early Church, or even by the gospel writer himself. We have already mentioned that there is a definite literary style for miracle-stories, controversy-stories, parables etc.,[4] and none of these patterns can be classified as 'pure reporting' from which all shadow of interpretation is absent. The historian who compares different versions of one event must therefore be alive to the influences which may have led the evangelists to include, to omit, to stress or to underplay different details.

The details are important, as details. Though they do not form the substance of the account, they certainly contribute substantially to its accuracy. An accurately exposed photograph may give a true picture of a person's face, but a painting of genius will often give a more faithful picture of the person by showing his personality or character. The painting, in short, is often more objective than the photograph; similarly, the gospel records are in their own way more objective

[4] See pp. 176–177.

than a filmed and recorded version of our Lord's life would have been. Everyone who has listened to political broadcasts on television must have asked himself after some of them, 'But what was he getting at? What did he mean?'

Each detail in the gospel story, then, has some importance, though its meaning may not be immediately evident. The parable of the Prodigal Son, for example, is not an allegory, and therefore we should not look for something corresponding with each detail: the pigs which are mentioned do not represent any class of persons, etc. On the other hand, there is a purpose in mentioning them: pigs were unclean to the Jews, and therefore the prodigal's presence in a land where pigs were kept tells us that he was an exile from the land of his fathers, and from the land where salvation would be found. To find salvation and forgiveness, he had first to return home.

We may now consider some of the details in the gospels, to see how the interests of the early Church or of the individual evangelist have led to certain modifications in the various accounts.

We know that the early Christians held the apostles in such veneration that they sought to cover up all their imperfections. The historian may reasonably infer that Mark, not Matthew, gives the more objective version of the story about the sons of Zebedee. Mark (10:35) says that James and John themselves asked for the places of honour in the future kingdom; according to Matthew (20:20), it was their mother who made the request. Mark's gospel, because it is based on Peter's preaching, never attempts to whitewash the apostles, but the gospels of Matthew and Luke often play down their imperfections (especially in the Passion story). Here, then, is a sound criterion for judging a wide range of passages where the apostles play a part.

In the gospel records of the trial of Jesus, great stress is placed on the guilt of the Jews, in order to lessen the guilt of the pagans involved: this creates acute problems for the historian. The Pharisees are never mentioned by name in the

Passion story, and it is no doubt true that as a group they played no part in the trial. The scribes, however, and 'the Jews' are often mentioned alongside the high priests: here the evangelists are obviously generalizing, not implying that every scribe and all the Jews had a part in the condemnation. Luke (22:63) says that Jesus was ill-treated by the guards during the night, whereas Matthew and Mark seem to imply that it was certain members of the high priests' caste who abused him (Mt 26:67; Mk 14:65). Here Luke's version seems preferable. This is all the more likely as Luke normally takes care to exonerate the Romans and is never afraid to state the case against the Jews; yet on the other hand, he passes over in silence the condemnation of Jesus by the Sanhedrin, and distinguishes between the Jewish high priests who had a part in the trial and the ordinary people, who had not (Lk 23:35).

There can be no doubt that Pilate was legally the one responsible for the death sentence, and for the subsequent crucifixion of Jesus. The trial by Pilate was manifestly a gross miscarriage of justice, and Jesus was manifestly innocent. Pilate, therefore, was morally guilty for yielding to pressure by the high priests, whether through negligence or cowardice. Caiaphas and his clique, however, were even more to blame, for they initiated the proceedings and spared no pains to force the governor's hand (*cf.* Jn 19:11). This is the essence of the story which the four evangelists recount, each from his own angle.

Theological preoccupations are rarely absent from the gospel record of any event in the life of Jesus. Indeed, they have affected the narratives so profoundly that many think they sometimes gave rise to the story. Thus the gospel account of the baptism of Jesus seems to some people a story made up to express and then to justify the Church's belief that Jesus was the Son of God. Against this interpretation, we may ask whether the early Christians would have made up a story which apparently showed Jesus as inferior to the Baptist. It is all the more unlikely if we recall that, at the time when the gospel tradition was taking shape, there was a sect which sought to exalt the Baptist above Jesus.[5] (This argument proves also the authenticity of Jesus' saying that John was 'the greatest of men', Lk 7:28; this phrase would hardly have been included in the gospels unless it had been considered authentic.)

So far, we have given examples of the way in which the theological interests of the early Church or of the evangelists influenced the presentation of facts in the gospels. But presentation was affected by a second factor also, namely, by the literary form in which a narrative was cast.[6]

The cure of the epileptic boy, recorded in Mt 17:14–21 and parallels, provides an excellent illustration of how one and the same event could be presented in three different ways. The reader may at first be startled by the discrepancies between the three accounts, but a close study of each version well repays the effort involved.

Matthew, broadly speaking, tells the story for a catechetical purpose; for him, it is primarily a lesson to the disciples about the need for faith (Mt 17:14–21). Luke (9:37–43) relates the same episode as a miracle story, stressing the distress of the boy (v. 39) and the astonishment of the bystanders at the sudden cure (v. 43); he never mentions that the disciples failed to heal the boy because of their lack of faith. Mark (9:14–29) combines two ideas in the one narrative: he gives a most vivid description of the boy's plight (vv. 18, 20, 22, 26) and of Jesus' triumph over the demon (v. 26), and then adds as a conclusion a lesson for the disciples, that this kind of miracle could not be worked except after prayer (v. 29).

If we now attempt to reconstruct the objective, historical happening, we must beware of simply linking together everything mentioned by each of the evangelists, as if this would give the historical fact. Instead, one must look at the three versions to grasp the underlying event. There are certain facts common to all three narratives, without which the story

[5] See above, p. 87.
[6] See above, pp. 175–177.

would fall apart: they are the presence of a large crowd, the appeal of the father, the plight of the boy, and the exorcism. But each of the gospel writers has taken these facts and adapted them to his own purpose. The evangelists were not concerned to put down verbatim the words of the boy's father; nor does Matthew imply that Jesus pronounced on this occasion the saying about faith moving mountains, for he cites it in 21:21 also. The evangelists were, however, most concerned to ensure that Christians grasped the truths revealed in this happening, about the person of Jesus, about the power of faith and about the need for prayer.

The infancy gospels of Matthew and Luke provide an even better illustration of a literary form which Western minds find strange, and which has often been misunderstood. A brief, and necessarily simplified, treatment of these chapters may not be out of place.

The infancy narratives did not, apparently, form part of the original preaching of the Church, which began with an account of the ministry of the Baptist (*cf.* Mk 1:1; Ac 1:22; 10:37). They are, in content and in style, utterly unlike anything else in the gospel tradition, and a critical reader may well wonder whether they are to be taken as history in the same sense as the narratives of the public life.

First of all, it must be clearly stated that neither Matthew nor Luke makes any attempt to conceal the doctrinal purpose of his writing. Matthew shows Joseph welcoming Jesus in the name of Israel, the Gentiles coming to adore him, and the leaders of Israel rejecting him. Luke is full of carefully balanced parallels between Jesus and the Baptist, leading in to the preaching of the Good News which he relates in Chapter 3. Both evangelists use Scripture extensively to show how Jesus has fulfilled prophecy.

From this, some writers have claimed that these infancy gospels are *midrashim, i.e.* edifying, homiletic commentaries on Scripture; this may be so, but it depends on how one defines a *midrash*. Though the infancy narratives certainly approximate to the midrashic style so often found in Jewish writing, their authors were concerned not with interpreting the Old Testament, but with interpreting an *event* in terms of the Old Testament. Hence it is an over-simplification to call these chapters *midrashim* without specifying any qualifications.

There are two factors, however, which enable us to compare the infancy narratives with the stories of the public life: the presence of the marvellous (what is commonly called, in non-theological English, the 'supernatural') and the use of Scripture. Each merits some attention.

If we except the story of the Temptations in Matthew and Luke, and the episode of Gethsemane in Luke, then angels are never mentioned in the public life of Jesus; nor does God ever reveal himself in dreams. Everything takes place in the ordinary, everyday, world—even the miracles recorded. In the infancy gospels, on the other hand, it is not miracles but 'marvels' (the 'supernatural') which continually come before our eyes. Zachary, Mary and Joseph, the Magi and the shepherds all communicate with the heavenly world through these messengers. The setting of the story is still Palestine, but the invisible world repeatedly intervenes in a most extraordinary manner.

The second feature which characterizes these pages is their use of Scripture. In the account of the public life, the Old Testament is cited from time to time to show that prophecy had been fulfilled; in the infancy narratives, both Matthew and Luke multiply their citations of Scripture, and compose their stories along the lines of certain literary forms found in the Old Testament. Thus the annunciations to Zachary, to Mary and to Joseph follow the standard pattern of biblical 'annunciations'—a pattern which can be recognizably defined. The person who receives the visit from an angel is addressed by name (Abraham, Sarah etc.); there is generally some difficulty to be overcome (*e.g.* the childlessness of the mothers of Isaac and Samuel), and the angel gives an assurance that it will be overcome. Lastly, the child is given a name full of significance. All these features are found in the infancy gospels, but we should beware of extreme conclusions. One is not justified in concluding, on the ground of the literary

form, that no real event underlies the infancy narratives; and
one is not justified in saying that the literary form had no
influence on the way in which Matthew and Luke presented
their story.

The story of the Magi, if we strip it of its biblical citations,
seems to have been patterned on a well-known *midrash* about
Moses which was widely popular at the time, and which is
recounted in the *Jewish Antiquities* of Josephus.[7] The texts
are too long to cite, but the principal parallels are as follows.
Amram, the father of Moses, was told in a dream about the
birth and future mission of his son (in some accounts, it is
Pharaoh who has the dream). Joseph is informed about the
child's mission in a dream (Mt 1:20–21), and Herod is informed by the Magi. Herod reacts as Pharaoh reacted: seeing
the child as a dangerous rival who will free the people of
Israel from his rule, he seeks advice (Pharaoh consulted his
counsellors and astrologers, Herod consulted the high priests
and the teachers of the Law). Both kings decide to put to
death all the little boys who might fulfil the prediction, but
in each case the child escapes because his father is warned in
time by God. Such is the substance of the story, but the
closeness of the parallel can be seen at its most convincing
by reading Ex 4:19–20; 'The Lord said to Moses in Midian,
Go, return to Egypt, for all those who sought your life are
dead. Then Moses took his wife and his children, put them
on an ass and returned to Egypt.' These are almost the very
words in which Joseph is instructed to return from Egypt to
Israel, when the king who sought to kill Jesus had died. It is
impossible to deny that the *midrash* about Moses had considerable influence on the story of the Magi and the Flight
into Egypt, in the form in which that story existed before the
many biblical citations were inserted.

Certain people have concluded from this that there never
was in fact any real, historical, objective visit by the Magi.
The historicity of the episode cannot be decided purely by a

[7] II, 9, 3–4 = II, 210 ff. = vol. 4, pp. 254 ff. in the Loeb edition,
London and Cambridge, Mass., 1961.

study of the literary form in which the narrative is cast: the problem is not settled by this—on the contrary it is opened. But to say that the historicity of the adoration of the Magi is opened as a problem is to accept the possibility of a negative answer. (Naturally, there are many who fear the pastoral consequences of denying that the Magi were real people, but the historical existence of such men would not seem to be a dogma by which the Christian faith stands or falls, as, for example, it stands or falls by the fact of the death of Jesus on Calvary. It could perhaps be that Matthew was trying to teach, in a popular form, a doctrinal truth, namely, that the message of Jesus was for all nations; but for the moment, it is safe to say that it has not been proved that the Magi never came to Bethlehem. Such a proof would only be forthcoming if it were shown that the episode was impossible, or that the *whole* of the story had been fabricated; and so far, this has not been done.)

It must be granted, therefore, that the literary forms used in the infancy gospels are very unlike those used in the public life. What are we to say about their historical value? These parts of the gospel do not rest on the evidence of eyewitnesses who saw what happened (unless we except Mary), as does the story of the public life, but one can affirm that they come from Jewish–Christian sources, as literary criticism shows.

Furthermore, it is evident that neither Matthew nor Luke made use of the traditions contained in the account given by the other—their versions are far too different. It is all the more significant, therefore, that they agree on the essential details. A virgin named Mary, the fiancée of a man named Joseph, conceived, by the power of the Holy Spirit, a child who (in accordance with a heavenly command, given by an angel) was to be called Jesus. After they had been married (Mt 1:24–25 = Lk 2:5), Mary gave birth to her son at Bethlehem, but in the end they settled at Nazareth.

In this story, there is one fact of cardinal importance: the virginal conception of Jesus. This cannot have been intruded into the gospel from pagan sources, such as describe the union of gods with mortals, for there is no question of any carnal union, but only of a new creation by the Holy Spirit. Nor could it have come from Palestinian Judaism, which does not seem to have entertained the idea of a virginal conception of the Messiah, or from Hellenistic Judaism, for the examples often cited are allegorical. It is very doubtful that it was suggested by Isaiah 7:14, and the early Church would have found it difficult to deduce from its own belief in the Resurrection or in the divinity of Jesus Christ. There seems to be only one possible source left—Mary herself, as has so often been suggested and so long believed.

We have given only a very few examples of the way in which different versions of an event must be compared with one another in order to grasp the historical kernel of an episode. To write a 'Life of Jesus' one would need first to have examined every single episode in the gospels along these lines, and to have examined them far more thoroughly than has been possible (or desirable) in a book of this type. But the principles at least should now be clear to the reader, and we may therefore pass on to attempt a reconstruction of his life in its broad outlines.

3. The Sequence of Events

Unlike present-day biographers, the evangelists were not scrupulously anxious to give the exact place and the precise date of an event or saying, and the historian must frequently admit that it will never be possible to discover them. One or two examples will be sufficient to demonstrate this.

Jesus must have preached several times in Jerusalem, for both Luke (13:34) and Matthew (23:37) record his saying 'How often I wanted to gather together your children!' Yet the Synoptics record only one visit, and place most of his ministry at Capernaum or around the Lake of Galilee. It is quite possible, then, that certain episodes said to have taken place in this area happened elsewhere, and were blocked together not because they happened in the same locality but for some other reason. (E.g. Mt 6:9 says that Jesus taught his disciples the Our Father at the very beginning of his ministry, during the Sermon on the Mount, whereas Lk 11:1 says that it was much later on, during his final journey to Jerusalem, in response to a request from a disciple. Matthew has inserted the words into a passage about prayer, to give a more complete account of Jesus' teaching on the subject, without meaning to say that the Our Father was taught at precisely that time.)

Another example of topographical confusion occurs at the end of the public ministry. According to Matthew and Mark (Mt 20:29 = Mk 10:46), Jesus gave sight to a blind man as he was leaving Jericho for Jerusalem; Luke says that the miracle took place as Jesus was entering Jericho (Lk 18:35). Here (it would seem) Luke has transposed the order of events for literary effect. By situating the miracle before Jesus' entry into the town, he is able to tell the story of Zacchaeus the tax collector (which happened in the town, and which he, alone of the Synoptics, relates), and then to give as a commentary on Zacchaeus' new generosity the parable about the ten talents (Lk 19:11). The parable itself contains hidden references to Jesus' impending departure from this earth, and to his Second Coming: 'Carry on your business until I return' (Lk 19:13). This literary crescendo, ending with the reference to the destruction of God's enemies (Lk 19:27), would have been considerably weakened, if not destroyed, had Luke put the healing of the blind man between the story of Zacchaeus and the entry into Jerusalem, which is the climax of his gospel.

Much more important than topography is chronology. It must be candidly confessed that it is almost impossible to fix an absolute date, even in terms of years, for any event in Jesus' life: we do not know the year of his birth, or of his death, and we are not sure how long his public ministry lasted. But it is possible to fix a few events of his life in a 'relative' chronology, *i.e.* to say that the Baptism took place before he began preaching, and so on. It is not merely useful but essential to fix the succession of events in this way, for upon it depends our appreciation of the gradual self-revelation he gave. We must therefore try to determine, as far as possible, the sequence of events in his life.

The fourth gospel presents a pattern of Jesus' life which diverges widely from that given in the Synoptics, but (as we have said[8]) it provides many illuminating historical details.

From the Synoptics we learn of the baptism of Jesus by John, and of the Lord's deep admiration of his work: 'Among those born of woman, there has never been a greater than John the Baptist' (Lk 7:28). The fourth gospel provides valuable supplementary information about Jesus' relations with the Baptist. It records that the first two followers of Jesus were disciples of the Baptist (Jn 1:35–40), and that the disciples of Jesus practised a rite of baptism very similar to that administered by John (Jn 3:22–23; 4:2), so that a certain rivalry arose between the two groups. Before Jesus began preaching in Galilee, then, there must have been a period of ministry by the banks of the Jordan, during which Jesus allowed himself to be overshadowed by the Baptist. Once this is admitted, the historian will feel compelled to pay great attention to the connection and contrast between the teaching of Jesus and that of the Baptist.

We have already mentioned that certain Synoptic texts clearly imply that Jesus visited Jerusalem more than once before his death (Lk 13:34–35 etc.). Even if we ignore the episode about the cleansing of the Temple (Jn 2:13–21), we can take it as assured that Jesus once visited Jerusalem in the autumn, at the feast of Tabernacles or Tents (Jn 7:14). He stayed three months, until the feast of the Dedication (in December), when he had to go into hiding in Peraea because an order had been issued for his arrest (Jn 11:55–57). The Synoptics do not mention this three-month stay in Jerusalem, but it must be dated in the early winter (September–December) preceding the arrest.[9] From St John, therefore, we can be sure that the public ministry of the Lord was not

[8] See above, pp. 111–112.

[9] For a detailed exposition of the arguments see M. Goguel, *Jésus*, Paris, 1950, pp. 318–323.

limited to Galilee: he began his public life beside the Jordan, and when the Galilean ministry was ended, he preached in Jerusalem before retiring beyond the Jordan to Peraea.

St Luke's Gospel, as we have seen, presents the life of Jesus as an 'Ascent to Jerusalem'.[10] The plan is attractive, ingenious, and skilfully executed; but it is also artificial, and therefore we must turn to Matthew or Mark for the general pattern of the succession of events in the Galilean ministry. Matthew, however, frequently groups episodes together because their subject-matter is similar (e.g. the series of miracles in 8:1–9:34); and in his accounts of the discourses of Jesus, he never hesitates to place together sayings which must have been uttered at very different times.[11] Mark, on the other hand, has completely omitted many of the sayings found in Matthew and Luke. Consequently, neither Matthew nor Mark permits us to determine with certainty the precise sequence of all the events in the Galilean ministry, but many scholars would agree with the following outline.

The preaching of Jesus in Galilee met at first with resounding success, supported as it was by impressive miracles: this is the theme of Mt 5:1–9:35. Jesus preached at this time about the imminence of the kingdom, and very soon sent certain chosen disciples to spread the same Good News throughout the region (Mt 10:5). The enthusiasm awakened by his message disturbed Herod, who began to sense that here was a troublemaker just as dangerous as the Baptist (Mk 6:14–16; cf. 3:6; 8:15 and Lk 13:31). But if Herod's hostility was one factor which induced Jesus to bring the ministry in Galilee to a close, there was another factor more potent still: the simple-minded crowds in Galilee were making the same mistake as Herod, and beginning to look upon Jesus as a potential king who would deliver them from oppressors and establish an earthly kingdom. Nationalist sentiment was winning for Jesus unwelcome political support; and the climax came after the feeding of the five thousand, when

10 See above, pp. 158–159.
11 See above, pp. 129–131.

'Jesus realized that they were going to take him and make him king' (Jn 6:15). When this moment came, he retired to the hill country and gave up public preaching in Galilee.

It is difficult to say precisely where he lived at this time. Some think that he lived almost alone, while his disciples continued their preaching, but since the gospels always picture him surrounded by his faithful friends, the suggestion may be discounted. It is more likely that when he himself ceased to preach openly, the disciples returned to join him (probably to hear his plans for the future). He certainly made one journey up towards the coast of the Lebanon ('the region of Tyre and Sidon'), and seems in fact to have moved around the northern borders of Herod's domains until he came eventually to Caesarea Philippi. He devoted these months to the formation of his disciples, but he no longer spoke of the imminence of the kingdom, because it was not necessary. Instead, he began to teach them that there would be a time of waiting before the kingdom was revealed in all its glory.

Towards the end of this period, Simon Peter confessed to Jesus openly, 'You are the Messiah!' Jesus thereupon began the final stage of his instruction of the disciples, seeking to persuade them that he would accomplish his messianic mission only by suffering and dying. He began his final journey to the cross, leaving Galilee and setting out for Jerusalem. This must have been in late September, in the year before his death.

Various motives have been suggested for Jesus' departure to Judea. There can be little doubt that the text in John 7:3 states a fact: Jesus' disciples pressed him to go and preach in the south of the country, in the capital. But Jesus went there from a different motive. The mission in the north had come to an end because the people of Galilee had only wanted Jesus to become an earthly king; Jesus, on the other hand, wished to focus attention on his own person rather than on the kingdom as such.

A second motive, which may have influenced Jesus, was the need to proclaim the Good News to all the Jews, including therefore those in Jerusalem. Jesus himself would hardly have expected to receive a warm welcome in Jerusalem from the scribes and Pharisees, and the substance of his teaching would no doubt have been known to them. This may account for a change in the content of his teaching: in John 5–10 we find that his discourses in Jerusalem all deal with his own position and person, not with the coming of the kingdom. This is exactly what one would have expected to happen in Jerusalem: the leaders of the people and the scribes would naturally have challenged Jesus' credentials. By whose authority had he been preaching new ideas in Galilee?

Lastly, Jesus must have known that by going to Jerusalem he was risking persecution and death. We shall show later that this was part of his plan for redeeming the world; for the present, it is sufficient to note that all three motives may well have influenced him to take the road to Jerusalem and Calvary.

These, then, are the broad lines of Jesus' life. He began his ministry alongside the Baptist, beside the Jordan, and then preached in Galilee about the coming of the kingdom. His preaching provoked hostility among the Jews and from Herod, and the ordinary folk failed to grasp his spiritual message. He therefore ceased to preach in public, and after a period on the borders of Galilee (during which he concentrated on the formation of his closest disciples) went to Jerusalem, where he stayed three months. Finally, after spending some time in Transjordan, he returned to Jerusalem a few days before the Passover.

This outline enables us to divide the ministry of Jesus into three periods. During the first, he spoke to large crowds about the imminence of the kingdom and the urgent need for repentance; during the second, he concentrated on teaching his disciples; during the third, he spoke in public once more in Jerusalem, but by then he was speaking mainly about his own person, his divine mission and his credentials.

In the light of this plan, it is possible to say that a particular saying was most probably uttered at such and such a time. To give but one example: the beatitude about 'those who suffer persecution' belongs (in all likelihood) not to the first sermon our Lord preached, but to the final period of his life.

With this framework of the Lord's life before us, we may now turn to the central question in our inquiry: what should men think of Jesus Christ?

CHAPTER 13

The Quest of
the Historical Jesus

ii: 'Who Do You Say That I Am?'

We enter now upon the final stage in our quest of the historical Jesus. From the literary analysis of the Gospel Tradition given in Part III, it is evident that the evangelists did not always arrange their material in chronological order; and from the last few pages it is clear that only the broadest chronological pattern of Jesus' life can be known. The historian must submit to the limitations imposed by the evidence, and therefore must not attempt to give a detailed account of the development of the earthly life of Jesus. But even though he cannot descend into details, and even though many questions remain unanswered (and perhaps unanswerable), it is certainly possible to make a valid synthesis of the teaching of Jesus, and to give a true account of his earthly life. We shall thereby see the originality of the Christian faith in all its splendour.

In this attempt to reconstruct what happened before the Resurrection, we shall rely mainly (though not exclusively) on the evidence given in the Synoptic Gospels. This is not to imply that the fourth gospel has nothing to contribute on this topic, but one must respect its peculiar literary form. In the next chapter we shall be concerned mainly with the fourth gospel, and there its testimony will be used to complete our reconstruction of the earthly life of Jesus.

Two further preliminary remarks are called for, because

there are two points on which many scholars would disagree strongly with the outline which will be proposed here. Much has been written about the development of Jesus' thought in the course of his ministry. Maurice Goguel, for example, has tried to trace the steps by which (he claims) Jesus became conscious of his messianic dignity. According to Goguel, Jesus became conscious first that he was in a very privileged way the Son of God, and then, little by little, that he was the Messiah.[1] Some Catholic scholars have argued in a similar fashion, though not about the messianic dignity of our Lord. They claim that until Israel rejected his message, Jesus did not think he would have to suffer and die on the cross: everything would have happened in a different way, they say, if the people had listened to his teaching, and the Kingdom of God did not come into being in the way Jesus had envisaged at the beginning of his ministry.[2] Others think that Jesus was not at first conscious that he was to be the Servant of the Lord who would redeem men by suffering; the Transfiguration would then have been a confirmation, by divine revelation, of the destiny which Jesus had begun to anticipate only after his rejection in Galilee.

All these approaches seem to the present writer equally unhappy, for although it is true that one can discern different periods in the life of Jesus, it is impossible to prove that these periods represent various stages in the development of his thought. Even if he did not speak publicly about his messianic mission or about his sufferings in the first part of his life, it does not follow that he never thought of himself at that time as the Messiah or as the Suffering Servant. Moreover, the exact dating of events and sayings is extremely problematical, as we have seen. Hence though it is in theory possible to discuss whether there was a real development in Jesus' thought, it would seem that the available evidence is insufficient to justify any firm conclusions. In the opinion of

[1] M. Goguel, *Jésus*, Paris, 1950, pp. 249, 250, 312.
[2] E.g. R. Guardini, *The Lord*, London, 1955.

the present writer, the historian must be content with more modest ambitions.

The second point on which many scholars would disagree with the present chapter concerns the manner in which we can learn about Jesus' messianic consciousness. Several Catholic writers, in their anxiety to defend the faith against rationalism, try to sketch a portrait of Jesus not by examining the general content of his teaching and his general behaviour, but by concentrating on certain very explicit statements which he is said to have made during his public life, and on the 'titles' he is said to have claimed for himself (*e.g.* 'Son of Man', 'the Son'). Certain Protestant authors contest the validity of this method, claiming that there is not a single authentic saying in the gospels in which Jesus presents himself as the Messiah. Now if the Catholic scholars mentioned have a tendency to overlook the distinction between what was said before and after the Resurrection, these Protestant scholars seem to be guilty of an equal exaggeration in allowing themselves to be guided (perhaps unconsciously) by philosophical or theological presuppositions: they seem at times afraid to admit that Jesus can be an 'object' of investigation unless one first takes up a stand for or against the authenticity of the disputed sayings.

In the opinion of the present writer, both these exaggerations can be avoided by prescinding from those statements in the gospels which concern the person of Jesus. We shall examine them later, but for the time being we shall restrict discussion to the message and the deeds of Jesus. They will inevitably raise questions about his person, and supply some of the answers. Once we have those answers, we can then examine the texts which concern his person, and the titles which are ascribed to him.

The last hundred years have witnessed the publication of several 'Lives of Jesus' in which the humanity of our Saviour is sensitively portrayed. These books tell how Jesus began to preach to a people which was quite sure that a glorious future lay before it. He preached to priests and scribes, to Pharisees and tax-collectors, to rich and poor, to pious people and to sinners. He presented himself as the prophet of the kingdom of God, and yet disappointed many of his hearers. In Old Testament times, it had been usual for a prophet to prove that he really had been sent by God, either by recounting the circumstances of his vocation, or by appealing to the traditional nature of his teaching. Jesus did neither: he never described any personal vocation by God, and never sought to justify his teaching by appealing to any authority other than his own.

Like the rabbis, he often taught in the synagogues, but unlike them, he also preached in the open air, or by the lakeside. The gospels record, too, that his manner of teaching was very different from that of the rabbis: they would justify their views by citing the opinions of teachers in previous generations, whereas Jesus would simply say 'Truly, I say to you . . .' Lastly, he differed from the rabbis in having among his disciples women, tax collectors and even public sinners.

This is the familiar pattern in the classical 'Lives of Jesus' (Renan, Edersheim, Farrar, Lagrange, Lebreton, Prat etc.). These works also fill in the geographical and historical background of Palestine under Roman rule (with varying degrees of success) in order to give the reader a vivid picture of the life of our Lord. Their style and their limitations are well known. It would be unjust, as well as ungracious, to underestimate the contribution they have made to our knowledge of our Lord, but it must be frankly confessed that a different treatment of the subject is needed today.

The originality of Jesus can be seen by considering his teaching on three topics. He speaks about his own coming as being the end of time, about his personal relationship with the Father, and about his relationship with men: in technical language, we may refer to his eschatology, his theology and his ecclesiology. These three themes form the core of his message, and if one or another is neglected or misinterpreted, then the whole message will be misunderstood or even distorted. We shall discuss these three topics in the order in which (in all probability) Jesus preached about them. Our order is certainly that in which the apostolic

Church learnt to understand them. First we shall discuss the teaching of Jesus about the end of time; secondly, we shall see that the end of time, the final epoch of history, is marked by the manifestation of the Father through Jesus; thirdly, we shall see how, through the knowledge of the Father, the kingdom of God is brought into being, to transform this world of time.

Each of the first three sections in the present chapter will reveal a new aspect of the person of Jesus. Each of them will raise the same question, 'Who do you say that I am?' The final section will be concerned with the answer given to that question by God.

1. God's Sovereign Rule and Kingdom in Action

Jesus began his public ministry, according to the gospels, by proclaiming 'The kingdom (or, 'reign') of God is arrived' (Mt 4:17; Mk 1:15). Exegetes have long debated whether he was referring to a kingdom (in the sense of a community) or to God's reign (in the sense of 'sovereign rule'). There is disagreement, too, about the meaning of the verb: in Greek, it stands in the perfect tense, but the perfect of this particular verb can mean either 'has already arrived' or 'is now arriving' or even 'is now imminent'. The general context seems to imply that the kingdom or reign of God had already begun, or was then beginning, but this is not indisputable. There are evidently many questions to be asked about this saying, and the following paragraphs will rely chiefly on a recent study entitled *God's Rule and Kingdom*,[3] by Dr Rudolf Schnackenburg. One of his main contentions is that we must carefully distinguish between the notions of the kingdom of God, the reign of God and the Church; it is, he contends, the failure to observe these distinctions which has led to such confusion in the past.

There is in the teaching of Jesus an apparent compenetration of the present and the future. Several writers have tried to explain this by claiming that Jesus 'felt' or 'saw' the future

[3] London and New York, 1963.

as already present. Others claim that at the beginning of his ministry, he thought of the kingdom as lying in the future, and at the end as already present. A third group thinks exactly the reverse, namely, that Jesus began by thinking of the kingdom as present and ended by thinking of it as still to come. Two very distinguished scholars have advocated different solutions again: Albert Schweitzer maintained that in the eyes of Jesus the kingdom was not present, but imminent: Professor C. H. Dodd holds that in Jesus' eyes, the kingdom was already realized by his coming. The fact that such contradictory conclusions can be drawn from Jesus' words at least shows that there is a certain tension in these words, a reference both to the present and to the future, which we must try to explain.

The Greek word *basileia* can of itself mean either a kingdom or the rule of a sovereign monarch, i.e. his 'reign'. The underlying thought in the gospels is that God's reign extends over the entire course of history, from the beginning to the end of time. But with the coming of Jesus, a new era of that reign opens; this era is itself divided into two stages, one of which extends over the earthly life of Jesus and the other over the period after the Resurrection. In the first stage, Jesus visibly lives and acts among men; in the second, the Church he founded inherits his authority and his mission. Salvation history, therefore, should not be divided into two epochs (one of preparation, the other of accomplishment), but into three. This is the arrangement so well described by St Luke,[4] in which we may distinguish a time of preparation (Old Testament times), a time of redemption (the earthly life of our Lord) and a time of fulfilment, when men are invited to avail themselves of their chance to encounter God in Christ (from the Resurrection to the end of history).

(a) The Kingdom as present in Jesus

By presenting himself as the herald of the kingdom of God, Jesus easily won a hearing, if not understanding, from his

---

[4] See above, pp. 161–162.

contemporaries, for they cherished the hope that God would one day make Israel the centre of a great earthly empire. There is ample evidence that this attitude was generally shared by all Jews in New Testament times: the Galileans wanted to make Jesus king (Jn 6:15), the crowds in Jerusalem welcomed him as the Son of David (Mt 21:9 and parallels), the disciples looked for the restoration of Israel's independence (Lk 19:11; 22:38; 24:21; Ac 1:6), the two sons of Zebedee wanted the first places in the kingdom (Mt 20:21), and even Peter apparently expected Jesus to be an earthly king (cf. Mt 16:22). Some Jews (e.g. the Zealots) interpreted the Old Testament promises in the most crudely materialistic way; others, like the authors of the apocryphal literature, had more spiritual ideas, but expected them to be realized through the establishment of an earthly kingdom. To all these men Jesus preached that the kingdom of God was a purely religious kingdom, open to Jew and Gentile alike, and that in the kingdom there was salvation, both now and in the future.

There are at least two texts unanimously recognized as authentic sayings in which Jesus speaks about the kingdom of God as present in time. When John the Baptist sent some of his disciples to ask Jesus whether he was 'the One who was to come', Jesus did not give a direct answer; instead, he asked John's disciples to draw the conclusion for themselves from the events they had witnessed. 'Go and tell John what you have seen and heard: the blind see, the lame walk, lepers are made clean, the deaf are hearing, the dead are being brought to life and the poor are hearing the gospel preached to them' (Mt 11:4–5; Lk 7:22). The treatment of Scripture, the indirect answer, the attention he draws to his person—all these are authentic proofs that Jesus, with his works, miracles and preaching, is the sign of the presence of the Messianic era. Hence he concludes: 'Blessed is he who is not scandalized by me!' (Mt 11:6; Lk 7:23). Jesus' role in the coming of God's kingdom on earth is unique.

The second text about whose authenticity there is no dispute occurs in Lk 11:20 and its parallels. When certain scribes from Jerusalem argued that the exorcisms performed by Jesus were the work of the devil, Jesus denounced the illogicality of their reasoning and said: 'But if it is by the finger of God that I am exorcizing devils, it means that the kingdom of God has arrived among you' (Lk 11:20). The Greek verb here translated 'arrived' leaves no room for doubt[5]: it means that a new era in the reign of God has started, the era of his kingdom among men. Here, too, attention is concentrated on the person of our Lord through the power he displays.

These two sayings are recognized as authentic by all scholars, and their meaning is clear. Other, more enigmatic, sayings may therefore be interpreted in the light of them, *e.g.* 'Truly I tell you, there has never been, among mankind, anyone greater than John the Baptist; and yet the least person in the kingdom of heaven is greater than he' (Mt 11:11; Lk 7:28); 'From the days of John the Baptist until now, the kingdom of heaven suffers violence, and everyone is trying to force his way into it' (Mt 11:12); 'The Law and Prophets lasted until John; since then, the kingdom of God is being preached, and everyone is trying to force his way into it' (Lk 16:16). These texts are generally interpreted as meaning that John, for all his greatness, stood outside the kingdom, and never entered it, and that the coming of Jesus spelt a rupture with that epoch, and the beginning of a new age.

The same thought probably lies behind the words ascribed to Jesus after the return of the disciples from their missionary preaching. When they mentioned that even the devils obeyed their orders, Jesus said, 'I watched Satan falling from heaven like lightning' (Lk 10:18). The sovereign power of God had broken the rule of Satan. This is the lesson implied in the many exorcisms which run like a thread through Mark's Gospel. The proclamation of the kingdom of God (Mk 1:15) is followed almost immediately by the exorcism of a devil (Mk 1:23–27), and several others are recorded later (3:11; 5:1–20; 7:24–30; 9:14–29). Jesus rightly claimed to have

[5] It is not the same verb as that used in Mt 4:17 or Mk 1:15.

defeated 'the Strong One' and to have robbed him of his possessions (Mk 3:22–30).

Yet, in spite of these extraordinary miracles, the coming of the kingdom did not correspond to the expectations of the Jews. The disciples sent by the Baptist were no doubt expecting the Messiah to be a judge who would exterminate all evil men; others were looking for signs which would herald his coming. When some of the Pharisees asked Jesus when exactly the kingdom of God would come, he told them, 'When the kingdom of God comes, it will not be something visible, and no one will say, It is here, or there. In fact, the kingdom of God is among you!' (Lk 17:20–21). Here Jesus states that the kingdom is not something still to be looked for in time or space, because it no longer lies wholly in the future. Then he tells the Pharisees to open their eyes to what is before them: the kingdom is already among them, i.e. within their grasp, if they will only recognize in the works performed by Jesus the signs of messianic times. Here again there is a summons to look at Jesus.

St Luke sums up this message admirably in his account of the visit of Jesus to Nazareth. Jesus, after reading from the Book of Isaiah the passage about preaching the gospel to the poor (Is 61:1 ff.), said: 'Today, this passage of Scripture has been fulfilled before you' (Lk 4:21). This text and many others are solid proof that Jesus was very conscious of having a special mission to perform, by which the kingdom of God was, in his mind, to be inaugurated. The reader may wonder why Jesus did not speak out more clearly, if he was so firmly convinced of his mission. Why did he merely hint at his own greatness in words like 'There is someone greater than Jonah . . . greater than Solomon here' (Mk 12:41–42; Lk 11:31–32)? Why did he not speak more openly?

One of the themes in St Mark's gospel is that Jesus tried to lead his disciples step by step to an acknowledgement of his divine Sonship.[6] As a result, Mark takes pains to show that Jesus, during his earthly life, did not openly declare from the

6 See above, pp. 145–146.

first moment of his ministry who he really was; the full revelation had to wait until Jesus had shown the meaning of his
mission by suffering and dying. This is certainly Mark's
theory; was it the common belief of the early Church, and
if so, does it represent what really happened?

That it is Mark's theory needs little proof. According to
Mark, Jesus forbade the unclean spirits to reveal who he was
(Mk 1:34; 3:12); he imposed the same prohibition on those
whom he cured by astounding miracles (1:44; 5:43; 7:36; 8:
26), and even on the disciples (8:30; 9:9). Mark tells how
the disciples did not really understand the truth about the
personality of Jesus (4:41; 6:51–52; 8:16–21; 9:33–34; 10:
35, 41–42) and implies that half the purpose of speaking in
parables was to conceal the mystery from those who were
unworthy to know it (4:11). Matthew has no parallel to most
of these texts (only to Mk 8:30 and 9:9), and even though
he has one text not in Mark which teaches the same lesson
(Mt 9:30), as a general rule he plays down the lack of understanding shown by the disciples. Luke also plays down the
disciples' lack of understanding, and he never mentions that
Jesus forbade them to speak about his messianic mission.
For these reasons, many scholars claim that the theory of the
'messianic secret' is a purely Markan invention.

At first sight, it looks as if Mark did invent this theory;
but there is one objection. Mark has included in his gospel
two passages (Mk 2:10, 28; 10:47–52) in which Jesus apparently did not order men to refrain from broadcasting
his identity. Mark presumably took these texts from his
sources without altering them; and therefore it may have
been Mark's fidelity to his sources which led him to state
so frequently that Jesus forbade men to tell everyone who
he was. In that case, the 'messianic secret' would not have
been Mark's invention but a datum of very old tradition.
Matthew, as we have seen, is less scrupulous in the treatment
of his sources,[7] and therefore it is more likely that he sup-

7 See above, pp. 119–120, 128–131.

pressed it (particularly in the light of his theology[8]); in one text, though, he has preserved an example of the same tradition which is not recorded by Mark (Mt 9:27–31), and which therefore cannot have been based on Mark.

The theme of the 'messianic secret' is therefore not something thought up by Mark, but a datum which Mark accepted from tradition. Matthew transposed the idea and presented it as the story of Jesus' withdrawal from public preaching (Mt 12:15–21; 14:1–16:12); John has transposed the idea in a different way, by presenting his dialogues as questions addressed to the reader.[9] Thus the common tradition underlying the gospels shows Jesus not merely as a Messiah who was in fact unknown, but as one who himself chose to conceal his identity.

We may take it, then, that Mark's presentation of the messianic secret is not a personal theory, but a view founded on a pre-Synoptic tradition. Is this tradition itself trustworthy? Two facts make it antecedently probable that Jesus would have shown restraint in his claims. First, the Jews of the time had far too material a concept of the messianic kingdom; secondly, if he had openly claimed to be God, he would most certainly have been put to death as a blasphemer. In short, it was practically impossible for Jesus to state his claims openly until he had, by his Resurrection, provided irrefutable proof that those claims were true.

In the opinion of the present writer, this attitude of Jesus was bound up with the very nature of revelation. It was impossible for Jesus to enclose the whole mystery of his person under any single title or name which could be grasped by human minds; so he had first to arouse those minds to a realization of their own incapacity by making them ask the question: 'Who are you?' Jesus wanted both to present himself as the Messiah and to veil his messianic dignity, at one and the same time. This double attitude of his reflected the two sides of a mystery: on the one hand, he could not allow

[8] See above, pp. 127–128.
[9] See above, pp. 93–99.

men to think they had grasped or fully understood who he was, and on the other hand he sought to give himself to them. Later, we shall note how the parables were heard both by the crowds and by the disciples, but only the disciples came to him to ask him to give them that understanding which was lacking to all. In short, the words and deeds and the very presence of Jesus are seen as an invitation to use our freedom, and they ought to move a man of good will sufficiently to make him want (and need) to ask the decisive question. That is why we said above that the portrait of Jesus should not be the 'object' of research without reference to his message; for his message is that Jesus makes men ask questions about himself before revealing himself as the answer to those questions.

Jesus compelled men to ask themselves questions about him by hinting that the kingdom of God had arrived. He frequently spoke of the kingdom as a present reality, in the sermon at Nazareth (Lk 4:18–19), in the Beatitudes (Lk 6:20–21) and above all in the text: 'Happy are your eyes, because they see! Happy your ears, because they hear! For I tell you truly that many prophets and virtuous men wished to see what you see and never saw it, to hear what you are hearing and never heard it!' (Mt 13:16–17). These and a host of other texts challenged the hearers to recognize that the reign of God had entered a new era with the coming of Jesus. They were therefore bound to ask themselves, 'Who, then, is this man?'

(b) The Establishment of God's Reign

In those parables which concern the kingdom of God, Jesus often speaks about its growth. He speaks of its beginnings, of various events which take place consecutively in the kingdom, and of a final consummation of the kingdom in glory at the end of history. It is quite certain that many of these texts have been cast into their present form by the catechetical practice of the early Church; but it is equally certain that

Jesus himself was sometimes asked for, and sometimes gave, an interpretation of a parable.[10]

Many of the parables tell how God rules the course of human history. In the parable of the Sower, for example, the hearer is asked to reflect on what happens to the seed: some is wasted or destroyed, but in the end the rest yields an abundant harvest. It is a picture of the ministry of Jesus, in which he, though rejected by many, found abundant success in the hearts of a few. The parable of the Tares or Darnel complements the story: even among the little band of disciples who followed Jesus, not all would find salvation in the end. The other parables which deal with the kingdom (*e.g.* the mustard seed, the leaven in the dough) all underline the truth that the reign of God extends over a period of time, during which the kingdom is destined to grow. When, therefore, Jesus spoke of the kingdom as present in his own day, he did not imply that it had also reached its final stage at that moment. His own day saw the establishment of the kingdom (the sowing of the seed); the end of the world would see the final perfection of the kingdom (the harvest); but between the two, there was to be a period in which the fruit could ripen, an age for the growth of the kingdom.

These parables were no doubt addressed to large crowds, but were understood only by the disciples, to whom Jesus explained their terms. It was a common practice among rabbis of the time to provide close disciples with a fuller explanation of their public teaching. There is a parallel, too, in the apocalyptic books which were so popular at the time: God was often said to have revealed his will to someone in enigmatic visions, and when the man confessed his inability to understand their meaning, an angel was sent to explain the significance of the vision (*cf.*, for example, Dan 7–12).

[10] The two classic works on the parables are C. H. Dodd, *The Parables of the Kingdom* (first published in London in 1935 and frequently reprinted with some revisions), and Joachim Jeremias, *The Parables of Jesus*, revised edition, London, 1963.

All the Synoptics, and especially Matthew, present some parables which are followed by a request for an interpretation; it must therefore represent a pattern of teaching which antedates the Synoptic tradition. When, therefore, Jesus is said to have explained these parables, the evangelists imply that the reader must not simply ask questions *about* Jesus' relationship to the kingdom, but must also put this question *to* Jesus himself.

(c) The Kingdom yet to come

If the kingdom is present in Jesus, and even if it is destined to grow, is there any sense in which it can be said to lie still in the future? Some authors, principally in England (C. H. Dodd, J. A. T. Robinson), have laid such stress on the theme of 'realized eschatology' that an inattentive reader might think they did not believe in any future manifestation of the kingdom greater than that which took place in the earthly life of Jesus.

The preceding parables are solid evidence that, in the mind of our Lord, there was yet to be a glorious consummation of the kingdom. He told his disciples to pray, 'Thy kingdom come!' (Mt 6:10); he frequently spoke about the need to belong to the kingdom at the end of time (Mt 5:20; 7:21; 18:3; 19:23; 21:31; 22:12 etc.), and about the danger of being thrown into outer darkness (Mt 13:42, 50; 22:13; 25:30 etc.). In fact, some of the parables he used to describe the kingdom are taken from classical eschatological texts of the Old Testament (*e.g.* the great tree where birds nest is taken from Ez 17:23 and Dan 4:17–18; the 'banquet' of heaven is, of course, a classical figure in Hebrew thought for the company of God).

Yet there is another series of texts which demonstrates even more convincingly that Jesus thought of a glorious consummation of the kingdom at some future date: they are those in which he speaks of the 'Son of Man'. Nowadays, no one interprets this title in the light of its usage in Ezekiel, where it means simply 'I'; and though it is not impossible that our Lord's contemporaries may have taken it in this sense, all modern writers agree that Jesus himself used the title in the sense it has in Daniel, where it denotes a heavenly being who brings salvation, and who embodies in himself the Kingdom of the Saints of the Most High (Dan 7). (There is a Jewish work called the Book of Enoch, which seems to contain pre-Christian traditions, in which the term is employed in the same way: in certain 'parables' recorded there, it is said that 'the Son of Man' will come at the last day to judge sinners and to reward the righteous.) In calling himself by this title, Jesus implicitly claimed a heavenly origin and the role of judge at the end of time; he also said he had come to inaugurate the messianic era (Mt 12:8) and to save sinners (Mt 9:6); but he toned down the glorious character of the Son of Man by insisting that he who would judge mankind at the end of history was, here and now, a Servant come to suffer and to die for love of mankind (cf. Is 53).

It is clear that the above argument holds only if Jesus identified himself with the Son of Man, and some modern writers have denied that he did: the sayings in which he refers to himself as Son of Man were placed on his lips, they say, by the early Christians in Palestine. This is hardly credible, for it implies that the early Christian community attributed to Jesus (without foundation) a title that quickly disappeared from its own usage. (Elsewhere in the New Testament, the phrase is found only in Ac 7:56; Apoc 1:13; 14:14). Some even claim that in speaking of the Son of Man, Jesus was referring to a person other than himself. Without entering into detail, we may simply cite two or three texts which should be sufficient to settle the matter.

'I tell you, if any man declares himself on my side when men are watching, the Son of Man will declare himself on his side when angels are watching; but he who denies me before men will be denied before the angels of God' (Lk 12:8–9; cf. Mt 10:32–33, where 'I' is substituted for 'the Son of Man'). It is theoretically possible to maintain that the Son of Man mentioned here is distinct from Jesus, but then the meaning of the whole sentence is lost, for it concerns the existential situation of men who take sides for or against Christ. Certain other texts bear the same meaning (Mt 16: 27; 25:31–46; Lk 11:29–30); we may cite in particular the reply of Jesus to the High Priest ('You will see the Son of Man seated at the right hand of the Power and coming on the clouds of heaven', Mk 14:62 and parallels), which certainly refers to the coming of Jesus at the end of time. In short, there are some texts, whose authenticity cannot reasonably be doubted, in which Jesus asserted that he would return as judge of the world at the end of time. This 'Second Coming' or *Parousia* would (he claimed) entail a general judgment of all mankind, and would bring to a close the kingdom as it exists on earth.

2. The Revelation by Jesus of the Father

By his preaching of the kingdom, by his miracles and exorcisms, Jesus proclaimed that a new era had opened in the religious history of mankind. But it was not until his death that he publicly revealed himself as the Messiah, because his messianic dignity could not have been understood correctly before then. The Israelites had never expected the Messiah to be the Son of God except in a metaphorical sense, in the same way as other men; and they certainly had never expected the Messiah to achieve his task by suffering and dying. In these circumstances, it was essential for Jesus to move gradually, leading his disciples step by step to the point where he could tell them that his mission was to be accomplished by suffering; only at the end could he reveal to them that he was the Son of God. He began not by stating openly that he was the Son of God, but by speaking about the fatherhood of God.

Jesus was not, of course, the first to speak of God as the 'father' of men: the idea is found in some ancient Greek writers, and in the Old Testament, where God is often called the 'Father' of Israel. But the originality of our Lord's teaching is seen best by comparing it with the teaching of other people, for then it becomes clear that his teaching rested on two principles, that God is Love and that he himself was the Son of God.

(a) The Presence of the Father

Jesus often spoke of God as a master to whom men owed service, and as a father who loved them all as his children. By placing equal emphasis on both these aspects, he gave a true idea of God as a being full of majesty and loving kindness. Today, it is perhaps particularly necessary to state that God is not only a loving father, but also a master demanding service; neither aspect must be allowed to conceal the other, or the resulting concept of God will be a distortion of what Jesus said.

There are many familiar texts in which Jesus speaks of God's fatherly love: our heavenly Father makes his sun rise upon wicked men and good men alike (Mt 5:45), and knows of all our needs (Mt 6:42). Is this just metaphorical or even poetical language to express God's love for his creatures?

It is possible to understand these words only if we start from the fundamental fact that God is the creator. Jesus expressed this idea by speaking of men as his servants, and by comparing God with the proprietor of a large estate. In Galilee, certain landowners, when they went on a journey abroad, would entrust the administration of their estates to bailiffs. Jesus often compares men with bailiffs who have to be faithful in administering an estate which is not their own, but only entrusted to them for a time by the true proprietor. Their task is to make profit for him, 'and when you have done everything you have been ordered to do, say: We are *merely* servants; we have done only what was our duty' (Lk 17:10; the Greek word *achreioi* is hard to translate, but the sense is that given here, that the servants have only done their duty). If, on the other hand, the servant betrays his trust, he becomes a debtor to his master. This is the background of thought to the phrase in the Lord's Prayer: 'Forgive us our debts, as we ourselves have forgiven our debtors'

(Mt 6:12). Man is not merely a servant of God, but also a debtor to him, because all men are disobedient and sinful in the sight of God.

This theme is developed in the parable of the Unmerciful Servant (Mt 18:23–35): the message of this parable is that the gross sinfulness of man only underlines the abundance of God's forgiveness. The parable itself is credible enough except for one detail: the sum of money owed by the servant to the king is 10,000 talents, *i.e.* 100 million denarii. It should be noted that the talent was the highest unit of currency known, and 10,000 the highest number used: so that St Matthew is saying that the debt is quite unpayable by any private individual. The servant asked for time to repay (Mt 18:26), but the king knew that he would never be able to find the money. The lesson taught in this parable is that men can never pay their debts to God by their own efforts; all they can do is to ask for forgiveness because they in turn have been forgiving to everyone who has injured them.

The same lesson of God's readiness to forgive is evident in the parable of the Prodigal Son: perhaps a more apt title would be 'The Father of the Prodigal Son', because the point of the parable lies in the father's welcome when his son comes home. Two other parables in the same chapter of Luke (Lk 15) present the same theme: they are the parables of the Lost Sheep and the Lost Coin, each of which ends with the refrain 'There is joy in heaven over one sinner who repents' (Lk 15:7, 10).

In preaching of God's readiness to forgive, Jesus was condemning the idea that men were to be judged by their external conformity to the Law. How can any man know that another person will never repent of his evil ways (Mt 21: 18–31)? And what right had any man to despise a tax collector praying humbly for forgiveness (Lk 18:9–14)? In the eyes of Jesus, God's fatherhood was most evident in his eagerness to forgive totally the debts which men had incurred. In short, God's fatherhood is seen most clearly in the way he does not insist on his rights as creator and master.

But if men are so readily pardoned by God, they too have

a heavy obligation to forgive their fellow men. The parable
of the Unmerciful Servant ends with the statement that our
heavenly father will deal most sternly with us if we refuse to
forgive our fellow men from the bottom of our hearts (Mt
18:35). The same principle extends even to our enemies:
God forgives his enemies, and therefore God's children must
do the same (Mt 5:43–48). In this, Jesus is not preaching the
Stoic ideal that one must not draw distinctions between persons because of their race or nation; he goes far beyond it,
and demands—without ambiguity or compromise—that those
who claim to be his disciples must accept every single human
being as their brother, because all of them without exception
are children of the Father who made and loves them all.

(b) 'Like Little Children'

One day, the disciples tried to prevent some people from
bringing little children to Jesus, presumably because they
thought it would be for Jesus a waste of valuable time: these
children were not old enough to observe the Law, and the
disciples probably concluded that they were too young to be
of interest to their Master. But Jesus was intensely interested
in them just because they were so innocent and guileless, and
said: 'It is to creatures such as these that the kingdom of
God belongs. I tell you truly, anyone who does not welcome
the kingdom of God like a little child will not enter it' (Mk
10:14–15). In this episode, Jesus seized the opportunity to
teach that the kingdom was not something which men could
enter by their own efforts; it was a gift, to be accepted grate-
fully, in the way little children accept presents. Children
have nothing to give, they can only receive presents; and that
is why they provide so perfect an image of the attitude Jesus
expected from his disciples. Matthew records a similar saying ('Unless you become again like little children . . .', Mt
18:1–4), in which there may be a hint also of the need to
be reborn by baptism, through which a man enters the kingdom as a little child (cf. Jn 3:3).

Jesus also said, 'Happy are the poor in spirit, for theirs is the kingdom of heaven' (Mt 5:3). Detachment from worldly goods is indispensable for possession of the kingdom, because the man whose life is dominated by concern for possessions does not have sufficient trust in his heavenly Father: this is a major theme of the Sermon on the Mount (Mt 6:32–34). In a time of peace and relative stability, such detachment may not seem unduly difficult, but Jesus said that his disciples ought to have confidence in their heavenly Father even in war and under persecution. 'Do not be afraid of those who kill the body, but have no power to kill the soul. Be more afraid of him who can throw both soul and body into hell. Are not sparrows sold at two a penny? Yet not one of them falls to the ground unknown to your Father. The very hairs of your head are all numbered. So be without fear, for you are certainly more precious than many sparrows' (Mt 10:28–31; Lk 12:4–7).

Nor is it only in extreme situations that Jesus calls for an unreserved commitment of oneself to God's care; he demands the same attitude in daily life. 'No man can be the servant of two masters at once; either he will hate the one and love the other, or he will be attached to one and will despise the other. You cannot serve God and Money' (Mt 6:24). Luke places this saying in a different context (Lk 16:13), and introduces Jesus' teaching on poverty with the parable of the Rich Fool who, when he thought he had enough money, died suddenly the same night (Lk 12:20). It is not that Jesus condemned men simply for being rich: he was most gracious to Zacchaeus the tax collector, who gave half his wealth to the poor (Lk 19:8–9), but our Lord did condemn in the strongest terms those whose lives were consumed with the pursuit of earthly possessions.

The spirit of total commitment to God which has been described as a spirit of detachment and childlike simplicity is called, in technical theological language, faith. The word 'faith', when it occurs in the gospels, does not mean primarily an acceptance of some proposition as true, or even obedience to divine revelation (though either of these meanings may be implied); the primary meaning of the word in the gospels is a total entrusting of oneself to God, as a child trusts his father. Jesus demanded that men should show this same unbounded trust towards himself, and when they showed it, he never failed to respond with generosity. Those who carried the paralysed man to him (Mk 2:5), the blind men who asked for sight (Mt 9:29), the centurion of Capernaum (Mt 8:10, 13), and the Canaanite woman (Mt 15:28) all showed unbounded faith in Jesus, and were rewarded correspondingly. In these and many other texts, the miracles of Jesus are presented not as a cause producing faith in men, but as the reward and result of their faith. This is the lesson taught in the passage about the sign of Jonah (Mt 16:1, 4; Lk 11:29–30): the doctrine taught by Jesus should have been sufficient to engender faith in anyone who was well disposed, and Jesus was unwilling to perform miracles for those who turned a deaf ear to his preaching. In other words, when Jesus asked for faith, he asked men to respond to God's call like little children, in simplicity and sincerity of heart.

(c) The Revelation of the Son

In inviting men to look upon God as little children look upon their father, Jesus was pointing to the goal they had to attain; in demanding that they should have faith in himself, he was showing them the way to attain it. By turning men's attention to himself, Jesus did not mean to turn them away from God; on the contrary, just as the reign of God was made manifest in the external activity of Jesus,[11] so the fatherhood of God was made manifest through the sayings and deeds of Jesus.

Accepting the sovereignty of God, or entering the kingdom, meant confessing that Jesus was the Messiah and the Son of Man; and accepting God as Father meant accepting Jesus as the Son of God. Yet just as Jesus never publicly proclaimed himself as Messiah until his trial, so he made no explicit claim to be the Son of God. Occasionally, it is true, he used words which implied that he was conscious of a unique rela-

[11] See above, pp. 248–254.

tion to the Father, as when he said he was 'the Son', but he never made any explicit claim to a unique relationship.

It is equally certain that the early Christian Church confessed that 'Jesus was the Son of God'. How are we to explain this belief? Are there any sayings of Jesus which could have given rise to it?

Some scholars (*e.g.* Bousset, Dibelius and Bultmann) claim that the title 'Son of God' stemmed from a Hellenistic, not a Palestinian, background, and that it was ascribed to Jesus at a relatively late date by the Greek-speaking Church. Others think the title represents both Hellenistic and Palestinian ideas about him: *e.g.*, Jeremias thinks that the Greek phrase 'Son of God' is a translation of the Semitic phrase 'Servant of God'. A third group (*e.g.* V. Taylor, Cullmann) holds that the title is of Palestinian origin, but that it is used in the gospels in some metaphorical sense (*e.g.* to express both the majesty and the humble obedience of the Lord).

To disprove these contentions it is necessary to show first that the texts in which Jesus calls himself 'the Son' are authentic sayings of the Lord. Three criteria are here of assistance. First, whenever Jesus calls himself 'the Son', the gospel texts are notably devoid of other appellations which, in the primitive Church, accompanied the title 'Son of God' (compare, for example, Rom 1:3). Secondly, Jesus never says he is 'the Son *of God*' (as one would expect if the saying had been made up by the early Church); and his claim to be 'the Son' is not couched in words which are direct or indirect citations from the Old Testament (as might have been expected if the early Church had placed these sayings on his lips). Thirdly, in these sayings there is no allusion to his Resurrection.[12]

If we wish to test the authenticity of sayings by these criteria, we must leave aside those texts like the accounts of the Baptism and Transfiguration where Jesus is called the Son

---

[12] *Cf.* B. M. F. van Iersel, *'Der Sohn' in den synoptischen Evangelien: Christusbezeichnung oder Selbstbezeichnung Jesu?* Leiden, 1961, pp. 173–180.

of God: Christian belief may well have influenced the expression here, and in any case it is not Jesus who calls himself the Son of God. We must turn our attention to other passages.

The most important are those in which Jesus addresses God as *Abba*, the familiar form of address to one's father. The Jews did not address their Creator in this way, but as *Abinu* ('Our father'), and generally added some other epithet (*e.g.* *Abinu malkenu*, 'Our father, our king!'). Now Jesus told his disciples to say 'Our father in heaven', and often spoke to them about 'your father' or 'my father'; but he never spoke to them about '*our* heavenly father', as if God were the father of him and of the disciples in the same way. Here there is a hint that he was conscious of a difference in his relationship to God.

In the eschatological discourse of Jesus there is one sentence whose authenticity is admitted by all scholars, and which could never have been thought up by the early Church, because in it Jesus denies any knowledge of the exact moment of the Second Coming. 'As for that day or hour, no one knows them—not even the angels in heaven, nor the Son, but only the Father' (Mt 24:36). Here 'the Son' is clearly distinguished from men on earth, and from the angels in heaven; he is also mentioned next to the Father.

Another text in Matthew and in Luke contains an affirmation of the utmost importance. 'I bless thee, Father, Lord of heaven and earth, for having concealed these things from the wise and intelligent, and for having revealed them to little ones. Yes, Father, such has been thy good pleasure. Everything has been entrusted to me by my Father, and no one knows the Son except the Father, and no one knows the Father except the Son and he to whom the Son has revealed it' (Mt 11:25–27 = Lk 10:21–22). Not all scholars admit this passage to be authentic, but many do; and those who do admit its authenticity must also admit that it places Jesus in an utterly unique relationship to that Father who is Lord of heaven and earth, and in an equally unique relationship with men, for he alone reveals to them the truth about the fatherhood of God. (One may cite in addition the parable in Mt 21:33-43.) Jesus, in speaking thus, made it clear that he thought of himself as belonging to the realm of the divine and as being, at the same time, very much in this world of time.

Jesus thought of himself as being in a quite unique sense the Son of God. That is why he could say that the reign of God had been manifested by his coming; why he could fulfil the messianic hope of Israel; why he could promise the coming of a heavenly kingdom at the end of history; and why he could speak so confidently about the fatherhood of God. He could do all this because he was speaking from complete conviction, based on personal experience. Professor Jeremias has shown that in his use of the phrase 'Amen I say to you', Jesus (who alone uses this phrase) was employing a formula as strong as the Old Testament phrase 'Thus says the Lord'. In all his sayings and in all his behaviour we find ourselves face to face with a man who did not claim, but rather asserted, a unique authority, because he was conscious that he possessed it.

3. The People of God

This section is entitled 'The people of God' and not 'The Church', partly because the term 'Church' occurs only twice in the gospels (Mt 16:18; 18:17), and partly because the Church as such represents only one phase in the reign of God. The expression 'people of God', by contrast, connotes both the people of Israel under the Old Covenant and the community of saints as it will exist after the general resurrection, when the Son will have delivered his kingdom to the Father.

Jesus, in founding his Church, looked beyond its boundaries. There are, as we shall see, texts in which he lays claim to sovereign rule over all nations, whether they accept his claim or not; and there are other texts in which he says he will judge all nations at the end of history. Many misunderstandings between Catholics and Protestants might be avoided if they could agree on a common terminology at this point: Catholics sometimes place so much stress on the intermediary stage ('the Church') that they seem to have forgotten about the final consummation of the kingdom, and Protestants are sometimes so concerned with the eschatological kingdom that they seem to regard the Church on earth as of secondary importance.

(a) The Future Kingdom

Jesus had spoken of a kingdom to be established at the end of time, but who were to be members of it? Did Jesus think of this 'eschatological kingdom' as identical with the group of disciples who followed him on earth, or was there a place in the kingdom for others too?

Jesus himself was a Jew, and remained so until the end of his life[13]; but he did not think of himself as being in all respects like the other Jews of his day, for he was conscious of standing in a very particular and close relationship to God. He thought of himself as the Son of the heavenly Father. His behaviour, therefore, was not based merely on the Mosaic Law, but also (and more so) on his personal conviction that he lived in immediate contact with God. At times in his life, there seems to have been tension between the demands of the Law and the imperatives of his own religious consciousness: we see it in the controversies with the scribes and Pharisees, and sometimes in the teaching ascribed to Jesus. From these gospel stories, it is possible to reconstruct the attitude of Jesus to Israel.

'Do not think that I have come to abolish the Law or the Prophets; I have come not to abolish them, but to fulfil them. And indeed I tell you truly, that if your virtue is not greater than that of the scribes and Pharisees, you will never enter the kingdom of heaven' (Mt 5:17, 20). When Jesus here

[13] Thus the Jewish scholar, J. Klausner: 'Jesus was a Jew, and a Jew he remained till his last breath' (Jesus of Nazareth: His Life, Times and Teaching. Translated from the original Hebrew by H. Danby, London, 1929, p. 368).

speaks of 'fulfilling' the Law, he means 'bringing it to perfection'. This purpose is illustrated by the five sayings which follow, on murder (Mt 5:21–24), on adultery (5:27–28), on oaths (5:33–37), on revenge (5:38–42) and on loving one's enemies (5:43–48). In his comment on each of these topics, Jesus sets out a code of perfect behaviour, and on each topic he appeals only to his own authority ('But I tell you . . .').

Jesus presented the Jews of his day with a new ideal, by insisting that the Law should be regarded as primarily an internal law. Every action, he said, was right or wrong according to the secret intention behind it; and every intention was good or bad according to the love, or lack of love, which inspired it; and that love which inspired good actions had to be absolute. These are the three characteristics of his new teaching about the Law.

Liberal Protestants of the last hundred years have sometimes claimed that Jesus abolished the ritual parts of the Mosaic Law, while confirming the moral precepts. To a Jew, this would have been unthinkable, and it is more correct to say that Jesus pointed to the necessity of a right intention in performing any work commanded by the Law. Almsgiving, prayer and fasting are not condemned, but praised, provided the intention is not to seek praise from men, but to behave as children of the Father (Mt 6:4, 6, 18). Only good trees produce good fruit; bad trees produce only bad fruit (Mt 7:15–20). For Jesus, all human actions are to be judged by the depth and sincerity of the religious intention behind them.

But how is man to decide whether his intention is good or not? The classical Judaism of the day tended to judge every intention by the external act: if a Jew observed the Law, his intention was presumed to be worthy. Jesus, however, told his disciples that though they were not to judge others (Mt 7:1), they should ask themselves whether their acts were dictated by a sincere love of God and their neighbour.

Lastly, Jesus set no bounds to this love which he demanded. 'You must be perfect, as your heavenly Father is perfect' (Mt 5:48). He made no distinction between the 'beginners' and the 'perfect', between 'commandments' and 'counsels'. All his followers without exception were summoned to give everything they had to give, in imitation of their heavenly Father. This was his 'New Law'.

But how was mankind to achieve this apparently unattainable perfection? Here we must stress that Jesus did not promulgate his Law from heaven as a series of precepts and prohibitions, for that would only have crushed all hope, and would have weighed on mankind more heavily than all the articles of the Mosaic Law. Instead, he presented his New Law as the imitation of himself, a man familiar with suffering, and therefore able to sympathize with all our human weaknesses.

If the New Law seems at times impractical, it is because men have reduced it to a written code, and have divorced it from the person of Jesus Christ. Christians who treat the message of Jesus in this way degrade it in exactly the same way as the Jews of the first century had degraded the noble message of Deuteronomy: in clinging to the letter of the law, they jettison its spirit. This is the attitude which Jesus condemned when he said, 'The sabbath is made for man, not man for the sabbath' (Mk 2:27), or that mercy is more important than sacrifices (Mt 9:13; 12:7). Jesus himself never shrunk from contact with lepers, with tax-collectors and notorious sinners, and there is no finer summary of his moral teaching than in the invitation to 'come to him', who alone can make the practice of the New Law possible. 'Come to me, all you that labour and are heavy-burdened, and I will give you rest. Take my yoke upon you and learn of me, for I am meek and humble of heart, and you will find rest for your souls. For my yoke is easy, my burden is light' (Mt 11:28–30).

Such was the invitation Jesus addressed to Israel. Once such a principle is accepted, then it must apply to all men without distinction of race. John the Baptist had warned the Jews that their descent from Abraham was no sure guarantee of salvation (Lk 3:8), but there are certain texts in the gospels which seem to imply that Jesus did not envisage the inclusion of the Gentiles in his kingdom. He said that he himself had been sent only to the lost sheep of Israel (Mt 15:24), and told his disciples not to travel into pagan lands, or into any Samaritan village (Mt 10:5–6). These sayings are certainly authentic, but their significance should not be exaggerated. Jesus, like the Israelite prophets of old, restricted his activity to the country of his birth, but he never repulsed any Gentile who came to him. He stated publicly that he had never found faith in Israel like that of the pagan centurion (Mt 8:10), and said to the Canaanite woman, 'O woman, great is your faith!' (Mt 15:28). And perhaps the most telling text of all is his prediction that the Gentiles would have places of honour in the heavenly kingdom. 'I tell you, many will come from the east and from the west to sit at the banquet table with Abraham, Isaac and Jacob in the kingdom of heaven, but the children of the kingdom will be thrown out into the darkness; there, they will weep and grind their teeth' (Lk 13:28–29). This text is too full of Semitic phrases to have been coined by the Greek-speaking Church, and its authenticity cannot be doubted.

For Jews and Gentiles alike, then, there is a place in the heavenly kingdom. In the tableau with which St Matthew closes the public preaching of Jesus (Mt 25:31–46), all the nations of the world are summoned before the Son of Man, and all alike are judged by their practice of charity. More particularly, their practice of charity to their fellow-men is there presented as charity towards Jesus himself: 'As long as you did it to the least of my brothers, you did it to me' (Mt 25:40). The 'brothers' here are not just the disciples of Jesus on earth, but all mankind, for all the nations of the world are judged by this standard, even those who have never heard the name of Jesus of Nazareth. The same lesson is taught in the parable of the Good Samaritan (Lk 10:29–37), in which Jesus affirms that the true disciple must show himself a neighbour to anyone who is in distress.

The future kingdom, then, in Jesus' mind, was not to be restricted to Israel; nor was it to be formed of all who acted kindly towards their brothers as far as was humanly practicable. It was to consist only of those who, throwing human prudence to the winds, would give themselves unreservedly to the service of love, without counting the cost.

(b) The Church of Jesus

The eschatological kingdom supplies the background against which we must consider the foundation of the Church by Jesus. The Church itself is not identical with the kingdom, and our next task is to see its relationship to the kingdom. Here two extremes are to be avoided. It is impossible to deny that Jesus chose to found a community which would endure during the intermediary period between his life and the final Parousia: this must be admitted if one admits the authenticity of those parables which speak of the growth of the kingdom. On the other hand, it is equally impossible to say that Jesus founded a Church which was recognizably similar to the Church we know, with its institutions, laws and so forth, separated from Israel in much the same way as the sect of Qumran was a non-conformist denomination in Israel. It is not easy to steer clear of both these extremes, and it is easier to criticize other positions than to set down a satisfactory account of one's own views. We shall, however, try to trace the stages by which Jesus moulded his band of followers into a community which eventually took to itself the name of 'the Church'.

From the beginning of his ministry, Jesus called men to follow him: this we know from all four evangelists. Throughout his public life he continued to call certain individuals to leave all things and follow him: the tax-collector Levi was summoned in this way (Mt 9:9), and Mark says that many tax-collectors and sinners followed him (Mk 2:15). St Luke mentions a group of women who followed him (Lk 8:1-3), and John tells us that Nicodemus was one of the disciples (Jn 3). It is clear, therefore, that the Twelve were not the only regular followers of Jesus.

On the other hand, Jesus did not invite everyone to follow him. He positively dissuaded the man from Gerasa who had been freed from an evil spirit (Mk 5:18–20), and did not, apparently, ask Zacchaeus to join him (Lk 19:10). Sometimes he even discouraged prospective followers by stressing the hardships his disciples would have to meet (Lk 9:57–58); and even though he once said 'Anyone who is not with me is against me' (Lk 11:23), on another occasion he said 'Anyone who is not against us is for us' (Mk 9:40). The different data in the gospels, then, though at times hard to harmonize, suggest that Jesus acted with great liberty in choosing those who were to form the 'little flock' to which his Father would entrust the kingdom (Lk 12:32). Perhaps the group of regular followers varied in numbers from time to time (*cf.* Jn 6:66–67).

This group, however, did not form an association in any legal or constitutional sense: its members were united only by their common devotion to the person of their Master. At the centre of it were the Twelve whom he had chosen, and who were later to be his witnesses, but another tradition tells us that there was also a larger group of about seventy men to whom he once entrusted a mission of preaching (Lk 10:1–2). Though Luke alone mentions the figure of seventy (or seventy-two), Matthew may have had this larger group in mind when he recorded that Jesus said: 'The harvest is plentiful, but there are not many workmen; pray, then, that the master of the vineyard may send workmen for his harvest' (Mt 9:37–38). According to Luke, these words were spoken to the seventy disciples.

Among this band of regular followers, Jesus chose the body of the Twelve to be his constant companions, to preach in his name, and to exorcize devils with authority (Mk 3:14–15). He chose them during his Galilean ministry, before the crisis which brought it to an end. His object in choosing the Twelve was to gather all Israel together: they, like the Twelve Patriarchs of old, were to form the nucleus of the new people of God. 'When the Son of Man is enthroned in glory, you also will have your places on twelve thrones, to be judges of the twelve tribes of Israel' (Mt 19:28 = Lk 22:30). Yet they are not to be thought of, at this time, as the leaders of a separatist movement, but rather as twelve representatives of the old Israel, which was not, at this time, in any way distinct from the people of God. In giving them, and especially Peter (*cf.* Mt 16:16–18), a share in his own authority and power, Jesus proclaimed his intention of working with and through them for the establishment of the final or eschatological kingdom. So, after his death and Resurrection, this body of men continued his work because they were conscious of sharing in that authority and of having had his mission entrusted to them. This is what we mean by saying that Jesus founded a Church, namely, that by choosing the Twelve Jesus intended them to form the nucleus of the people of God who would one day inherit the heavenly kingdom, and to bear his authority and power.

(c) The Sacrifice of the Servant: the New Covenant

The new people of God is said to have come into being in and by the sacrifice of Jesus. This raises two questions for the historian. (1) Did Jesus in fact embrace death voluntarily, thereby transforming his own execution into an act of sacrifice? (2) Did Jesus, before his death, institute a sacramental sign of his sacrifice? These two questions can be formulated in biblical language as one: Was Jesus conscious of being the Servant of the Lord who by his sacrifice founded a New Covenant?

The Synoptics record that three times Jesus foretold his Passion and Resurrection (Mt 16:21; 17:22–23; 20:18–19 and parallels), but the wording of these prophecies is such that few critical historians would care to accept them without qualification as authentic sayings. They do, however, rest on sound tradition, for elsewhere in the Synoptics we find traces of sayings in which the references to his sufferings are allusive and imprecise. Thus Luke records that Jesus once said 'It is impossible for a prophet to die outside Jerusalem' (Lk 13:31–33), and that the Son of Man would have to suffer much and be rejected by this generation (Lk 17:25). Mark mentions, after the Transfiguration, this saying: 'How was it written

that the Son of Man would have to suffer and be despised?';
if this saying had been coined by the early Church, it is surprising that the allusion is not clearer and that there is no
hint about the Resurrection. Finally, we may mention also
the text of Matthew in which Jesus says (in a context of
sayings about the Baptist) that 'the bridegroom will be taken
away from them' (Mt 9:15). All three Synoptics, then, have
preserved sayings from the time of the Galilean ministry in
which Jesus hints at his future suffering and death.

In the weeks preceding his arrest, these references become
more common. He asked the sons of Zebedee whether they
could drink the cup he was going to drink (Mt 20:22); again,
it is unlikely that the early Church would have made up a
story which reflected so little credit on two of its most revered
leaders. The parable of the Wicked Husbandmen also speaks
of murder (Mt 21:33–43), and perhaps the whole meaning of Jesus' life is most accurately summed up in the words:
'The Son of Man did not come to have men serve him, but
to be a servant and to lay down his life as a ransom for
many' (Mt 20:28 and parallels). If all these texts are considered together, then it would seem certain that Jesus went
voluntarily to his death. The references to his fate are not
expressions of a merely human presentiment, but are so
phrased that he would seem to have envisaged this death as
a redemptive sacrifice, as foretold in the Book of Isaiah
(Is 53).

On the night before he suffered, Jesus took a farewell
meal with his disciples. According to John (Jn 13–17), Jesus
spoke at length to his disciples about their destiny and their
vocation in the years to come, and there are some echoes of
the same teaching in the Synoptics (Lk 22:15–20, 21–38; Mt
26:29; Mk 14:25). But the Synoptics place more emphasis
on the institution of the eucharistic rite (Mt 26:26–28; Mk
14:22–24; Lk 22:19–20, cf. 1 Cor 11:23–25). In each of
them Jesus speaks of his 'blood' in connection with a Covenant, i.e. of his death as connected with a Covenant. Luke
interprets this saying as the establishment of the New Covenant foretold by Jeremiah (Jer 31:31–34), but under all the

texts there runs the theme that Jesus is the Servant of the Lord come to make atonement for the sin of men by the shedding of his blood. And by this sacrifice, the New Covenant and the new age in the Reign of God is finally sealed.

One last remark is called for: was it Jesus himself, or the early Church which identified him with the Servant of the Lord described in Is 53? In spite of some dissentient voices, the majority of scholars think that Jesus himself made the identification, for the simple reason that the early Church never worked out what might be called a 'systematic theology' of the Servant-theme. There are a number of references to the Isaian text in the New Testament, but there is not one explicit citation from this chapter in the story of the Passion. Its theme is everywhere felt, but nowhere cited; and the most reasonable explanation of this fact is that Jesus had hinted at his role as the Servant of the Lord without putting it in so many words. This was characteristic of him; he spoke with the same reserve about himself as 'the Son' and as the Messiah, and the very absence of a direct claim is therefore an indication of his thought.

4. The Resurrection: God's Final Word

The life of Jesus on earth brings us face to face with a man who preached a message of comfort, salvation and peace, of a man who faced persecution and death bravely, in the assurance that through his suffering he could make atonement for sin. But did this noble life end forever in tragedy, when he was crucified on Calvary?

The problem facing the historian is here at its most acute, since it is impossible for him to assess any evidence for the Resurrection without first making a personal option about the possibility of a man's rising to life from the grave. Moreover, the historian cannot test the evidence for the Resurrection at first hand: he can only judge evidence presented nineteen hundred years ago, and is unable to interrogate witnesses. Those who believe that Jesus Christ really did rise to life from the grave may tend to minimize the philosophical and historical objections to what is the very foundation of their faith; those who cannot believe that a resurrection is possible can hardly approach any historical evidence with an open mind. Yet to assess the evidence fairly and impartially, a man must be free both from credulity and from dogmatic rationalism.

In our own day, the principal evidence against the fact of the Resurrection is thought to lie in the contradictory versions of events which the gospels contain. Many think that the early Christians began by believing in a purely spiritual triumph of Christ: by the nobility of his bearing during the Passion, he had proved that the good man is victorious over evil even in suffering and death. From this early belief (so the argument goes) the Christians passed on to believing that Jesus was still alive; and then, pressed for proofs of this assertion, they made up stories about apparitions of Jesus after his death. Finally, they made up stories according to which his tomb had been found empty on the third day, and the apologetic argument for the bodily Resurrection was complete.

Unfortunately, it is said, the apparition stories and the stories about the empty tomb were at many points contradictory. According to Matthew, Jesus appeared to his disciples only in Galilee; according to Luke, he appeared to them only in Jerusalem, and indeed ordered them to stay in Jerusalem until they had received the Holy Spirit (Lk 24: 49 and Ac 1:4). According to John, he appeared both in Jerusalem and in Galilee (Jn 20–21), but Mark, the earliest of the gospels, does not record any appearances at all. Many other points could be mentioned in which there are alleged discrepancies in the gospel accounts, but there is no need to list them. Rather, we must ask whether it is possible, by purely historical methods, to reconstruct the events of Easter Day.

It must be clearly asserted that it is not possible to provide the same kind of 'proof' for the Resurrection as for the death of Jesus. Death is something which is natural to man, and which is physically observable. The Resurrection or glorification of Christ's body is not natural, and in the strict theological sense, is not physically observable. (It would theoretically be possible to say 'This is a man whom I know died, and whom I now see alive before me'; but this would express only a part of the mystery of Christ's Resurrection. It is not possible to observe by the senses that this living man is sharing the glory of God the Father, and that is the principal assertion in the doctrine of the Resurrection.) 'Proofs' of the Resurrection, then, can only be comprehended and accepted through the gift of faith, and this is why the Church has always preferred to call it a 'mystery'. Without going into detailed exegesis, however, it is possible to set down the main testimony upon which the Church's faith in this mystery is based.

The earliest evidence attesting the fact of Christ's Resurrection is found in the first Epistle of St Paul to the Corinthians, which was written about A.D. 55 or 56, *i.e.* some twenty-five years after the events it purports to relate. It is particularly significant that Paul introduces this passage with a reference to 'the tradition' he had himself received: the argument, then, had been in use several years earlier. The text is well-known (1 Cor 15:1-11).

It is equally interesting to note that Paul mentions these appearances not because he is concerned to prove the truth of Christ's Resurrection, but because he is anxious to convince the Corinthians that all men will rise from the dead. He appeals, therefore, to what is undisputed ground—to the reality of Christ's Resurrection and the appearances he made in the flesh. It is also noteworthy that Paul never mentions in support of his argument the finding of an empty tomb, or the evidence of the women who claimed to have discovered it. He does not seem concerned with these matters, with what we may call the 'material' aspect of the Resurrection, and concentrates all his attention on the 'spiritual' aspect, *i.e.* on the 'mystery' rather than the 'history'. This certainly creates a problem for the historian, but it should also place the sincerity of Paul's witness beyond all doubt.

The problem becomes more tangled when we pass from

the writings of Paul to the gospels, in which the discrepancies seem, on close study, to be insurmountable. What are we to make of them?

First, it should be noted that the gospels do not state that on Easter Day the tomb was found to be empty *because* Jesus had risen from the dead; they simply state that it was found empty. This in itself is not a proof that Jesus rose from the grave; it was meant as a kind of 'negative apologetic', like the story about the soldiers in Matthew (Mt 27:62–66; 28: 11–15), and as an assertion that the disciples had not stolen the body. Two other traditions (Jn 20:1–2 and Lk 24:12) tell us that Peter himself went to investigate and confirmed what the women had said. There was, then, a straight assertion that sincere and honest witnesses had found an empty tomb.

This was not a proof of the Resurrection, but it was a rather curious fact, and it raised a question. Why was the tomb empty? The answer is given in the reply ascribed to the angels: Jesus had risen, as he had promised.

The narratives of the appearances of the risen Christ fall into two classes. When Christ appears to anyone other than the apostles, the disciples are shown to be reluctant to believe and slow to recognize him, but in the end they see that he is the Jesus they had known before, though living a different life. This is the pattern in the accounts of the appearances to the holy women (Mt 28:9–10; Jn 20:11–18; Mk 16:9), to the disciples at Emmaus (Lk 24:13–35) and even to Thomas (Jn 20:24–29). On other occasions, he appears to the group of apostles (Mt 28:16–20; Lk 24:36–49; Jn 20: 19–23; Mk 16:14–18), and here the pattern is different: as soon as the apostles have recognized him, Jesus tells them something about their new mission. These accounts are stories about the foundation of the Church by the Risen Lord.

The main and classical objection against the historicity of these narratives lies in the chronological and topographical discrepancies between the various accounts. The classical reply of orthodox Christians has been that Jesus appeared in

Jerusalem on Easter Day (Luke, John) and also eight days later (John), then in Galilee (Matthew, John) and finally in Jerusalem at the moment of his Ascension (Luke). This harmonization of the gospel data, though superficially attractive, does not stand up to a critical examination. According to Lk 24:49, the disciples were ordered to remain in Jerusalem until Pentecost (and this would preclude any apparition in Galilee); according to Mt 28:7, Jesus told his disciples he would see them in Galilee (and this would exclude any previous appearance in Jerusalem).

The only satisfactory way to resolve the discrepancies is to examine the literary form of each narrative. Luke, in his final chapter, would seem to have put together several stories in order to keep the reader's attention firmly fixed on Jerusalem, from which salvation would come to the entire world[14]: we know that he composed a similar tableau about the first visit of Jesus to Nazareth (Lk 4:16–30). In addition, Luke himself, in Ac 1:3, speaks of Jesus' having appeared to his disciples 'over many days', whereas according to Lk 24 it would seem that the Ascension had taken place on Easter Day. And if Lk 24 is an artificial composition, there is no good reason to deny that there may have been appearances in Galilee, too, as Matthew and John affirm.

But it would seem that John did not wish to assign precise dates to the events he records; rather, as a theologian, he wanted to show that the Spirit had been given by the Risen Lord in person,[15] and he spread the apparitions over a week, following a scheme he had adopted for the Passion (Jn 12:1) and perhaps for the first 'week' of the ministry (Jn 1:19–2:11). The justification of these statements would of course require a whole book by itself, but for the present it is sufficient to say that the interest of the evangelists lay not in the location or dating of appearances, but in what the Risen Christ did.

And this is the fundamental fact about the Resurrection:

14 See above, pp. 158–159.
15 See above, pp. 90–91, 96.

that the Risen Christ founded a Church. This was the cardinal belief of the early Christians, that the Church they knew and loved was founded by the Risen Christ: 'if Christ has not risen, then our preaching is worthless, and our faith is worthless' (1 Cor 15:14). This conviction they held by faith, but there were two observable facts to justify that faith: the tomb of Jesus had been found empty, and the timid apostles had been transformed in character. The empty tomb poses a question; the transformation of the apostles gives a clue to the answer.

That is all history can provide—a question, and a hint or indication of where to look for the answer. Historical study cannot 'prove' the fact of the Resurrection, because the essence of the doctrine is that Jesus is enthroned at the right hand of the Father; and there can be no apodictic proof of contingent fact which belongs to another world. But if history cannot prove the fact, it does record that after Jesus' death a group of Galilean nobodies suddenly started a movement which has affected the world ever since. And that raises a disquieting question: how did it succeed?

CHAPTER 14

Jesus Christ as Lord

The last chapter ended with a question which demands an answer, even though the answer cannot be found by human reason alone. Was Jesus of Nazareth merely a religious genius, or was he something more? Traditional Christianity has always insisted that it is impossible to prove by merely historical methods that Jesus was more than human, because this cannot be known to any man unless the Father in heaven reveals it to him. It might seem, therefore, that all the historian can say about Jesus is that he died, that his tomb was found empty, and that soon afterwards his disciples, transformed, began to preach a new religion centred on him. There is, however, one further fact which is a legitimate subject of historical inquiry, and without which any study of Jesus would be incomplete. We shall end this book by showing that the early Christians regarded Jesus as more than human, and adored him as Lord and Son of God.

1. The Enlightening Presence of the Holy Spirit

So far, we have tried to examine the gospels by purely rational methods. This is in itself a legitimate enterprise, but it has one defect: it takes no account of the mental attitude which moved the evangelists as they were writing, for everyone who contributed to the writing of the gospels saw Jesus with the eyes of faith. To complete our examination of the gospels, therefore, it is indispensable to look at them from the au-

thors' standpoint; otherwise, we shall never fully understand
their message. In a word, the gospels cannot be properly
understood except by the light of faith.

The last event in the earthly life of Jesus which is capable
of empirical verification is the finding of the empty tomb; the
first event after his death which can be similarly verified is
the transformation of the characters of the disciples. With
this transformation, the history of the Church began, and
therefore if we can grasp the cause of the transformation,
we may find the ultimate key to an understanding of the
gospel.

St Luke places the event which transformed the disciples
on the fiftieth day after the Resurrection (Ac 2:1), whereas
St John says that Jesus bestowed the Spirit on his disciples
on Easter Day (Jn 20:19–20). There is every reason to think
that Luke's dating of the event is correct, for the Passover
and Pentecost were the only two Jewish feasts observed as
holy days in the early Christian Church (1 Cor 5:7–8; 16:8;
cf. Ac 20:16; contrast St Paul's attitude to Jewish feasts in
general, Gal 4:10; Col 2:16). This conclusion is supported
by what we know about the date of the Ascension.

Luke (chapter 24) and John (chapter 20) seem to imply
that Christ ascended into heaven on the day of his Resurrection, whereas the Book of Acts (1:3) tells us that he frequently conversed with his disciples for forty days after his
Resurrection. It was this latter text which led the Church to
fix the feast of Christ's Ascension exactly forty days after
Easter, but the feast was introduced only during the fourth
century. Before this date, there was no unanimity among
Christian writers about the precise day of the Ascension:
some held that it had taken place on Easter Day, others that
it had happened between Easter and Pentecost, and some
even thought it had taken place on the afternoon of Pentecost. It is evident that these Fathers of the Church did not
consider the 'forty days' mentioned in Ac 1:3 as denoting a
precise date in the calendar which it was heretical to question,
and Luke himself, in the same book, speaks rather vaguely
of the appearances of Jesus 'over many days' (Ac 13:31).

Now, if St Luke's mentioning of the forty days did not lead, at an early date, to the observance of a Christian feast commemorating the event, why did Christians keep Pentecost as a holy day? The only possible answer is that some notable event took place on that day, as on Easter Day: the dating of the Resurrection 'on the third day' and of the manifestation of the Spirit fifty days later can therefore be regarded as historically certain.

Yet according to John, Jesus appeared in the evening of Easter Day, 'the first day of the week', and said to his apostles, 'As the Father has sent me, I in turn am sending you out. Saying this, he breathed upon them and said to them, Receive the Holy Spirit' (Jn 20:21–22). Some authors think that one must choose between this statement by John and Luke's assertion that the Spirit was bestowed on the apostles fifty days after the Resurrection. In fact, there is no reason to reject either statement, for the evangelists were not referring to the same event. Luke certainly describes a public manifestation of the Holy Spirit in the preaching of the apostles at Pentecost, but he nowhere states that Pentecost was the first occasion on which they had received the Spirit. Indeed, he records that a similar manifestation of the Spirit took place after the arrest and release of Peter and John: 'While they were praying, the place where they were meeting began to shake, and they were all filled with the Holy Spirit and began to preach the word of God with confidence' (Ac 4:31). Later, Luke writes that when St Paul had laid hands on twelve disciples of the Baptist at Ephesus, 'the Holy Spirit came upon them, and they began to speak in (foreign) languages and to prophesy' (Ac 19:6). Luke's description of the first Pentecost, therefore (Ac 2), is concerned with the outward manifestation of the Spirit through the public preaching of the apostles, whereas John's account of Christ's appearance on Easter Day is concerned with what we may term their 'interior consecration'. Thus consecrated by the abiding presence of the Spirit (John) and commissioned to preach the message of salvation publicly (Ac 2), they become 'apostles', *i.e.* men 'sent out' in the name of God to broadcast the Good News of salvation.

2. The Interpretation of History

We have already shown, in Part II, that each of the four evangelists presents his own interpretation of the events in the life of Jesus. There, however, we were concerned only to show that this is evident from a comparison of the four gospels as literature; here we may reconsider their differences of approach in order to see how the faith of each evangelist has brought out a different aspect of the mystery of Jesus' life. It is, of course, impossible to reconsider the whole of the four gospels, but we may take as an example the narratives of the Passion, in which the four gospels are closest to one another in the facts they relate, and yet distinctly individual in their interpretation of these facts.

The main theme of St Mark's Gospel is that Jesus only gradually unfolded to his disciples the secret of his own personality, and that the disciples were slow to comprehend his teaching. It was only at the very end of his life, when he was on trial before the Sanhedrin, that Jesus revealed his true identity: when the high priest asked 'Are you the Christ, the Son of the Blessed One?', he replied with an astonishing directness, 'I am' (Mk 14:62). From this point onwards, Jesus made no secret of his claims: he admitted to Pilate that he was a king, and Mark stresses several times that it was the king of the Jews who was crucified. Yet he died abandoned by all, by his disciples in Gethsemane (Mk 14:50–52) and by everyone on Calvary, except for a few women who watched from a distance (Mk 15:27–41).

It is all the more surprising, therefore, that *Mark* alone groups together two events which happened at the death of Jesus, the rending of the Temple curtain and the exclamation of the centurion that Jesus was the Son of God (Mk 15:38–39). Luke places the rending of the curtain before the death of Jesus, and Matthew mentions in addition an earthquake and the resurrection of some holy persons. Moreover, according to Matthew it was 'the earthquake and the other events' which impelled the centurion to exclaim that Jesus was the Son of God (Mt 27:54), whereas according to Mark it was 'the way in which Jesus died' (Mk 15:39). According to Luke, the centurion confessed that Jesus had been an innocent man (Lk 23:47); according to Mark, he confessed that Jesus was the Son of God (Mk 15:39). For Mark, then, the rending of the Temple curtain symbolized that from the moment of Jesus' death the presence of God was no longer the privilege of the Jews alone; and the pagan centurion who confessed the divinity of Jesus was speaking on behalf of all the Gentiles who were to profess belief in his name.

Mark's Gospel ends with the finding of the empty tomb. The women 'went out and fled from the tomb, for they were seized with fear and beside themselves; and they said nothing to anyone, for they were afraid' (Mk 16:8).[1] They had a promise from the angel that Jesus would meet his disciples in Galilee, and here Mark ends, on a note of interrogation, leaving the reader in suspense, wondering when Jesus will appear. The whole life of Jesus is a proclamation of the mystery of man's union with God in him at the end of time.

Mark's Gospel, therefore, culminates in the life-giving death of the Son of God, who came to save men from the snares of death in which Satan had trapped them, and who reveals himself to the man who confesses his divinity. All history is recapitulated in that 'present' event of Jesus—as if revelation took place at a given time and as if, henceforth, our union with God could be achieved only in that 'present'. The mystery remains; and yet it is entrusted to any man who embraces the Good Tidings of Jesus, the Christ, the King of the Jews and the Son of God.

But the whole of history is not restricted to the temporal

---

[1] Mk 16:9–20 is accepted by Catholics as canonical Scripture, but did not apparently form part of the original gospel of St Mark. It is a summary of details from the other gospels, and was added later. Whether the summary was added by Mark or by another is irrelevant to the fact of its inspiration.

event of God's union with men in Christ. *Matthew*, more than any other evangelist, brings out this point. Like the scribe of ancient Egypt, he has captured the lessons of the past; the object of his work is to be a 'remembrance' of the union that God brought about—and still brings about—with men. Matthew is the historian of God's fulfilment of his promises. It is from this angle of salvation history that he edits the material of his gospel, and while he makes use, even more than Mark, of catechetical material, he subordinates it to a portrait of the Lord Jesus.

Thus Matthew gives a different interpretation of the Passion story. There is no need to stress how often he uses the phrase 'All this happened in order that the Scriptures might be fulfilled', but one cannot help noticing how frequently he uses the name 'Jesus', especially at the beginning of a new passage. Matthew's version of the Passion was written for those who already believed that Jesus was the Son of the living God, and therefore he emphasizes the supreme liberty of Jesus, who controlled every single incident that happened. Jesus himself gave the word for the chain of events to start (Mt 26:2, no parallels); he announced that 'his time was near' (Mt 26:18, no exact parallel except in Jn 13:21–30). In the Garden of Gethsemane, he knew that he had at his disposal more than twelve legions of angels, and during the trial even the false witnesses acknowledged that he had claimed the 'power' to destroy the Temple (26:61). Astounding miracles accompanied his death (27:51–54), so that the centurion and his detachment were terrified and acknowledged that Jesus was truly the Son of God. The whole story ends with the solemn, liturgical proclamation 'All authority in heaven and on earth has been given to me . . . and I will be with you through all future ages, even to the end of the world' (28:18–20). The Passion of St Matthew is a text composed for the assembly, the '*ecclesia*' of Matthew. All history is given its ultimate shape in the Person of the Risen Jesus who, having received all power from the Father, remains amidst his followers until the end of time. The story of Jesus' life is told against the background of the history of Israel, to reveal God's fidelity in the past and to guarantee that same fidelity in the future.

This future, which the past prefigures and with which the present is charged, is one that neither Matthew nor Mark contemplates for its own sake. Their reader finds himself before the future as it were before a mystery—the mystery of the Person of Jesus, and since he has reached the end of time, he does not think of the duration that still separates him from the Last Day. *Luke*, on the contrary, is directly interested in the future—in the era that succeeds the Event of Easter. His version of the Passion is different again, for he was writing at a time when the Church was acutely conscious that an indefinite future lay before it. The expectation of an early Parousia had receded, and Luke was therefore anxious to tell the story of the Passion not as a fact of the past (like Mark), nor as a lesson for the present (like Matthew), but as a guide for all future time. The theme of Luke is that all Christians must share in Christ's Passion if they are to share in his glory (*cf.* Lk 24:26, 46). Luke, alone of the Synoptics, has recorded in the setting of the Supper the words of Jesus advising the disciples of the persecution which will await them when he has left them (Lk 22:35–38). His theme is of the combat between Jesus and the powers of darkness.

After the Temptations, Satan had left Jesus 'for a while' (Lk 4:13), but in the Passion story he re-enters on the scene. Satan entered into the heart of Judas (22:3), and was set to tempt Simon Peter (22:31) because it was then 'the hour of darkness' (22:53). In Gethsemane, Jesus overcame the weaknesses of his human nature by insistent prayer and by being prepared to resist unto blood (22:40–46): in this episode, Jesus showed himself the model for all his disciples. Throughout his sufferings, he never showed himself as a zealot or a revolutionary like Barabbas (23:19, 25), but always as the gentle, forgiving Saviour: he accepted the embrace of Judas the traitor (22:48), healed the servant who had been wounded by Peter (22:51), and simply looked at Peter after his denials (22:61). He retained his dignified bearing before the Sanhedrin (22:67–70) and before Herod (23:9); he uttered words of compassion for the mothers of Jerusalem (23:28–31), prayed for his executioners (23:34) and spoke words of hope to the repentant thief (23:43). In his death agony, he commended himself to his Father (23:46).

The portrait given by St Luke is that of the Servant of the Lord described in Isaiah 53. Pilate never ceased to proclaim that Jesus was innocent (23:4, 14, 22); Herod implicitly acknowledged the same (23:11); the women of Jerusalem said the same, in their own way (23:27–31), as did the repentant thief (23:40–41). Even the centurion protested that Jesus was an innocent man (23:47).

In Luke's account of the Passion, the reader is not merely invited to make an act of faith in the God who fulfils the Scriptures, and in Jesus, who was manifested as Son of God at his death: Luke (like Matthew but unlike Mark) explains to the reader the mystery he wishes to expound. Where Matthew had asked his reader principally to adore Jesus as the Son of God and the all-powerful Lord, Luke asks him to identify himself with the persons in the drama—to recognize his own weakness in Peter's, and his own wickedness in that of all who took a part in accomplishing Jesus' death. Luke calls upon the reader to adore the limitless mercy of Jesus, which is so human and so appealing, and thereby to learn how to share his patience; for on the Last Day, it is through patience that he will possess life (Lk 21:19). Jesus is not put forward simply as an example to be followed; rather, he is the prototype of all who suffer in the cause of righteousness, for he sums up in his person the sufferings of all who are persecuted down the ages, and by his own triumph reveals the future victory of all who believe in him.

Thus the life of Jesus retains its value for all future ages of the Church. That life was the first act of God's design in the Church, and it has been stamped and sealed as the prototype for the future. Whatever is to come in future time will depend on that life, because although it was a factual event in the past, it remains forever present.

If the above analyses are correct, then we find history presented in its threefold chronological dimension of present,

past and future. Man does not yet know history in its eternal
dimension, which has nevertheless been a constitutive element of that history from the moment of the meeting between the Eternal and man, the moment where time and
eternity intersect. By going back to the beginning, to the
creative Word, *John* did not blur, but rather recapitulated
this threefold dimension of history. An example of this is
found in his account of the Passion, where he assembles and
integrates (though in another key) the doctrinal riches contained in the Synoptic Gospels.

The conspiracy of the Jews (Jn 11:47–53) was part of
God's eternal design 'to bring together the sons of God who
had been divided'; the agony of Jesus (12:27) did not come
and find him unprepared—it was for this that he had come
into the world of time. The betrayal of Jesus, the denials of
Peter and the cowardly flight of the disciples had all been
foreseen by God. John does not describe the trial before
Caiaphas, because he has already described how the Jews had
in their own minds found Jesus guilty (Jn 5:7–10), even
though it is obvious that Jesus had there put them on trial.
In the trial before Pilate, it is Jesus who is judging Pilate as
the symbol of the State. And in the story of the crucifixion,
John omits every detail which would make the cross into a
gallows rather than a royal throne: he omits the story of Simon of Cyrene, the mention of the word 'robbers', the mock-
ing, the darkness over the earth and Jesus' cry of abandon-
ment 'My God, my God, why hast thou forsaken me?' Jesus
carried the cross (or perhaps even 'embraced' it), and the
inscription which Pilate refused to alter can best be interpreted as *regnavit a ligno Deus*. The sharing out of Jesus'
clothes and each of his words from the cross are seen as the
fulfilment of prophecy; and the story ends with the piercing
of his side, out of which flowed blood and water, symbols of
the cleansing power of his sacrifice.

John, therefore, like St Luke, presents the Passion as a
struggle between Jesus and the powers of darkness, and, like
Matthew, stresses that Jesus was in unfettered control of
every incident throughout. Like Mark, he puts forward his

account as that of an eye-witness. John therefore is the summit and crown of the gospel tradition. The reader of St John is not asked simply to make an act of faith (as in Mark), nor simply to adore Jesus (as in Matthew), nor simply to share in his sufferings (as in Luke). St John summons his readers to do all three things at once, in the conviction that by his suffering he is sharing in the destiny of the Incarnate God.

3. Jesus Christ Our Lord

Christians who read the gospel story in the light of their faith penetrate into the minds of the four evangelists, and find no difficulty in believing that in the person of Jesus they have the key to the history of the world. In Jesus, God came on earth to meet man. Mark describes this encounter from the time when Jesus began to preach; Luke describes it from the moment of Jesus' birth; Matthew traces God's intervention back to Abraham; and John begins his story with creation itself. 'In the beginning was the Word, who became flesh and lived among us.' All four gospels, therefore, present the Incarnation as God's coming to meet man. John, however, has a complementary theme, that every man born into the world must go out of himself to meet God.

In the fourth gospel the earthly life of Jesus extends over the whole of Palestine—Judea, Samaria, Galilee and Jerusalem. But whatever the place, every meeting with Jesus symbolizes a meeting between humanity and the Incarnate Word. According to the Synoptics, Jesus first made himself known to certain disciples, then to the Jews in Galilee, and even to some of the Gentiles (e.g. the centurion of Capernaum). John develops and extends this notion by showing Jesus face to face with different classes of men. First, Jesus is pointed out to the disciples of the Baptist as the Messiah (Jn 1: 19–2:11); then he presents himself to the Jews in general as the one for whom Israel has been waiting (2:13–22). He introduces himself to Nicodemus, the type of the Jewish intellectual, as the one who brings eternal life (3:1–21), and to the poor sinner of Samaria as the Messiah who was to bring her and her countrymen salvation (4:1–42). Finally, he reveals himself to the pagan world (4:43–54). In these first four chapters, Jesus reveals himself not only as the Messiah but also as the Saviour of the world.

In the same chapters, Jesus puts forward a new order of religion. There is perhaps a symbol of it in his changing of the water into wine (2:1–11); it is certainly implied in his teaching about the new temple (2:19), about rebirth through water and the Spirit (3:5), and about the eternal life which all who listen to his word will enjoy (4:14, 50). The question is therefore raised: who is this man? The debates and discussions about his mission and his message occupy chapters 5 to 11 of the gospel.

The Synoptic Gospels had set down various conditions for entry into the kingdom—a spirit of poverty, of chastity, of sincerity, and self-denial, for example. St John sets down only one condition, 'believing in Jesus' (6:29). The reason for this difference is that the Synoptics viewed Jesus' life as something taking place within time, whereas John saw that life as the irruption of the eternal into time. The Synoptics thought of heaven, and the end of world history, as lying in the future; John had a different perspective, in which the timeless Word dwelt among men. Certainly, John did not deny that the 'Last Day', the general resurrection and the final Parousia were still to come; but eternal life was already present for all who desired it.

The Synoptics speak about the final judgment at the end of the world; for John, judgment takes place in the here and now of this world of time. Jesus had been sent from the Father, and 'whoever believes in him is not condemned; anyone who does not believe is already condemned, because he has not believed in the name of the only-begotten Son of God. Judgment lies in this: That the light has come into the world and men loved darkness rather than light, for their works were evil. Everyone who does wicked deeds hates the light and refuses to come to the light, lest his deeds should be revealed for what they are; but those who follow the truth do come to the light, that their deeds may be openly seen as done by the power of God' (3:19–21). John's assertion that men must choose between light and darkness, between good and evil, is the same as the statement that 'You cannot serve God and Money' (Mt 6:24), but in John the choice is between believing in Jesus and rejecting the light. For St John, there is a stark choice between alternatives, which can be summed up in the words of Jesus: 'I am the light of the world. Anyone who follows me will never walk in darkness, but will have life-giving light' (Jn 8:12).

Judgment takes place here and now because men are brought face to face with the co-eternal Word. The Synoptics only give hints of the true personality of Jesus by recording his miracles, his exorcisms, his forgiving of sins and so forth; they think of the glory of Jesus as something which will be revealed at the Parousia. For John, the glory of the Incarnate Word was manifested throughout his earthly life: 'we caught a glimpse of his glory, the glory as it were of the only-begotten of the Father, full of grace and truth' (1:14). That is why John usually calls the miracles worked by Jesus not 'acts of power' (*dunameis*) but 'signs' (*semeia*) of the invisible reality. The reader of John is asked to recognize in him who gave sight to the blind the light of the world (8:12) and in him who raised Lazarus from the tomb, 'resurrection and life' personified (11:25). Jacob had dug a well near Samaria on which the people of the region had lived for over a thousand years (4:12); Jesus was ready to provide men with water which would lead to eternal life (4:14). Moses had given the Israelites manna in the desert (6:31); Jesus claimed that he himself was the true heavenly food given by the Father for the life of the entire world (6:32–33, 49–50). In the end, Jesus spoke in such a way that the Jews accused him of making himself out to be greater than Abraham (8:53); he replied, 'Before Abraham was, I am' (8:58).

In St John's Gospel, the reader's entire attention is directed towards the person of Jesus, but as a general rule, when Jesus is asked about himself, he replies that 'he has come in the name of the Father' (Jn 5:43). Twenty-four times in the gospel Jesus repeats this message: 'I have not come on my own initiative . . . (7:28) . . . My food is to do the will of him who sent me, and to achieve his work' (4:34). If the 'signs' done by Jesus direct our attention to him, he himself directs our attention to the Father.

There is no need to develop this theme by citing references to the gospel, for almost every page of the fourth gospel is replete with allusions to it. St John's theme is that those who believe and follow the light encounter in Jesus a person who dominates time and is master over life and death, without thereby being any less human. John therefore invites the reader to 'believe in Jesus', to recognize in him a man who really is the incarnation of God. This recognition is, of course, only possible to those who accept an interior enlightenment from the Father: 'no man can come to me unless the Father who sent me attracts him' (6:44). But those who accept this enlightening grace will never be separated from the Father and Son (6:37–39; 17:2, 6–7, 12, 24), for in welcoming Jesus as the Son of God, they are brought face to face with God in his eternity. 'He who sees me sees the Father' (14:9).

Epilogue

At the end of this examination of the historical value of the gospels, one question will surely be in the reader's mind. If the arguments set out in this book are even approximately valid, why is there such profound disagreement among scholars over the trustworthiness of the gospels?

The disagreement stems ultimately not from dissension over the literary methods employed, but from other presuppositions which have nothing to do with literature. Every man who studies the gospels either believes that Jesus is the Son of God, or does not believe it, or is on the way to belief or unbelief. Most people who study the gospel carefully, however, have already made up their minds, before they examine the text, about the possibility or impossibility of supernatural happenings in this world. Here we are not concerned to defend the possibility of these happenings, but merely to point out that just as religious faith may lead a Christian to be less than rigorous in his examination of the historical evidence, so a dogmatic rejection of the supernatural may influence a rationalist to be less than fair to the evidence before him. Everyone who writes or speaks about Jesus should openly admit whether he is a believing Christian or not, because no one can speak about him without being influenced either by faith or by unbelief.

Should one therefore conclude that it is impossible for any man to produce an impartial, scientific assessment of the life of Jesus, and that all the historian can do is to present the facts about 'the Christ of faith'?

1. The Historical Jesus or the Christ of Faith?

Over the last seventy years it has become customary to draw a distinction between 'the historical Jesus' and 'the Christ of faith'. Though the terms can be used with varying nuances, 'the historical Jesus' generally denotes Jesus as he can be known by the historian, and 'the Christ of faith' stands for the concept of Jesus as the co-eternal Son of God, adored by the early Church. The issue debated among theologians revolves round this distinction: some maintain that the early Christians created the idea of the Christ of faith by idealizing and deifying Jesus of Nazareth, and that it is impossible to discern from the early Christian writings what Jesus of Nazareth was really like. Can this position be maintained?

It is clear that the whole case turns on the validity of the distinction between 'the historical Jesus' and 'the Christ of faith'. This distinction originated towards the end of the last century, at a time when many historians believed with passionate sincerity that absolute objectivity and complete impartiality were humanly attainable. They envisaged a future in which history would be studied with the same cold objectivity that men bring to the natural sciences, and in which all the personal feelings, prejudices and presuppositions of the historian would have been eliminated. Their objective was to isolate the raw material facts of the past, and then to combine them in chronological succession; one would then have 'true history'. When these principles were applied to the historical figure of Jesus, the main care of historians was to isolate the material events and sayings of his life. This, they thought, would present a true picture of 'the historical Jesus'.

At the turn of the century, this quest of the historical Jesus led Harnack, the most brilliant representative of 'Liberal Christianity', to conclude that the essence of Christianity lay in the moral teaching of Jesus, and therefore principally in the sayings attributed to him by the evangelists. Few agnostic humanists would have any difficulty in accepting this version of the Christian religion, which makes no demands of dogmatic belief; but was that what Jesus really preached and was it for this that he was crucified? A second school of thought, of which Loisy was the leading figure, saw in Jesus an itinerant preacher who was convinced of his own role as a prophet, and who genuinely believed that the end of the world was imminent. If that was what Jesus taught, then his disciples made a remarkable recovery after his death, when it should have shattered their last illusions.

Neither Harnack's theory nor Loisy's is sufficient to account for the facts related in the gospels, and after the First World War two theological giants began to question the presuppositions on which both theories were based. Karl Barth and Rudolf Bultmann demanded that those who studied the Scriptures should not be content with literary or historical criticism of the texts, but should turn their minds to theology.

Barth has insisted, in his earliest works, that God's revelation is spoken directly to each man. It leaves no trace in the visible world, but is communicated only at the moment of preaching. Consequently, the true Christian does not direct his attention to the 'historical figure of Jesus' rediscovered by exegetical and philological labour, but only to the Lord whom Christians adore. What Jesus actually said to the crowds in Galilee two thousand years ago is irrelevant for *my* salvation; what I read in the Bible today is of eternal importance to me. Bultmann was at first profoundly influenced by this message of Barth, and even though other considerations (*e.g.* the philosophy of Heidegger and the literary methods of Form Criticism) have led him to modify it somewhat, his position is still basically that what matters in the end for Christians is sharing the faith of the primitive Church, not an anxious search for the actual words Jesus spoke before his death.

There is obviously tremendous truth in the positive contentions of Barth and Bultmann. It *is* more important for the

Christian of today to apply the biblical message to himself than to spend his life in an effort to reconstruct the earthly life of the Lord he adores. It *is* more important to enter heart and soul into the faith of the apostles after Easter than to be a master of the *formgeschichtliche Methode*. Where both Barth and Bultmann go astray is in the negative part of their theology, in their assertions that knowledge of 'the historical Jesus' is in no way profitable for salvation.

During the last fifteen years, many German scholars who were formerly pupils of Bultmann have abandoned this uncompromising doctrine of their professor. By using those literary methods of Form Criticism which Bultmann has developed so splendidly, they seek to advance from a knowledge of the religion of the early Christians to a knowledge of Jesus himself, because he must surely have been a greater figure than anyone in the early Church. This development cannot but be welcomed by all who believe in traditional Christianity, but it should also make people ask whether there has not been a fundamental error in drawing a distinction between 'the historical Jesus' and 'the Christ of faith'. Does not the Risen Christ belong in some way to history? And did the disciples have no kind of 'faith' in Jesus until after the Resurrection? The continuity of the disciples' faith before and after the Resurrection, and the identity of the Risen Christ with Jesus of Nazareth can be denied only on *a priori* grounds, because of philosophical or theological presuppositions, not because there is *historical* evidence to the contrary.

2. The Mystery of Jesus

The nineteenth-century belief that men would one day be able to write about history as impersonally and as dispassionately and as impartially as they write about chemistry or mathematics is now universally abandoned. Modern historians are more conscious of their own limitations and are prepared to circumscribe their ambitions accordingly. To acknowledge these limitations of human nature is by no means equivalent to asserting that history can teach us nothing for certain; it is, however, a recognition that history cannot teach us everything about the past.

Throughout this book, the author has tried to keep strictly within the limits of historical method, and has tried not to appeal in support of his argument to that knowledge which comes only from faith. The aim has been to rediscover, as far as possible, the 'objective truth' about Jesus of Nazareth; and the objective truth about him is that he confronts all mankind with a question demanding an answer. And the answer cannot be given except by faith.

Are we then to say that Bultmann is right after all, that history cannot teach us anything for our salvation, and that we must rather try to recreate in our souls the faith of the early Church? Karl Barth has put his finger on the flaw in Bultmann's theology, which stems from the philosophy of Heidegger. Theology (the study of God) becomes mere anthropology (the study of man) when it despises the objective fact which is the transcendent element in existential knowledge. And it is only because the faith of the early Church was based on an objective fact that we can say Christianity is more than mythology. This event is the foundation of all early tradition and of all faith, and it is this which the historian uncovers at the end of his investigation. The apostolic preaching is all about 'the things which happened among us'.

There is a living and indestructible link between the tradition of the infant Church and the course of events which made up the earthly existence of Jesus of Nazareth—a kind of ebb and flow between the kerygma which the Christian believes and the life of Jesus before Easter Day. The kerygma which is accepted by faith derives from Jesus, and the full meaning of his life can be known only through the 'pattern of apostolic preaching'. Thus the historical research of the exegete should not be concerned solely with the tradition of the infant Church, but also with that other tradition, from which the Church's tradition derives, and which comes from Jesus. This is the precise relationship between the kerygma and the events of Jesus' life. While it may be necessary and right to distinguish the one from the other, they are in fact inseparable; they are two dimensions of the one truth whose meaning is ever the same.

In this way history and faith may walk hand in hand, each making its own contribution to our knowledge of Christ Jesus. History provides the facts, and a question; faith provides the interpretation of those facts, and the answer to the question. Nor are there two different fields of interest: just as the historian is concerned both with the earthly life of Jesus and with the faith of the early Church, so the committed Christian should be concerned with both, because both have religious significance for him here and now. There is no discontinuity between the two periods, either for the historian or for the believer.

The problem with which Jesus confronts mankind cannot be resolved by historical research alone, because human reason can never be a substitute for God-given faith. It is possible, though, by historical studies to bring men into contact with the living Word of God as revealed in the gospels. This was the purpose with which the evangelist wrote: they were not concerned merely to set down a record of certain events, but above all to introduce their readers to a living person. The only faithful interpretation of the gospels, therefore, is that which reveals Jesus as a living person, speaking not only to his own generation, but to all future ages. Our inquiry has shown that the factual events of his life—even though they include the answer which becomes evident only in the light of the Holy Spirit—are, first and foremost, a question addressed to mankind; 'And you—who do you say that I am?'

For Further Reading

GENERAL WORKS

E. HOSKYNS and N. DAVEY, *The Riddle of the New Testament*, London, 1931 (several reprints, with an excellent bibliography up to 1947).

R. H. LIGHTFOOT, *History and Interpretation in the Gospels*, Oxford, 1935 (several reprints).

C. H. DODD, *The Apostolic Preaching and Its Developments*, London, 1936 (several reprints).

———, *History and the Gospels*, London, 1938.

H. E. W. TURNER, *Jesus, Master and Lord*, London, 1953.

V. TAYLOR, *The Life and Ministry of Jesus*, London, 1954.

O. CULLMANN, *The Christology of the New Testament*, London, 1959.

A. ROBERT and A. FEUILLET (ed.), *Introduction to the Bible*: vol. 2, New Testament, New York and Tournai, 1965.

INTRODUCTION

On the person of Jesus:

A. SCHWEITZER, *The Quest of the Historical Jesus; A Critical Study of its Progress from Reimarus to Wrede*, London, 1910 (reprinted 1963).

L. DE GRANDMAISON, *Jesus Christ: His Person—His Message—His Credentials*, 3 vols., London, 1930, 1932, 1934.

T. W. MANSON, *The Servant-Messiah*, London, 1953.

J. M. ROBINSON, *A New Quest of the Historical Jesus*, London, 1959.

On literary criticism and inspiration:

C. CHARLIER, *The Christian Approach to the Bible*, London, 1958.

J. LEVIE, *The Bible, Word of God in Words of Men*, London, 1961.

J. L. MC KENZIE, *Myths and Realities*, London, 1963.

Part I

1: THE GOSPELS AND THE GOSPEL

L. CERFAUX, *The Four Gospels*, London, 1960.

M. R. JAMES, *The Apocryphal New Testament*, Oxford, 1924.

E. HENNECKE, *New Testament Apocrypha . . . An English Translation* edited by R. McL. Wilson: vol. 1: *Gospels and Related Writings*, London, 1963; vol. 2: *Apostolic and Early Church Writings*, London, 1965.

A. GUILLAUMONT *etc.*, *The Gospel according to Thomas*, London, 1959.

B. GÄRTNER, *The Theology of the Gospel of Thomas*, London, 1961.

2: JESUS AND THE THEOLOGIANS OF THE NEW TESTAMENT

L. CERFAUX, *Christ in the Theology of St Paul*, London and New York, 1959.

3: THE BACKGROUND TO THE GOSPELS

G. DALMAN, *Sacred Sites and Ways*, London, 1935.

D. DAUBE, *The New Testament and Rabbinic Judaism*, London, 1956.

J. T. MILIK, *Ten Years of Discovery in the Wilderness of Judaea*, London, 1959.

M. BURROWS, *The Dead Sea Scrolls*, London, 1955.

——, *More Light on the Dead Sea Scrolls*, London, 1958.

M. BLACK, *An Aramaic Approach to the Gospels and Acts*, Oxford, 3rd ed., 1967.

C. F. D. MOULE, *An Idiom Book of New Testament Greek*, Cambridge, 2nd ed., 1955.

W. F. ALBRIGHT, *From the Stone Age to Christianity*, Baltimore, 1940 (Reprinted).

Part II

4: THE GOSPEL ACCORDING TO SAINT JOHN

E. HOSKYNS, *The Fourth Gospel*, London, 1940 (several reprints).

C. H. DODD, *The Interpretation of the Fourth Gospel*, Cambridge, 1953.

——, *Historical Tradition in the Fourth Gospel*, Cambridge, 1963.

C. K. BARRETT, *The Gospel according to Saint John: A Commentary on the Greek Text*, London, 1955.

R. H. LIGHTFOOT, *Saint John's Gospel: A Commentary*, Oxford, 1956 (several reprints).

R. E. BROWN, *The Gospel according to John* (I–XII), Anchor Bible (29), New York, 1966.

5: THE GOSPEL ACCORDING TO SAINT MATTHEW

G. D. KILPATRICK, *The Origins of the Gospel according to Saint Matthew*, Oxford, 1946, 2nd ed., 1952.

K. STENDAHL, *The School of Saint Matthew*, Uppsala, 1954.

G. BORNKAMM, G. BARTH and H. J. HELD, *Tradition and Interpretation in Matthew*, London, 1963.

6: THE GOSPEL ACCORDING TO SAINT MARK

R. H. LIGHTFOOT, *The Gospel Message of Saint Mark*, Oxford, 1950.

V. TAYLOR, *The Gospel according to Saint Mark*, London, 1952.

J. M. ROBINSON, *The Problem of History in Mark*, London, 1957.

7: THE GOSPEL ACCORDING TO SAINT LUKE

H. J. CADBURY, *The Style and Literary Method of Luke*, Cambridge (Mass.), 1919.

——, *The Making of Luke-Acts*, Cambridge (Mass.), 1927, new ed., 1958.

H. CONZELMANN, *The Theology of Saint Luke*, London, 1960.

Part III

9 and 10: THE FORMATION OF THE GOSPEL TRADITION

V. TAYLOR, *The Formation of the Gospel Tradition*, London, 1933 (several reprints).

M. DIBELIUS, *From Tradition to Gospel*, London, 1934.

——, *A Fresh Approach to the New Testament and Early Christian Literature*, London, 1936.

R. BULTMANN, *The History of the Synoptic Tradition*, Oxford, 1963.

——, *The Theology of the New Testament*, 2 vols., London, 1955, 1956.

C. H. DODD, *The Apostolic Preaching and its Developments*, London, 1944.

——, *According to the Scriptures*, London, 1953.

W. L. KNOX, *The Sources of the Synoptic Gospels* (ed. by Henry Chadwick), 2 vols., Cambridge, 1953 and 1957.

T. W. MANSON, *The Sayings of Jesus*, London, 1937.

11: THE ULTIMATE SOURCE OF THE GOSPEL TRADITION —JESUS OF NAZARETH

H. RIESENFELD, *The Gospel Tradition and its Beginnings. A Study in the Limits of Formgeschichte*, London, 1957.

B. GERHARDSSON, *Memory and Manuscript. Oral Tradition and Written Transmission in Rabbinic Judaism and Early Christianity*, Uppsala, 1961.

Part IV

12 and 13: THE QUEST OF THE HISTORICAL JESUS

R. SCHNACKENBURG, *God's Rule and Kingdom*, London, 1963.

C. H. DODD, *Parables of the Kingdom*, London, 1935 (several reprints).

J. JEREMIAS, *Rediscovering the Parables*, London, 1966 (a non-technical abridgement of his work *The Parables of Jesus*, revised ed., London, 1963).

T. W. MANSON, *The Teaching of Jesus*, Cambridge, 1931 (several reprints).

V. TAYLOR, *Jesus and His Sacrifice*, London, 1957.

INDEX

INDEX OF BIBLICAL TEXTS

(Comprising only those references where some comment or inference is made)

INDEX OF AUTHORS AND SUBJECTS

OTHER IMAGE BOOKS

OTHER IMAGE BOOKS

OTHER IMAGE BOOKS

ST. JOAN OF ARC – John Beevers (D131) – 75¢

A HISTORY OF PHILOSOPHY: VOLUME 1 – GREECE AND ROME (2 Volumes) – Frederick Copleston, S.J. (D134a, D134b) – $1.25 ea.

A HISTORY OF PHILOSOPHY: VOLUME 2 – MEDIAEVAL PHILOSOPHY (2 Volumes) – Frederick Copleston, S.J. Part I – Augustine to Bonaventure. Part II – Albert the Great to Duns Scotus (D135a, D135b) – $1.25 ea.

A HISTORY OF PHILOSOPHY: VOLUME 3 – LATE MEDIAEVAL AND RENAISSANCE PHILOSOPHY (2 Volumes) – Frederick Copleston, S.J. Part I – Ockham to the Speculative Mystics. Part II – The Revival of Platonism to Suárez (D136a, D136b) – $1.25 ea.

A HISTORY OF PHILOSOPHY: VOLUME 4 – MODERN PHILOSOPHY: Descartes to Leibniz – Frederick Copleston, S.J. (D137) – $1.45

A HISTORY OF PHILOSOPHY: VOLUME 5 – MODERN PHILOSOPHY: The British Philosophers, Hobbes to Hume (2 Volumes) – Frederick Copleston, S.J. Part I – Hobbes to Paley. Part II – Berkeley to Hume (D138a, D138b) – $1.25 ea.

A HISTORY OF PHILOSOPHY: VOLUME 6 – MODERN PHILOSOPHY (2 Volumes) – Frederick Copleston, S.J. Part I – The French Enlightenment to Kant (D139a) – 95¢. Part II – Kant (D139b) – $1.25

A HISTORY OF PHILOSOPHY: VOLUME 7 – MODERN PHILOSOPHY (2 Volumes) – Frederick Copleston, S.J. Part I – Fichte to Hegel. Part II – Schopenhauer to Nietzsche (D140a, D140b) – $1.25 ea.

A HISTORY OF PHILOSOPHY: VOLUME 8 – MODERN PHILOSOPHY: Bentham to Russell (2 Volumes) – Frederick Copleston, S.J. Part I – British Empiricism and the Idealist Movement in Great Britain. Part II – Idealism in America, the Pragmatist Movement, the Revolt against Idealism (D141a, D141b) – $1.25 ea.

THE WATERS OF SILOE – Thomas Merton. Account of the Trappists (D144) – $1.25

WE WORK WHILE THE LIGHT LASTS – Dom Hubert van Zeller, O.S.B. Meditations on contemporary problems (D146) – 75¢

MARY MOTHER OF FAITH – Joseph Weiger. A beautiful meditation on Our Lady (D148) – 85¢

TRANSFORMATION IN CHRIST – Dietrich von Hildebrand. Analysis of the Christian experience (D152) – $1.45

CATHEDRAL AND CRUSADE (2 Volumes) – Henri Daniel-Rops. A history of the Church between the eleventh and fourteenth centuries (D154a, D154b) – $1.35 ea.

OTHER IMAGE BOOKS

PRAYER IN PRACTICE – Romano Guardini (D157) – 85¢

THE PROTESTANT REFORMATION (2 Volumes) – Henri Daniel-Rops (D159a, D159b) – $1.35 ea.

ON THE LOVE OF GOD (2 Volumes) – St. Francis de Sales. Translated and with an Introduction by John K. Ryan (D164a, D164b) – 95¢ ea.

THE CHURCH IN CRISIS: A History of the General Councils, 325–1870 – Philip Hughes (D168) – $1.25

ISRAEL AND THE ANCIENT WORLD – Henri Daniel-Rops (D169) – $1.55

THE SPIRITUAL EXERCISES OF ST. IGNATIUS – Translated by Anthony Mottola, Ph.D. Introduction by Robert W. Gleason, S.J. (D170) – 85¢

A NEWMAN READER: An Anthology of the Writings of John Henry Cardinal Newman – Edited with an Introduction by Francis X. Connolly (D171) – $1.45

THE GOLDEN STRING – Bede Griffiths, O.S.B. (D173) – 75¢

THE WAY OF PERFECTION – St. Teresa of Avila. Translated and edited by E. Allison Peers (D176) – 85¢

REFLECTIONS ON AMERICA – Jacques Maritain (D177) – 75¢

THE CATHOLIC REFORMATION (2 Volumes) – Henri Daniel-Rops (D179a, D179b) – $1.25 ea.

WE HOLD THESE TRUTHS: Catholic Reflections on the American Proposition – John Courtney Murray, S.J. (D181) – $1.25

LETTERS FROM VATICAN CITY – Xavier Rynne (D182) – 95¢

LIFE AND HOLINESS – Thomas Merton. Exposition of the principles of the spiritual life (D183) – 75¢

THE EMERGING LAYMAN: The Role of the Catholic Layman in America – Donald J. Thorman (D186) – 85¢

THE SOCIAL AND POLITICAL PHILOSOPHY OF JACQUES MARITAIN – Selected Readings – Edited by Joseph W. Evans and Leo R. Ward (D188) – $1.45

AMERICAN CATHOLICISM – John Tracy Ellis. A comprehensive survey of the American Church (D190) – 85¢

THE CHURCH IN THE SEVENTEENTH CENTURY (2 Volumes) – Henri Daniel-Rops (D191a, D191b) – $1.25 ea.

THE WORLD'S GREAT CATHOLIC LITERATURE – Edited by George N. Shuster (D192) – $1.45

THE CRISIS OF WESTERN EDUCATION – Christopher Dawson (D194) – 95¢

SOCIETY AND SANITY – F. J. Sheed. An explanation of Christian sociology and ethics (D195) – 95¢

THE COUNCIL, REFORM AND REUNION – with a new Introduction by Fr. Hans Kung (D198) – 95¢

OTHER IMAGE BOOKS

OTHER IMAGE BOOKS